UNTYING the KNOT

A Husband and Wife's Story
of Coming Out Together

David L. Kaufman, M.D.

Addicus Books
Omaha, Nebraska

An Addicus Nonfiction Book

ISBN 978-1-936374-88-5
Cover design and typography by Jack Kusler
Cover photo by Michael's Studio, Lansing, Michigan

Library of Congress Cataloging-in-Publication Data

Kaufman, David, 1959 June 6-
  Untying the knot : a husband and wife's story of coming out together / David Kaufman.
      pages cm
Includes bibliographical references and index.
  ISBN 978-1-936374-88-5 (pbk.)
1. Kaufman, David, 1959 June 6- 2. Gay men—Biography. 3. Lesbians—Biography. 4. Coming out (Sexual orientation)—United States. I. Title.
  HQ75.2.K38 2013
  306.76'62092--dc23
  [B]

                          2012044689

Addicus Books, Inc.
P.O. Box 45327
Omaha, Nebraska 68145
www.AddicusBooks.com

Printed in the United States of America
10 9 8 7 6 5 4 3 2 1

Contents

Part III — Later

Part IV — Acceptance

Acknowledgments

I would, first and foremost, like to thank Cathy Kaufman, my companion for so many years, my best friend. There's no clear label for our relationship, probably because of its rarity, but it's mutually supportive and very strong. We have taken such good care of each other for more than twenty years and particularly so through these tumultuous times.

Also, I thank Rod Colvin and Jack Kusler of Addicus Books for their unfailing support and multitude of wonderful ideas.

Additionally, I would like to thank the rest of my family; you have all been so supportive and that's a huge blessing. Specifically to my father, Lee, thank you for understanding me, and thank you for the help with this work.

I also want to thank my colleagues and coworkers, you have all also been very understanding and very patient with my wild phases. To my mentor Robert, I couldn't have done this without you, you've been incredible. Kenneth, thank you for being such a faithful and supportive confidant. For the rest, thank you all for your support and the gift of understanding that there's nothing wrong with me.

Bobby, Jason, and Manuel, thank you for what I've learned from you.

Introduction

I've had, at times, a bizarre life, but by far the greatest bizarreness occurred in 2009. The following is an autobiographical account of the struggles, tragedies, and triumphs that both Cathy, my wife of eighteen years, and I have encountered along the way. Cathy and I were a romantic couple for twenty-two years and are now the very best of friends. In recent years, we both found profound insight about who we are as individuals. We've explored our amazing new lives together and also with newfound friends. I couldn't have come this far without their support and counsel.

This book is an attempt to present, as accurately and honestly as I can, what our lives have been like since our epiphanies, and how we feel about them. The issues presented here ultimately represent not only the most fundamental crisis of my entire life but also profound opportunity for both of us. This undertaking was not taken lightly; I am writing, sometimes desperately, for my life and sanity. It has at times been very intense, but frequently also humorous; I hope some of the humor comes through, as well.

The year 2009 brought incredible changes and challenges to our marriage; the following account depicts the roller-coaster ride we found ourselves on. In the end, it's really all good, all very good. The year 2012 finds me emotionally stronger than I've ever been in my entire life up to now. I'm also much more confident and much happier than I've ever been. I'm truly a different person.

The normal adjustment of the average, common-sense, well-adjusted man implies a continued successful rejection of much of the depths of human nature.

—Abraham Maslow
—*Personal journal entry 6/20/08*

Part I
Personal Background

My cup is overflowing
I don't know where I'm going
The world is slowly spinning
No losing and no winning
The road is never ending
My compass point is bending

"Compass Point" by Lowen and Navarro

This song, "Compass Point," woke Cathy and me up one morning in San Francisco on one of our first trips to the Bay Area. I knew somehow that it was talking to me, personally, without having any idea of what was in store. I did know something big was up, though. The turns my life have taken since that trip are reflected more in these lyrics than I ever thought possible.

—Personal journal entry 10/7/09

1

Elementary School

I have a deep-seated unconscious assumption that people won't like me.
—Personal journal entry 11/11/05

"Faggot! Faggot! Faggot!"

Forty years after elementary school, those words still sting. Tears still form. There was often more than mere name calling—hitting and punching often accompanied the verbal harassment. Being nonviolent and very passive, I even had bullies who occasionally were much younger than I.

Although I tried hard, it was difficult to find a route walking home from school that would avoid them. There was really no escape from the mocking; it continued in the halls at school, in classrooms, anywhere I might encounter other boys even close to my age. At times I was physically attacked in school.

The school administration either didn't understand what was happening or didn't care. Usually, when they did get involved, the situation was twisted into being at least partially my fault; I was seen fighting with another student (on rare occasions I tended to at least try to fight back), therefore I must be guilty of something. I tried to be strong, to not let it bother me. There was only so much I could do, however, to counter the effect of an assault that was pretty much continuous.

As time passed, I began to walk more and more hunched over, trying to hide within my own body, not understanding that it wasn't my fault, ashamed and embarrassed to even exist at all. The insults were compelling in their constancy and difficult

1

to ignore. I didn't understand why this was happening to me; to the limited extent that I understood it, I was convinced of my heterosexuality.

Over time, the insults and put-downs became more and more internalized. Although I didn't and couldn't identify myself as "homosexual," I always knew there was something really wrong with me. Why was I so different? Why was I so bad?

To a small child, the world revolves around them, everything relates to them, and when something negative is perceived in their environment it becomes internalized as, "there's something wrong with me; I'm a bad person." Sensing at a very early age that I was very different primed me for the shame that would come with these insults. Even though at the time I could not see any truth to their taunting, deep down inside I sensed there really was something wrong with me.

I did what I could to try to stave off the attacks. I developed a keen sense of humor; making my attackers laugh might prevent a beating. Probably also related to this suffering, I developed an insightful ability to discern what people around me are feeling. It was often necessary to be able to tell if someone was about to hit me. The ability to read others' emotional states was critical to survival. I've often attributed the perceived emotions to the wrong cause, usually taking something personally when it has nothing to do with me, but I've learned to be very aware of the emotions of the people around me. The combination of sense of humor and emotional sensitivity has resulted in diplomatic skill, which has served me well.

My mother struggled with her own demons, left by her husband with three small children at a time when divorce was rare had left her with many challenges. Raising children alone is very difficult, and trying to piece together something resembling a complete life while balancing children, finding romance, and keeping the bills paid was difficult.

Nevertheless, she was still somewhat sensitive to my situation.

"Let the insults roll off you like water off a duck's back," she would frequently say. Unfortunately, that's much, much easier said than done. My innate sense there was something wrong with me, deep down inside, made it all that much harder to believe her. Believing that I was a bad person responsible for my parents' divorce and feeling a strong sense of shame at being so different made it very difficult to even stick up for myself. "Jesus says you should turn the other cheek," my mother also said often. Well, I'm sorry, but I'm not Jesus; not even close. That takes a strength of character far beyond what the average school-age child is capable of, and was far beyond my ability at that point (probably beyond it at any point in my life). My father was also supportive. We saw him very regularly, every other weekend, but he was hard for me to understand when I was a young child. Intellectually powerful and emotionally strong, he was also very eclectic; his sense of household cleanliness was significantly less than what I was used to with my mother. He also tried to support me with advice, but there was little anyone could say to me that would actually stop the bullying. Attempts to comfort me were limited in the face of continued oppression.

Through the hardest years, I had one or two friends. They were on the periphery of the social scene, but they were not bullied like I was. Being a bit removed from my personal struggle, and not suffering from harassment themselves, they were probably not completely able to understand it. In any case, they were powerless to do anything about it. Only much more recently has bullying begun to be understood for the scourge it is. Many, many young people fall victim to this epidemic and suffer emotional scars that last a lifetime. I recently read an article on bullying and was startled to see that the description of the typical victim's emotional response fit me perfectly. Victims of bullies frequently have difficulty trusting others and often lack self-confidence.[1] It's not surprising.

The negative feelings that surround being beaten up and teased were internalized, producing profound shame and emotional pain. Humans are social animals; we're inclined to accept what others think or say about us. My feelings of inferiority, worthlessness, and shame started from an early age, probably long before the bullying started.[2] I had begun to feel different from the other boys; there was a sense that I didn't belong with them, that I was somehow weird. This started at an early age and contributed to profound feelings of inferiority and the feeling that I was being left out. Feeling left out has had a powerful hold on me since those early years. I was an easy target for the bullies.

Although by the time the harassment started taking place I perhaps should have been old enough to rationally counter it, my long-held feelings of worthlessness didn't allow me to see that I didn't have to accept what was being said about me. In an effort to help, my mom also often quoted the old adage, "Sticks and stones may break my bones…." But the statement "…but words can never hurt me" isn't true; insulting words can be powerful and deeply hurtful. That's why we use them.

Even so, I couldn't accept the core truth of the accusations until much later in my life. I could not accept or even understand the insults at that time; I didn't even know what homosexuality was until my late teens. By puberty I thought "homosexual" meant a guy who liked to wear women's clothing; the idea of a man who prefers sex with other men was totally outside my realm of understanding. It was understood during puberty that all guys like girls; presumably even the "homos" who dress like women still like women sexually (and in fact, some cross-dressers do). Before puberty I wouldn't have even recognized the word "homosexual." I didn't hear the word "gay" in this context until much later. At puberty I had no knowledge of any individuals who would fit under the heading of "queer." I only knew of males born in a male body attracted to women, and females born in a female body attracted to men.

So what was all this harassment for? Why did they do it? In retrospect, I wonder now: Did they really even know what I was? Or were they just a pack of dogs, going for the weakest, attacking any way that worked to counter their own insecurities or perhaps just to enjoy someone else's suffering? I actually suspect the latter. By the time I was old enough to know the words "homosexual" and "faggot," I understood even less why I was a target. Believing I must be straight only increased my indignation. Why did they pick on me for something that wasn't even true? I liked girls, I loved girls. I strongly preferred hanging out with girls.

Attempts were made to toughen me up, but ultimately they didn't help much. My mother arranged for karate lessons, but it wasn't of much use. I just wasn't much of a brawler, I'm more a peacemaker. I've always been conciliatory rather than confrontational. Years later I considered law school, but realized I don't have the constitution for adversarial conduct. I've always been more of a diplomat.

I couldn't understand then, and don't totally understand now, why I was victimized. But I didn't talk about these experiences much over the years; being the school punching bag, for whatever reasons, is not something to brag about. Discussing it would open old wounds, and the scars go very deep. But I had no idea then how these experiences would affect me later, no idea of both the turmoil and triumph that would ultimately result.

...but the poor duckling, who had crept out of his shell last of all and looked so ugly, was bitten and pushed and made fun of, not only by the ducks, but by all the poultry...

The ducks pecked him, the chickens beat him, and the girl who fed the poultry kicked him with her feet.

—*The Ugly Duckling*, Hans Christian Andersen[3]

2

The Neighborhood

As a child, I lived in a very poor neighborhood in an extremely conservative part of the country, even for the Midwest. Although both my parents had graduate degrees, they were not in high-paying fields, and multiple marriages and divorces on both sides ate away at family finances. A big old house in a poor neighborhood on the edge of the inner city was all we could afford. But we always had enough to eat, although it was simple and finances limited how much we ate. Later, when this was no longer true, I had to face that bit of my history and learn to control my weight. We had basic inexpensive clothing and an old car. We never had color TV or a microwave. The house was old, but had a lot of character. It was spacious, with plenty of room for running around and playing games.

I lived there with my younger brother and occasionally my older sister. She had run away from home in her mid-teens following a beating by a mentally ill stepfather. My younger brother moved out in his mid-teens to live with a friend. I lived with my mother until I married the first time; I didn't have the fortitude to strike out on my own.

My brother and sister and I played together endlessly. We played the usual games, built forts, and spent a lot of time cooking in the kitchen. The neighbor kids were fun to play with, and in that era, we could safely wander all over the neighborhood.

Our mother worked during the day as a high-school English teacher, and was often grading papers or out on dates in the evening. My older sister filled in somewhat as a maternal figure. As much from our father as our mother, we learned some basic cooking, nothing fancy. To this day, that style cooking represents comfort food to me: macaroni and cheese, peanut butter sandwiches. I learned to cook well with basic ingredients—ground beef, potatoes, rice, and macaroni. We essentially never went out to restaurants or to the movies. In early adulthood, I was very intimidated by restaurants, not having had any experience with them. I never even saw cooked lobster until my mid-teens while working in a restaurant; steak was also unheard of in our household. Chuck roast was as close as we came to that.

I have many happy memories of fooling around in the kitchen with my sister and brother, creating this or that from the basic staples my mother was willing and able to purchase. I'm amazed at people who say they don't know how to cook. To me, cooking is a fundamental human skill, like reading and writing. To not know how to cook seems a form of illiteracy.

For kids our age, the house was pretty special. The kitchen was warm and inviting, but the dark basement had a gigantic gravity furnace that had been converted from coal to natural gas. This huge octopus was foreboding and lent a particular scariness to the basement. In the yard were gigantic oak trees so the house was perpetually shaded, like deep woods, helping stave off summer heat, but also contributing to a sense of gloom that frequently matched my mood.

This was a very conservative neighborhood. Many of the neighbors were ultraconservative Dutch Calvinist—the kind of people who believe drinking is wrong and oppose liquor licenses for restaurants, but drink in their homes where no one can see them. Any visible activity on Sundays could invite criticism for "working on the Lord's day." Anyone not of their way of thinking was suspect, but there weren't many of these. The saying was, "If you're not Dutch, you're not much." I had been brought up fairly liberal protestant, with a strong sense of social justice, so there was a general feeling of religious oppression in this environment.

The neighbors were otherwise reasonably sympathetic and supportive to us and generally with each other. Danger, however, was only a few blocks away. It wasn't north toward the black inner city; the black kids left me alone. It was the poor white kids a few blocks away who caused all my torment.

3

Always Different

Although I always knew I was different from other boys, I couldn't quite fathom why. I was very passive and non-aggressive. In general, as a child, I'd rather play with girls than boys. I wasn't into playing with dolls so much, playing house was better, but in general I found the girls much easier to understand and get along with. They just thought the same way I thought and were so easy to talk to. I truly didn't understand boys.

I didn't understand the masculine attraction to things like firecrackers, guns, or pointless destruction. I didn't enjoy any kind of rough play and tended to avoid it as much as possible.

I had a total lack of interest in any competitive athletics, particularly those involving some kind of ball. And I was completely clueless regarding team sports. I still don't even know the rules of football or basketball, and couldn't have played them if I'd been asked. I was somewhat familiar with baseball, but found it ridiculously boring. Instead of watching a sporting event on TV, I would rather be in the kitchen cooking. Actually, I'd really rather be in the kitchen even if I'm just washing dishes. Dismal performance in every aspect of gym class generally meant I was intentionally left out of any neighborhood ball games. I wasn't particularly sorry about that, but the inevitable humiliation during physical ed was excruciating. I recall that during high-school volleyball, my nickname was "statue" because all I'd do was stand there, whether the ball was coming at me or not.

As a child, I played with cars and trucks, but not the way the other boys did. I didn't actually play with them, I took the mechanical and electrical ones apart to understand how they worked. At least that seemed manly; engineers and mechanics are usually men, right? I have always had an intense fascination with machines and electronics and that's usually a man's world.

So I generally tended toward hanging with the girls, and then later with women. I assumed, of course, that this was because I was attracted to them sexually. Actually, I now realize that I have always been drawn to women, generally preferring their company to that of men, at least straight men. This probably has a lot to do with conversation. Women tend to talk about things that are interesting to me. Straight men, less so. Straight women have an approach to life that's similar to mine, much less competitive than straight men; they seem to exhibit less need to prove themselves.

Other factors contributed to my introversion. Starting around the age of six, I developed extremely severe environmental allergies and asthma. I was basically allergic to everything alive outdoors except possibly reptiles and insects. We had to get rid of the cat that I loved, and my father ultimately had to get rid of his beloved Siamese cat. Outdoor play often meant an exacerbation of asthma, and therefore resulted in my being confined indoors for a while. This only reinforced my dislike for team sports; they could literally make me sick. At the time, the medical advice for those with exercise asthma was, "Don't exercise."

My bedroom was a semi-sterile environment; there was no carpet and there were bags over the mattress and pillows. Cheesecloth filters covered the furnace vents. Owing to these health problems, I spent most of my childhood in that nearly sterile bedroom, alone with my books. Because my parents were both English majors, I had a rich supply of literature, mostly science fiction. I was intrigued by space exploration; this was the era of the Apollo moon landing. This cloistered aspect of my childhood greatly enhanced an existing tendency toward shyness, and a feeling of vulnerability not shared by my male peers.

At least, I thought, that's why I was always alone. Hanging around with boys made me uncomfortable, as hanging around with men as an adult would also make me at least as uncomfortable. But it took me a while to realize this. Not until after my awakening could I face how I really feel. I'm sure I have some natural tendency toward shyness, possibly that shy gene recently discovered, but I think my fear of exposing what a flawed being I thought I was had a lot to do with it. The more time I spend with others, the greater the chance someone will pick up on how I'm not right. It was a lonely existence, wanting human contact, but being afraid of it at the same time.

I never understood the point of my peers' enjoyment of senseless destruction and violence. It seemed like a dog marking its territory. I despised war, partly because of my parents' pacifism I guess, but its violence seemed totally pointless. War to me is another form of male competition. I was a child during the later part of the Vietnam war, and watched the news footage and the body counts on the evening news. There was a draft at that time, and I was terrified of what would happen to me if I were drafted. I knew I could not shoot another person; I couldn't even shoot in the general direction of where people might be. I never had, and still don't have, any attraction to the machines of war. Peaceful machines are fascinating to me; machines for violence are very disturbing. As an adult it seems to me that some men must actually like war. Why else would it keep happening?

I believe some people pay lip service to the idea that war is bad, but they keep engaging in it because for them it's fun. And some war instigators, like generals, aren't even generally in harm's way. I don't think our civilization is really that far removed from the ancient Romans and their gladiators. On a trip to Peru as an adult, I visited ruins where the people practiced human sacrifice. How barbaric, I thought, but then remembered that we do, too. We call it war. We also sacrifice young men in their prime.

As the realization was growing that I was different from other boys, I wondered where did I fit in? And what was wrong with me? Why didn't I want to be with the guys? Much more recently I've realized I'm generally uncomfortable around any group of (straight) guys. One on one is not so bad, but with larger groups I get uncomfortable. I want to fit in, but I just don't and I don't know how to. For young children this feeling is particularly difficult to process. As children we see our environment as connected to us, a part of us. This is a learned response from when we're infants and sense how the world seems to function.

Unfortunately, when a young child perceives something negative around them, it's internalized to mean, "There's something wrong with me." Any feeling of negativity must somehow relate to me as a person; if I see badness around me, there must be badness within me. My grandfather was very much into photography, particularly involving his grandchildren. Prior to my parents' divorce and before I realized that I truly was different from other boys, there were many photos of a happy, bubbly, smiling Davey. Maybe he's still in there, somewhere.

In my youth's restrictive and conservative environment, homosexuality was simply not an option; it was completely unthinkable. It wasn't just wrong, it was impossible. In my era, no boy at puberty would ever think to admit a difference such as this to anyone, and probably not even to himself. To be attracted to boys was too far outside the box, so I just forced myself to be as much like other boys as I could. To even admit to masturbation was to be reviled by my peers. I still remember the taunt, "If Jack was stuck on a roof would you help Jack off?" So I just held that secret in, accompanied by guilt and shame, feeling I was somehow inferior even for that. During puberty I'd heard of group masturbation and wondered why my peer group didn't do this; I think I knew I might have liked it. At the same time, however, the idea of masturbating with someone else still felt wrong somehow.

It was the first in a long series of thoughts, feelings, and desires I couldn't share with anyone; and there were quite a few I couldn't even admit to myself. The emotional cost of this inward deception was enormous. Rarely actually feeling attracted to a man, I unknowingly but completely forced that desire from my consciousness. I simply blocked any interest in men. Any boy or man I unconsciously found attractive would be perceived as annoying, an irritant. So this left girls as my objects of desire, which is, after all, who I'm supposed to be chasing after. I went through the motions of liking girls and was able to convince myself that I really meant it.

As a young boy, I always had "girlfriends." Of course, there was no sense of romance or sex before puberty; the girlfriends were really just close friends, playmates. But I still called them girlfriends. The need for this kind of attachment would come back to haunt me in later years.

My peers, even before puberty, announced their affections and desires for girls (and later, women) profusely. So, in imitation, so did I; peer pressure is a very powerful influence. Of course I believed it; if we say something often enough, we will begin to believe it. I learned to admire what other boys admired, say the things they said, and believe it. The desirable physical attributes of femininity were repeated over and over by other boys. Parents and schoolteachers encouraged us to understand we were all going through the same thing. So if I felt I was different from the other boys in any way relating to puberty and sex, I suppressed it completely.

Girls and sex could even be a common bond; I couldn't join the boys in their love for team sports, but I could profess the same adoration of girls they did. I learned what was and wasn't attractive to males. Only much later did I realize how much I was fooling myself. These habits were learned in puberty when I was too young to know any better and old habits are very persistent. For years, I felt satisfied that my interest in girls, and later, women, was "normal" and I truly felt romantic interest in girls after puberty.

In retrospect I'm not sure whether it would have helped or hurt me then to know that I was gay. On the negative side, there are definite negative connotations and associations in being labeled "gay." On the positive side, it was still a group and to know I was not a singular freak could have been helpful. Around puberty, things changed with me in a dark and dysfunctional way. Coincident with the move to a conservative neighborhood shaded by giant oak trees, my mood darkened considerably. It was as if the sun never shown. Dark brooding clouds always gathered over my head. I wondered what the point was of anything. My depression probably started at this point; my first suicide attempt was at age thirteen. Was it a coincidence that my depression started around puberty, when I would have to more actively suppress the real inner me? I often wonder. I still had "girlfriends," but there were a few new twists. I understood sex and was physically mature enough to want it in some form. The girls who had been singled out by me usually didn't know they were supposed to be my girlfriend. Eventually, they'd figure out my interests and then make it absolutely clear that a relationship wasn't going to happen. I'd mourn briefly and move on.

Rarely was my interest in a girl reciprocated. Occasionally there'd be a brief relationship, and then pretty quickly a breakup. In retrospect, I realize I wasn't able to give them what they wanted or needed, possibly because I didn't understand romance. Chasing after the wrong gender may explain my lack of romantic understanding, but it could have just as easily been naiveté. Profound lack of self-confidence related to self-doubt probably also contributed to my lack of attractiveness. Either way, I was usually without an actual relationship, but virtually always with some girl in my head I considered to be my girlfriend.

Most of my later romantic relationships with girls or women were somewhat dysfunctional. To some extent, after puberty I may have even picked girls to like who I knew wouldn't like me back; that way I was safe. I could go along with the idea of heterosexuality without actually having to act on it.

In high school, I had been encouraged to take typing, even though few boys did, on the promise that it would help me later. This was a significant skill, and provided employment opportunities in computer data entry. In one job, in the summer heat, I got to work indoors, in the air-conditioning, with the women and heat-sensitive computers. The men at this company all worked in an outdoor warehouse, exposed to the elements, working with noisy and dangerous power tools. This seemed an amazing deal to me at the time: work in comfortable surroundings, with women—way more comfortable and fun than being out in the heat and humidity with the men.

In college, I preferred jobs, such as office work, that were traditionally considered feminine. In medical school, before starting clinical rotations, we were all counseled that there would be patients we would be attracted to. This is a normal part of human nature and is no cause for guilt. However, acting on these feelings would, of course, be a profound ethical violation. But throughout my medical training I never felt really attracted to a female patient. But there were a couple of male patients who affected me in a way that in retrospect I now know was as attraction. Early on, I couldn't remember ever being attracted to a man. But then I remembered one, then another, then another. But my attraction to men felt more like a distraction, a disturbing pull in a direction I didn't want to go. I recall a man at work who always bothered me; I just never liked him. Now I realize that he made me uncomfortable because he was really cute and highly likely to be gay.

Although, as I got older, I experienced feelings toward men that I interpreted as irritation, I was never aware at that time of consciously, outwardly falling in love with a man. I was obviously not ready to accept it. Even now, getting used to being different is hard enough. Then, it could have been catastrophic for me.

But I realize now that I've always been attracted to men. For example, if I had been asked as a young man to sketch how specific body parts of an ideal woman should look, from breasts to bottoms to arms and legs, as a series of separate exercises so I could not see how the whole person would look, the composite image, when assembled, would have been a man's body. The sexiest woman's butt I've even seen was on the Internet, and she had a man's butt, with essentially no hips.

15

David L. Kaufman, M.D.

Although I preferred hanging with women, I was always afraid it looked bad, that people would think, Who is that guy always hanging out with the girls? What's wrong with him? I always felt aware of that at parties or other events. Sometimes, a group of men could be having a perfectly normal conversation about flowers and gardening, and then one of them would bring up sports, hunting, or fishing, or some such demonstration of machismo. I'd suddenly become silent. Although I never considered these activities bad or wrong, I had absolutely no interest in them, knew nothing about them, and couldn't converse about them. Sports were the worst. Professional sports teams would be mentioned with adoration bordering on flat-out worship, and I wasn't even sure if they were talking about basketball, football, baseball, or hockey. I would try to guess, based on the time of year, knowing at least that baseball is a summer sport and football a fall thing. I knew only that the general idea with these activities is to get the ball, or puck, past the other team into a net, past a line, or in a basket.

By early adulthood, I realized consciously that I was different from other young men in at least a small way. Given any group of women, there were always certain ones most likely to be singled out by my peers as attractive. I had learned, and could easily recognize, what feminine characteristics were most desirable to men. I could tell immediately which women the average guy would be attracted to, but they were never the same women I was attracted to. I was attracted to women whose bodies most closely resembled men's bodies, but I was not consciously aware of it at the time.

Early on I realized I wasn't attracted to women with large breasts. Other guys often made preposterous statements regarding how large a woman's breasts should be; there is apparently no limit on how big is enough. No matter how big, bigger was always better to other young men. Since my teens, the women I was attracted to usually had smaller-than-average breasts, actually they were pretty flat-chested. But not being attracted to large breasts doesn't automatically mean someone is "queer." Although I've heard some men say, "Breast reduction surgery should be illegal," I also knew that my father would disagree, saying, "More than a handful is unnecessary."

I suspect I wasn't alone in my pretending to like what the other guys did. I imagine there are straight guys who are attracted to different types of women than the average guy but that they go along with the crowd, too, in order to fit in; they may not even realize themselves how much they're pretending. Growing up and living in the Midwest as a young man, I was not aware of knowing any gay men. I'm not exactly sure what I thought gay men were like. Presumably, to me at the time, there was something very different and inferior about them. I carried a great deal of homophobia with me from puberty on until early adulthood when I finally realized that gays are people, too, and deserve respect. This homophobia had been taught to me by my peers. Much later, in Sonoma County, when I was finally exposed to gay men willing to admit their orientation, I discovered I was particularly drawn to them. After moving out west, there were a few openly gay men at work, and at job-related parties and functions, Cathy and I just tended to gravitate to them. Yet that didn't register as a clue to my preferences at the time either.

4

First Marriage

The girls I was interested in rarely reciprocated the feeling. During my senior year in high school, I found myself sitting next to a beautiful girl, a junior. Barbara was of partly Irish descent with full dark hair and a fair complexion. She was also quite curvaceous; this didn't particularly appeal to me, but I knew it made her quite a catch. She readily conversed with me and we quickly struck up a friendship.

Things progressed rapidly toward a romantic relationship and she informed me that she was trying to become a member of the Church of Jesus Christ of Latter Day Saints, a Mormon. Her parents wouldn't let her be baptized. She indicated that she wouldn't seriously consider a boyfriend unless he was also Mormon. I agreed to consult with the missionaries, two clean-cut and enthusiastic young men who were very happy to explain basic things about the Mormon Church. More-detailed information about the church's beliefs is reserved for a later orientation.

I was informed about the Word of Wisdom, prohibiting alcohol, tobacco, and beverages containing caffeine. No problem, I figured; I didn't smoke, partly because of asthma, and I couldn't drink because I was too young. I wasn't a huge caffeine fiend at that point and I felt I could give that up. The Word of Wisdom also prohibits eating meat except in times of famine but no one seems to follow that rule for reasons I've never been clear on. The missionaries explained that I had to give 10 percent of my gross income to the church, also not a problem because I didn't really have any income.

During our dating period, Barbara and I did a fair amount of necking and petting. Nothing too serious but we both seemed into it at the time. I thought at the time that it was good, it felt right. I was eager for more. Barbara had already clarified that sex outside of marriage was totally taboo. This didn't bother me and I wanted to marry her anyway; she was beautiful and she liked me. There were so few girls who liked me, and she would be quite a catch. I also felt comfortable with her and enjoyed her company.

Barbara and I at some point after turning eighteen were both baptized and confirmed as members of the Mormon Church. The church then pushed me to go on a mission, like all good young Mormon men do, but I resisted. I didn't want to go on a mission; I wanted to marry Barbara.

Barbara accepted my marriage proposal, although with some trepidation, and we planned to get married as soon as possible after she graduated from high school. We arranged to be married in the Washington, DC Mormon temple, giving us an advantage in the promise that this meant we would still be married in heaven. The idea is that if you're married in the temple, the marriage isn't "until death do us part," but "for all time and eternity." This sounded like a good deal to me at the time.

One problem that plagued me throughout my eight years as a Mormon was the church's rules regarding masturbation. The Mormon Church forbids any sexual activity outside of conservative sexual positions with your spouse. Masturbation was forbidden. This was especially difficult for me. Sex with a woman wasn't as good to me as sex with myself, partly because I could do things that most women wouldn't want to do in bed. I never thought about it overtly, but I think I saw my identity as a kinky, weird straight guy with a butt fetish. My parents had instilled in me the idea that masturbation was a good thing, that it prevents men from sexually harassing women. But my peer group's belief that masturbation was wrong had made me think it was not okay. Now the Mormon Church was telling me I couldn't masturbate and if I didn't follow all the rules they wouldn't let us be married in the temple. So I managed to quit masturbating long enough to get married, but it continued to be a frequent activity throughout my first marriage.

As a married couple, Barbara and I both worked entry-level full time jobs while I attended junior college part time. In my first semester in junior college I took math, physics, and English and my GPA was 1.9. I then realized that this school cost money, the government was paying for it because of my family situation, and that I should probably actually try to succeed. I vowed to start actually doing assignments, reading the textbooks, and studying for tests. A guidance counselor at the school suggested I change my focus to biology, since I wasn't doing well in hard-science courses. Given both changes, my grades went to As and Bs. I completed JC in three years and was unsure what to do next. I could not have attended a typical four-year college right away even if I'd wanted to, as my GPA in high school was below 2.0. I actually had to take high school algebra four times before I passed.

My social relationship with Barbara was good and we loved and respected each other. However, she wasn't very interested in sex. That was very hard for me because I was a man in my early twenties and a Mormon who wasn't supposed to masturbate. We didn't have sex very often and when we did she was very passive. My sex life was very unsatisfying. The chemistry we had while dating seemed to have disappeared. I was very frustrated, and it didn't seem that things could possibly get better. I thought about continuing my college career at a local university for a bachelor's degree and then a PhD in crop science, but I wasn't really sure it was what I wanted to do. Further, I was enjoying married life to some degree and having a regular income. I had grown up poor, with basic needs met but no money for anything else. The minimum-wage jobs we had allowed for a decent apartment and a small amount of discretionary income. The extra money was a real treat to me.

So I put college on hold and we both continued with full-time work. This lifestyle continued for a few years. Our interest and participation in church activities waxed and waned during this time together. I became close friends with a man I met through the church who had a very cute two-year-old daughter, which got me interested in having children and Barbara and I decided to go for it. The Mormons encourage large families but don't strictly forbid birth control, which we had been using.

Barbara had some medical difficulties during her pregnancy, but our daughter finally arrived and I was ecstatic. She was so beautiful, I don't think my feet touched the ground for weeks. It was all so cool. It was also a lot of work. About two years later Barbara became pregnant again. Michael was feisty and very cute. I have fond memories of time spent with our children when they were very little. It's difficult to appreciate what being a parent feels like unless you are one. I've heard childless friends criticize how some people parent their kids but a childless couple really has no idea what being a parent is like. It's very hard and there are no breaks. I've come to believe that "falling in love" is actually just a trick our brains play on us to get us to reproduce. I think if people could be totally objective about parenthood, few would opt for it; it's just too much work.

Notwithstanding how cute our kids were, Barbara and I were having trouble. We didn't connect anymore romantically and I thought she was too aloof, too cold. We never had sex and that was still a big thing for me as a young man. I wasn't really sure what her problem was with this, so I assumed that proper women just don't generally like sex and I should just deal with it, somehow, without masturbation. We discussed marriage therapy but never really got any. There were other issues affecting me as well.

I became severely depressed. I had tried to sell life insurance, but I am not a salesman. I couldn't sell firewood to an Eskimo in a blizzard. When I couldn't make any money doing this, we ended up losing the little house we had managed to buy and we were forced to move back to a less-expensive apartment.

As my life seemed to be spiraling down, I worked a succession of minimum-wage jobs, even spending some time driving a delivery van for a vending machine company. I wasn't even high enough in the hierarchy to actually fill the vending machines; I could only drive the delivery truck. The people who actually filled the vending machines had to pull every product that had expired (those highly processed pastries actually do have an expiration date) and I was supposed to return the food to the warehouse. It was allegedly then donated to old-folks homes, but we were so poor I kept a lot of it for us to eat. We practically lived on expired Suzy Qs for several months.

My depression grew worse, as did my desperation. When I was depressed I felt worthless (I actually felt pretty worthless even when I felt well, on a good day), and I often contemplated suicide. I really felt that I was not an asset to the human race and that everyone would be better off if I wasn't around. The depression skewed my thought process so that I couldn't see how my untimely death would obviously be a bad thing for my wife and children.

After one suicide attempt, as close to lethal as I ever got, I spent four days in the hospital recovering from an aspirin overdose. Somehow, in the aftermath of recovering from serious physical illness, I felt a little better, at least able to go on with life.

A close friend with counseling experience was trying to help, but ultimately the best advice she gave was suggesting I go back to school. She said I was too smart to drive a van for a living. She also said that I was doing so much with the little Radio Shack computer I had bought (with money borrowed from relatives) that I should go back to school for computers.

I took that advice and applied to the closest big school, Michigan State University, for computer science. I was accepted to MSU, but not to the college of engineering because I hadn't taken enough math classes in junior college. They suggested I pick another major and try again. Admissions advised me that I could be accepted to other colleges that were part of the University, like The College of Social Science. Actually, they

22

said I could enter the university as a sophomore and take math classes, then apply to the college of engineering. But I wasn't sure financial aid would cover me as a sophomore after going to junior college for three years. Also, at the time, I wasn't keen on taking a bunch of math classes, believing that math was really hard and I wasn't good at it.

I looked through the course catalogs and came across biochemistry. I had no idea what it was, but it sounded cool so I applied for that college with that as a major and was quickly accepted. I had to pick a major other than engineering because those spots were limited only to students who could qualify for them and I didn't. Wondering just exactly what it was I had been accepted to, I read more about the subject in the school catalogs. "Biochemistry is a good background for medical school," it said and suddenly I was seized by the idea of being a doctor. "Yeah, that's what I want to do," I thought; I want to go to medical school. That would likely give me job security and a reasonable income, both of which were lacking in my earlier career attempts. Plus, medical school could be fun because it's such a challenge. I'm not the most financially savvy person and the idea of having a good income left room for financial mistakes without compromising the grocery budget. This turned out to be a wise decision financially.

I later changed to psychology as a major because it seemed an interesting subject and I also hoped to learn more about what had gone wrong in my life. It turned out that I wasn't really personally interested in biochemistry, but I was interested in psychology. My particular area of interest was social psychology, which I still find fascinating and very practical. I gained some profound insights into human behavior that have served me well since. For example, social psychology has shown, from countless experiments, that our beliefs actually follow our actions, not the other way around. We may think we believe what's right and that belief influences our actions, but actually we believe what we have to in order to support our actions. These insights helped me much later understand how I had lived so much of my life unaware of a fundamental understanding of who I am.

David L. Kaufman, M.D.

My junior year, my first year at MSU, I got a perfect 4.0 GPA, the highest possible GPA, while taking classes in organic chemistry, physics, and calculus. My grades at the junior college had been pretty good following the first semester, and I credit my academic success at MSU to learning how to study and apply myself as well as maturity and a strong sense that it was this or drive a delivery van for the rest of my life. This time around, I found math to be straightforward, and not all that difficult. It was elegant and powerful. I changed my major a few times, never losing sight of the goal to be a doctor, and graduated with high honor with a degree in psychology.

After I arrived at MSU and began to make friends who weren't Mormon, I began to see my life in different terms. There was nothing left in my relationship with Barbara to even closely approximate a viable marriage. We were barely even friends anymore. We were both so jaded by each other's behavior that we couldn't see past that. It was obvious to me that I couldn't stay married to her anymore. Barbara and I were divorced shortly after my arrival at MSU.

I had felt during my time as a Mormon that I believed all their teachings sincerely and wholeheartedly, but very soon after my arrival at MSU, my religion become unnecessary and a hindrance. I've often wondered since how I could think I believed in it. The answer, in part, lay in my psychology classes. We think we believe what we do because of our principles and values; that we believe what's right and true. Actually, people believe what they have to in order to survive. A multitude of practical research bears this out. I had wanted to marry Barbara and stay married to her so badly that I accepted the Mormon teachings in order to keep her. This is similar to how brainwashing works, and shows to what extent we can deceive ourselves. Realizing this has helped me to understand how powerful self-deception can be.

The truths I later learned about myself probably reflect on some of my issues at this time: difficulty being married to a woman and always feeling out of place among men. Having to leave my two children behind was hard, but they turned out

24

to be wonderful people and I am immensely proud of them. I can console myself now that although the road I have chosen has been hard one, it has been rewarding and a blessing for me to have children.

After our divorce, I mostly worked on my studies to get into medical school, but I allowed some time for socialization and recreation. Never having really been alone for more than a month or two, I dated several different women in short succession. For extra money, I learned that I could sell my blood plasma twice a week for a total of $25 a week. For me, this was a great deal of money at the time. Because blood plasma rapidly regenerates and the red blood cells are returned to the donor, blood plasma can be donated much more often than whole blood or red cells. There was a plasma donation center across the street from the MSU campus. The pharmaceutical products made from blood plasma are big business and college students usually have high-quality plasma and empty wallets. For a short time, I worked at the center.

Many of my coworkers there were gay men, but I never associated with them or really hung out with or talked to them much. When one of them actually asked me out, I was so startled and embarrassed that I just stammered "No" and he let it go. It never occurred to me to wonder why he thought I was gay. But I think I was also flattered that he found me attractive enough to ask out. One of the gay employees I worked with was clearly a "bottom" man and occasionally, in that open and accepting college-town atmosphere, made comments at work regarding his desire for rectal stimulation. Once I suggested that if he didn't do what I wanted I'd stick my foot up his ass. He responded, "Oh, please, would you do that." I was amazed to hear anyone admit that they liked anal stimulation and realized that he and I had something in common. But I never even got close to thinking I could actually be gay and I largely suppressed any feelings of camaraderie with him. In my head, I was still just a kinky, weird straight guy with a butt fetish. Recreation at MSU mostly meant going to the bars and particularly good bar nights were Thursday and Sunday, not traditional party days. I learned to drink beer; it was cheaper than mixed drinks or wine coolers and not watered down. I had a little trouble with depression and anxiety then, but mostly I felt good about what I was doing and accomplishing. Making progress toward long-term goals was sustaining.

5

Marriage to Cathy

Cathy and I met at Michigan State University; we had both attended two-year local colleges in our hometowns and then transferred to MSU for bachelor's degrees. I was out of school for five years between junior college and MSU. Cathy went straight through. She is younger than I am. We both worked in the microforms section of the large campus library. The area was darkened to enhance viewing microfilm and microfiche; perfect to enhance the romantic mood. We got to talking. We started out as friends, probably because of shared interests and ideals. I thought she was very cute and was strongly drawn to her as a person, as well as physically attracted. I knew I was going to medical school but Cathy wasn't particularly impressed by that.

Cathy had been dating a real catch, a prior captain of the football team, when he unceremoniously dumped her. So I started pushing a little and our friendship soon turned into romance, although not a typical one. We accepted each other out of practicality as much as out of being passionately in love. We were already good friends, with an uncanny appreciation of each other, and neither of us had anybody else and we didn't think the other was bad looking, so why not? As a romantic couple, we did very well, caring for and taking care of each other. We bickered fairly frequently, but didn't really fight very often. Over the years we developed a deep and abiding appreciation of each other. As expected, there were many tests of our love for each other, but we always survived, usually stronger for having had the challenge. We've always maintained a strong friendship starting from when we first met.

I had been taking a psychology class about relationships and was learning about how couples can sabotage things. Particularly, the class professor said that people always hide the bad parts of themselves, the "shit," and the other person doesn't find out until later. On one of our first dates, Cathy and I discussed this and decided to put all our "shit" out front for each other to see. At the time it seemed funny, but it probably helped us a lot. We were, from the beginning, probably more pragmatic about our relationship than most college couples are at that stage. We both had had a number of prior relationships, and we didn't have stars in our eyes. Although we had traditional in-love-type feelings for each other, it was more a case of us each rationally accepting that the other would make a good romantic companion.

Things progressed pretty quickly and we decided to get married before I entered medical school. As Cathy's mother became quite excited about planning the wedding, I simultaneously discovered that being married significantly limited my financial aid in medical school; they assumed my wife would pay for it. My family was unable to support me at all financially and I relied completely on financial aid. I was even paying child support from student loans. With Cathy as a roommate I received a much better aid package, and so we decided to just live together for now. Also, we had had some conflicts that made us feel we weren't ready to be married just yet. We planned to marry after medical school graduation.

Given my academic success up to that point, medical school seemed an intriguing challenge. I was on a high from finally having real success in undergraduate school after multiple repeated failures in various endeavors. In truth, during medical school my self-doubts often returned and I frequently wondered if I was going to make it.

I have mostly fond memories of medical school, time having erased the painful parts. Cathy, however, remembers it as a time of my endless bitching. I attended medical school in inner-city downtown Detroit. Even growing up on the edge of the Grand Rapids inner city hadn't prepared me for this. The inner city of Detroit is like a third-world country. One night in the downtown emergency department I worked on three different men, all conscious, with blood alcohol levels that should have been fatal. I had close contact and long conversations with prostitutes, gang members, and drug addicts. It was enlightening and very rewarding, resulting in a fundamental shift in how I see other people. I learned how bad some people really have it and how strongly the odds can be stacked against them. Drug dealers were often smart and ambitious, and some did what they did because they thought they had no other options.

I spent a large part of my time at the local VA hospital, which has since been replaced. At the time, it was a place of such limited resources that only people with no other options would go there. The physicians I worked with were virtually all young, bright, and idealistic, struggling to provide the best care they could in a difficult situation. Practicing there was something like taking a vow of poverty, nobly agreeing to work in very ascetic conditions. Medical students like me specifically asked to work at the VA hospital because of the excellent teaching that takes place there. Med students had to draw blood, do EKGs, and take chest X-rays. Amazing to me at the time, the patients I saw were always incredibly grateful for the care they were receiving. That's likely what drew the physicians who chose to practice there. I found it gratifying to be able to help people who needed it so badly.

For residency training, I chose Grand Rapids to be closer to my two children from my first marriage. I don't remember this time so positively. For reasons that remain unclear to me, I was singled out as being unpopular among the three of us in training. It only took a couple of people not liking me to make my entire residency experience unpleasant. Fortunately, over time, I was able to impress a number of my attending physicians and my program director.

Cathy and I had been talking about having children. I had been willing to have more kids early in our relationship, but at that time Cathy was adamantly opposed to it. Her position on the matter softened considerably later and now she wanted a child. I felt at the time that if I didn't agree to have a child with her, I would probably end up having another divorce, and, anyway, I wasn't that against having more children. Cathy became pregnant in my last year of residency. Andrew was born a few weeks before I took my oral board exams. He turned out to be a delightful addition to our marriage. I decided to do a fellowship, an extra year of training, to enhance my job prospects, which at that time weren't that good. At that time in the country, there weren't a lot of jobs for radiologists, so extra training made me more attractive as a candidate.

In a fellowship in interventional procedures and angiography, my coworkers and I worked as a team, with appreciation and support for one another; it was a very collegial atmosphere and I was treated like part of the family. The difference from residency was striking.

However, during my fellowship, even with the support of my teachers and coworkers, I experienced profound depression. I believe now that it was male postpartum depression, the realization of everything that can no longer be because of having a child. My depression was so severe and not responding to antidepressants that I was given electroconvulsive therapy. In this procedure, while under general anesthesia for only a few minutes, a patient has an electrical current sent through their head and brain that causes a seizure. The anesthesia prevents the patient's body from moving during the seizure. For reasons no one really knows, after a seizure depression tends to lessen. For me this actually worked better than antidepressants and really helped.

Unfortunately, there is one side effect: amnesia for events that occurred around the time of treatment prevents memories from forming. There are a few weeks of my life that are simply gone; I have no memory of them. Cathy and I made a trip to Ohio to look for a house for the job I found, and I even made notes on index cards of properties. But I have absolutely no memory of any aspect of this trip. I can recognize the handwriting on the cards as mine, but I don't remember writing it. Nevertheless, the treatments helped. With my depression somewhat under control, Cathy and I gratefully moved from my medical training to practice. Even though I was technically employed during residency and fellowship, the pay was so low that, coupled with big student loan payments, we had a meager existence. Finally, starting to practice meant we would be making decent money.

During my initial years of practice, I worked, gained experience, and became a better doctor. Cathy and I took care of Andrew and our home. In the winter, which in the Midwest is long, cold, and dark, we escaped to Orlando, Florida, for a week or so every year, usually going to Disney World. We did all the usual family/couple things that people do, and lived very normal lives. Cathy remained the most beautiful woman in the world to me, both physically and personally. I don't think it ever occurred to either of us that there was anything out of the ordinary about us.

6

Survival

How did I go from puberty through the next thirty-five years never realizing I was gay? That's a big question, but the answer is simple. I just went through the stages of life, doing what I was expected to do, doing what everyone else did. I simply forced my own experiences and feelings into that straight framework. In school, during our eighth-grade science class, during "reproductive system" lessons (this part of the curriculum was the sexual education offered by my school) we were all told, both boys and girls, that we would be experiencing many new and unusual feelings, but that we boys were all feeling the same things. In an attempt to bolster my understanding about these important events, my mother provided me with age-appropriate books about sex and puberty. The books said basically the same things and neglected to mention the possibility that some of us weren't like the others. The books also said we were all feeling the same things; it never occurred to me that they might be wrong. At puberty, I didn't even know what homosexuality was. Homosexuality and gay issues just weren't talked about or probably even thought about in the Midwest at that time. Gay rights was starting to make some progress nationally, but in the Midwest gay issues were not much in people's awareness at all.

Men sexually attracted to men didn't reach my consciousness as even a possibility until my late teen years when my older sister explained what homosexuality really meant. I do recall being intrigued by the possibility, though. Still, all my fantasies and minor attractions were forced to fit in a straight framework. I just assumed that of course I must be straight, probably weird or kinky, but still straight and I tried to live my life that way. I had to be straight: I loved women.

> "You don't understand me," said the duckling.
> —*The Ugly Duckling*, Hans Christian Andersen.[4]

All those years living in the fear of what I might be, suppressing it with overwhelming powers of denial, took a toll. My lack of self-esteem and self-confidence were profound and obvious. My lifelong struggle with depression probably started at least around the age of ten, around the time of my mother's second divorce and our subsequent move to Grand Rapids. Somewhere around the age of thirteen, I was exposed through literature to the concept of suicide as an answer to suffering. My first suicide attempt was at about that age. There were many more to follow. I often tried counseling and psychiatry to deal with my depression, but they didn't help much. The constant and recurring theme in my therapy was poor self-esteem and feelings of worthlessness. These were probably related to a deep sense of shame about feeling like a freak or aberration of nature and to my feelings of inferiority regarding my sexuality. I realize now that even pre-pubertal, I had a sense of what my preferences were. Even pre-pubertal children are exposed to sexual mores, and all during my pre-pubertal years it was assumed I'd marry a woman and probably have children. Internalized negative feelings related to my parents' divorce is probably also a secondary factor in my feelings of worthlessness.

My self-loathing was deep and long-lasting, but the reasons why hovered somewhat below my conscious awareness. The result of these feelings was almost always evident. The simple inability to even tolerate seeing my own face in a mirror demonstrates the degree of discomfort I felt.

David L. Kaufman, M.D.

In college, at MSU, in my psychology classes I was exposed to the work of Daryl Bem and others who showed that, contrary to what we usually think, our behavior shapes our values rather than the other way around. The innate power of denial enables us to deny things that can be blindingly obvious to others. How often have we known someone in a bad relationship and although it's readily apparent to us what's wrong, the person involved can't see it? I've been very reluctant to discuss my involvement with the Mormon Church with anyone over the years because I'm embarrassed to have to admit that I really thought I believed all their teachings.

At the time, I genuinely accepted everything they stood for. I insisted, repeatedly, "I know the church is true." I tried hard to convince nonbelievers (including members of my family) that it was true. I supported it wholeheartedly. Now, looking back, my acceptance of the Mormon Church is an example of how blind we can be to truths that affect us deeply. Tragically, there are international examples of groups of people denying the rights and feelings of others, believing they're justified in stealing, maiming, and killing. The Nazi movement in Germany, the country my ancestors are from, is a profound testimony to how warped people's beliefs can be, both individually and collectively.

While I was still living a straight life, from my strict homophobic milieu I gradually became more and more acclimated to a gay-friendly mind-set. Gradually I stopped finding homophobic humor funny, and I became more supportive of gay issues, even though I didn't know any openly gay men or women.

One evening, just as the sun set amid radiant clouds, there came a large flock of beautiful birds out of the bushes. The duckling had never seen any like them before. He knew not the names of these birds, nor where they had flown, but he felt towards them as he had never felt for any other bird in the world.

—*The Ugly Duckling*, Hans Christian Andersen.[5]

34

Part II
Revelation

Who/What am I?!?!?
—Personal journal entry 4/18/09

7

Heading West

Content to leave conservative values and cold weather behind, Cathy and I moved west after I had eight years of private practice in Michigan and Ohio. Initially, I found it quite a shock. Sonoma County is like another country entirely compared to conservative southwest lower Michigan. A Sonoma County conservative could be a liberal in southwestern Michigan! The cultures are totally different. There is a different accent and what people say can mean something else from what I thought it did. Even driving is different: pedestrians in California have the right of way over cars and they use it. In Michigan, only an idiot would step out in front of an oncoming car.

People and coworkers in Sonoma are much more likely to do things that Midwesterners would find risky. Every season people free-dive for abalone, even though several drown every year. Ask someone on crutches what happened and they're as likely to say they were hang-gliding, surfing, or base-jumping as they are to say they stepped wrong off a curb. In the Midwest, travel to Florida was a big deal. In northern California, West Coast mind-set, travel to Africa is not uncommon. At one point, hobbling around the hospital in a special shoe, I was repeatedly asked what happened and wanted to say I was hang-gliding off Goat Rock, but I felt compelled to admit I broke my toe tripping in the bathroom in the middle of the night after getting up to use the toilet.

The weather and scenery are nice in California, but the social–political climate is remarkable. There is so much diversity, so many different points of view, that no single vantage point is dominant. This means we all have to learn to get along. It doesn't mean everyone agrees about everything, just that differences can be accepted. This single point is worth repeating, *Differences can be accepted.*

The first few years living in Sonoma County went by with me feeling, well, like a Midwesterner living in northern California. Slowly, things began to change. At some point, I noticed that my Midwestern mind-set was gradually being replaced by a West Coast, Bay Area California way of looking at things. It had taken almost four years living there to learn to think for myself. Part of the Midwestern view not shared by Bay Area Californians is the whole conformity thing; at least in this part of California, few feel compelled to live according to someone else's values. No longer do I play by other people's rules.

8

Sick in Peru

Initially, our time spent in the Bay Area was largely uneventful. We learned to enjoy the great restaurants and fine wine. We explored the new area and all the amazing scenery.

Four years after moving west we had the chance to visit Peru through a friend of Cathy's who had lived there for much of her life. During this extraordinary vacation opportunity, an odd thing happened. In Cusco, Peru, walking from the tour van into a restaurant, I became light-headed and wobbly. My legs went limp but I didn't lose consciousness. Had it not been for the quick thinking and physical strength of one my tour-mates, I would have hit the floor. Medically, this is a condition generally referred to as orthostatic hypotension, or orthostasis.

Given that we humans originally were quadrupeds, but now walk upright, evolution had to devise a method for blood pressure to remain constant to critical organs, like the brain, between lying, sitting, and standing. The neurovascular response to standing is complex, and many things can render it ineffective. I had experienced dizziness on standing many times in the past and didn't think much of this one episode. Perhaps I was dehydrated; possibly the extreme altitude had something to do with it. I had found the altitude change from Lima, at sea level, to Cusco, at 11,000 feet, very difficult, and much worse than expected.

On returning home, the episodes of orthostasis were recurring, and gradually over the following several months became somewhat more frequent, and of greater intensity. I consulted a gifted cardiologist, and we tried every treatment he could think of: thigh-high maximum-strength compression stockings, tilt training maneuvers, standing up really slowly, and literally eating salt. I even stopped my high blood pressure medications, but still got no relief. Over time, I would have five to ten episodes of dizziness daily, and no matter what I did to prevent them, I would end up on the floor, somewhere, at least once a week. This could be any floor: at work in the hospital, at a local store, or in the meeting room for a medical conference. I quickly learned that people in public places get really freaked out when someone goes down like that. It often took a lot of reassurance on my part to prevent a call to paramedics.

I was at a loss to explain why this was suddenly happening to me, and there was no way I could find to stop these episodes. They were gradually increasing in severity, but I hadn't considered that it could be ominous.

I saw several physicians, mostly my internist and a cardiologist. It seemed that because the only symptom I'd had so far was blood-pressure related, cardiology studies was the direction to pursue. I actually saw the chief of cardiology, a brilliant and compassionate physician, but he was at a loss to explain what was wrong and had only limited success in dealing with my symptoms.

It would be a few months before I would be diagnosed and treated.

9

Transgenders

Several months after the onset of these symptoms, I was coincidently feeling more secure and less guilt about my sexuality, a little less guilt anyway. I knew I wasn't a typical straight man, I believed I was straight and maybe a "little" bisexual or just kinky. I had been struck by the homophobic notion that anyone born a man could never be an attractive-looking woman, no matter how many hormones or how much surgery he had. A man who believes he is a woman in a man's body and wishes to become a woman is called a transsexual or transgender. The term "tranny" is somewhat derogatory slang.

I had developed the habit of checking transgender Websites, ostensibly to prove my theory, when I came across an extraordinarily beautiful woman, shown initially on my small computer screen from about the belly button up. She was truly a very beautiful woman. Surely, I thought, she was born a woman, because there's no way a man could be made to look this gorgeous. I initially studied her face, looking for clues of a masculine origin, but there was no evidence of anything remotely manly about her face.

Scrolling down the image, to prove to myself she was born a woman, I encountered the full-on image of her male genitalia. My reaction was immediate and undeniable. There was no way I could deny what I felt; it was one of the most intensely positive sexual reactions I've ever felt from an image. I think I just about melted into the chair.

Just as immediate as my strong attraction was the realization of what it must mean. I was completely expecting to see women's genitalia, but when I saw men's instead I had a very positive response. Because my immediate reaction to the image was undeniable, it could mean only one thing: I realized, in an overwhelming way, that I really wanted a partner with a penis, not a vagina. And that must mean I'm gay. What?!?!?

I had passed off my craving for anal sex as the receiver as kinky, but not gay, even when sometimes the urge has been so strong at night that I couldn't sleep. And when I fantasized about servicing multiple men, wondering if I should follow up on it, somehow the urge faded and my worries faded as well. I can't be gay: I'm drawn to women. In public settings, I seek out women, not men. I'm not attracted to men, I've never been attracted to men. I can't possibly be gay.

In the very repressive culture I grew up in, it was simply unthinkable to be something so abhorrent, so obviously wrong, so against nature and "God's will." Any of my feelings of masculine attraction were always carefully recast by me in terms of what a straight man might occasionally feel. I got used to doing this early until the habit became deeply ingrained. Any of my direct sexual interest in men was so carefully and thoroughly suppressed that it took months after my awakening to begin to be able to even fully realize it. Since my epiphany on seeing that beautiful transgender on my computer, there is no way I could ever again really believe that I'm not attracted to men.

Yet, months after my awakening, I could still sense those walls, still have my guard up. "Don't be attracted to men, it's wrong" runs so deep through me I wonder if I'll ever completely get over it. Some of my gay friends don't seem bothered by these thoughts, but I suspect some gays are still troubled by thinking how wrong these feelings, and, therefore, they themselves must be.

When I can let my guard down, which sometimes requires conscious effort, I'm amazed at how attracted to men I can be. Like the powerful attraction to the transgender woman, it can be overwhelming, greater than any attraction to women I've managed to feel over the years.

In my pre-awakened life, the desire for sex with a male partner became stronger, but the denial and lies still held. I told myself I didn't want sex with an actual man, I just wanted "rectal stimulation." I didn't fantasize about any particular man, just a generic faceless man. A straight man could feel those things, right? I'm still only attracted to women, never men. Right? More denial. My fantasies were carefully concocted to include women and the possibility of straight sex. In my mind, though, that never happened. I had many dreams of gay sex or, at least, receiving anal sex. I haven't had dreams of straight sex in years. It was always gay sex, every time. Again, though, I'm just kinky, I'm not gay. Right?

A few years back, I read some talk of a "G" spot for men. Of course there is, I thought immediately, I know exactly where it is. Around the time of puberty, around the time I discovered my penis, I also sexually discovered my anus. Yet after all the anal play over the years, and all my fantasies about it, were carefully recast by me in the context of straight man with unusual desires. Straight men can enjoy anal stimulation. So I'm not gay.

So, when I first saw that transgender's image in its entirety, I was absolutely stunned. I walked around in a fog for twenty-four hours, hardly speaking to anyone. I'm gay!? That's ridiculous. Is this even possible? If so, how could I not know? How can this be? I'm 49½ years old. How could I get to half a century and not know something so basic, so fundamental about myself? Could I be, is it possible, might I actually be really gay? Really?

The following day after I had found that transgender's image, I found the exact same photo again and repeated the experience exactly, with exactly the same result: an overwhelming draw when I got to her lower body, more attraction than I could remember ever feeling for any picture of a naked woman. Then I *am* gay?!?

If I was straight, on seeing the rest of the image, I would have been disappointed. Had I seen female genitalia, it could also mean she was born a man, but had also had gender reassignment surgery. Some time later, I sheepishly realized that there are many gorgeous transsexuals, I just don't know who they are, I don't recognize them, so I only notice the unattractive ones.

Also much later, I realized I was blurring the distinction between transsexual/transgender individuals who actually want to look like women and gay men in drag who may be trying to look like women, but in a gaudy, tacky, way-over-the-top outrageous way that would not likely leave them mistaken for an actual woman. I now know men who do drag who've actually grown beards just to be more outrageous. Drag is about entertainment, not identity.

If I was somewhere in the vicinity of bisexual, my reaction would have been positive, but not more so than seeing a naked woman. I wouldn't have been surprised and would have had no strong feelings one way or the other. Clearly, the reaction I had was potentially troublesome; at the very least it meant I was wrong about transgenders. My reaction had resulted in so many ramifications that it didn't occur to me until much later that it destroyed my sick homophobic belief. I was really attracted to a penis; this can only mean I must actually be gay! Previous to this epiphany, I had realized on some level that I like penises, but I assumed it was because I had one! It was my learning to want what I have rather than have what I want.

I also realized much later that just because I realized I was gay didn't mean I had lost all my homophobia and tendency to stereotype; actually, unconscious ideas about what gay is are pervasive. Just because someone's gay doesn't mean they're completely open-minded about the whole thing. There are, for example, many gay men and lesbians who are, on some level, suspicious of the whole idea of transgender; that is, I can be gay, but you can't possibly be a woman in a man's body. Somehow that just seems too weird even for some gays to believe. A small percentage of gay men like to do drag, yet another percentage of gay men don't get that at all, don't understand why anyone would want to, and are a little suspicious of that whole thing. Straight-acting gay men can be put off by effeminate gays and vice versa.

It occurred to me much later also that I was probably looking at transsexuals because I liked looking at naked men's genitalia but I could only accept it on women's bodies. It's "safer" and "less gay" to look at transsexuals than to look at men; looking at men would be too obvious. I've come to believe that this entire experience with the transgender image was crafted by my unconscious to lead me toward men without scaring me or invoking my filtering mechanisms. I'd seen pictures of naked men before; they're often included with pictures of naked women (I've actually heard that some straight men won't accept porn that shows any depiction of male anatomy). But I can't recall ever before being consciously aware that I was strongly attracted to male anatomy. I can see now in retrospect that I have been all along. I'm sure my subconscious walls would never have let that through. I needed a safer, sanitized way to realize it and accept it openly. My ability to unknowingly filter out any interest in men or men's body parts would have blocked me, had already many, many times blocked me, from accepting my interest in men. This was my subconscious way to gently lead me to male anatomy, bypassing my filters, see just the penis and scrotum, and then truly know I found them insanely attractive. Wow, I actually am gay!!

The suggestion that being gay represents an actual choice occurs to me. The most obvious rebuttal to that preposterous idea is that no one in their right mind would choose to be a member of a minority group that's discriminated against and often despised. No one would willfully choose to be hated. With everything I've gone through in my life up to this point, through this transition and the aftermath, wouldn't it have been so incredibly easier to not choose this? I tried to be straight for thirty-five years after puberty; if it were a choice I think I would have succeeded in making myself straight. I tried too hard for too long to be straight and I failed. What I've gone through isn't all that unique; I think many gay men have had or still have a similar struggle. It's insane to think we'd do this on purpose. What I do with this knowledge is, of course, a choice. I could choose to continue to try to be straight, to consciously continue the deception that up to now had been unconscious. Given how much I had suffered up to this point while unconsciously trying to be straight, I couldn't consider trying it any longer. By the time I finally thought I was gay, I was pretty much incapable of straight sex; my body just wouldn't cooperate. It's also grown harder to fight the aspects of gay culture I see in me. I really am not competitive; I can't make myself like professional sports or even games of any sort. I've gradually, over decades, been coming closer and closer to just being overtly gay. Now I can be attracted to men, openly and with acceptance. I no longer feel compelled by the dictates of society as to what a man should be or be like. I can be who I really am, finally. It's such a relief!

10

Conversation with Cathy

After a twenty-four-hour period of self-imposed silence after viewing the beautiful transgender's image, I returned to somewhat more-normal interactions. But I started thinking more about events from my past, and the pieces of the puzzle began to fit together, and over time, with dramatic clarity; it was astonishing to me that I had not seen this before.

The harder and closer I looked at myself, the more obvious my sexual orientation was. It took me some time to even begin to understand how I could have not been aware of this. In part, I think I needed to have reached a safe place in my mind not only for me to come out to others, but even to come out to myself. It would have been hard for me to accept this had the epiphany happened even a few years earlier. Yet now, my West Coast friends and coworkers are so accepting of my being gay that I think it's hard for them to understand what a big deal this was to me.

A year or two before we moved out west, I had spent a few days contemplating the idea that I could be gay. I thought about what would happen if I was gay, the consequences with my family, my friends, my career, and my marriage. Overall, my career wouldn't have been that big a deal, but the main consequence was to my marriage. I couldn't see how I could be gay and stay married to Cathy. I came to the conclusion, at that time, that I couldn't possibly be gay because I was obviously attracted to women. Once again, I believed I was straight but kinky. I now realize my attraction to women is as companions, not lovers.

As time passed over the next few weeks, I began to really think about what should come next, what did I want to happen, what did I need to happen.

I began to realize that I really needed to pursue this. This wasn't just some passing thought or quaint realization; this fundamentally changes who I am and how I need to live my life. It was obvious that I needed to live gay, because just realizing I'm gay was incredibly liberating. I knew even then that pretending to be straight sexually would be next to impossible. I was getting to the point of realizing I needed to be free of the marital commitment of fidelity because, after all my false starts and serious longings, this time I felt I had to actually follow through. This wasn't going away; every morning I wake up, I'm still attracted to men. But this was a really big thing for my marriage; after more than twenty years together, I was actually thinking our marriage may have to end. I couldn't see it any other way. All the fine details had not occurred to me, just the idea that I needed to be sexually free. I was only beginning to understand the ramifications beyond my sexuality.

One day about two or three weeks after my awakening, Cathy and I were helping make wine with a group of people at a private winery. On our way home Cathy suggested we get something to eat and said that she wanted to talk to me. We settled on a brewpub that served food. In the hectic noisy atmosphere of the boisterous restaurant we sat at a small table for two and ate in relative silence. Finally, she said she had something she knew she needed to say, but wasn't sure she should. She was concerned that I'd be angry. She looked upset. I could see the tension on her face. She was biting her lip. She knew she was going to be dropping a bomb. For some reason, although I knew something big was up, I wasn't really all that worried. Maybe because she had been so hard to live with the last few weeks, I was expecting that she would tell me something that would somehow resolve that. I remember feeling very calm about whatever it was she wanted to talk about. I guess I didn't really expect anything *that* big.

Tentatively, carefully, she said, "I'm really sorry, but over the last several weeks I've come to realize that I'm a lesbian and I know that I need to pursue it."

"I'm sorry about what this means to our marriage," she continued when I interrupted her.

"What? You're a lesbian? No way! Get out!" I was dumbfounded.

I blurted out, "I've just realized I'm gay and I really need to pursue it!!"

We looked at each other, now both of us suddenly and totally astonished.

"What?" we both said together.

"I'm a lesbian," she said.

"I'm gay." I said.

I think at that point we both said, "Wow!" simultaneously.

Her face brightened considerably and we both smiled.

We each repeated that we each knew we were gay and that we both really felt the need to live our newfound identity. Strangely enough, we had both, simultaneously and independently, within several weeks of each other, realized we were gay.

We discussed how we both came to this realization. I mentioned the transsexual picture experience and she said she had been developing feelings for a lesbian she works with. She had been talking to Judith, the woman, for several weeks about lesbianism, but had not specifically told Judith that she had feelings for her.

We talked about how we both realized now that we each had fantasies involving gay sex for some time without realizing the significance. We asked each other if either of us had any inkling what was going on with the other and we didn't. She was totally surprised by my declaring I was gay and I was totally surprised by her saying she was a lesbian. We discussed, in rather vague terms, what we thought would happen to our marriage in a practical sense. At some point one of us would move out, but we expected that we would be on good terms with each other. We would sell the big house when the market was conducive to recovering what we had put into it. Although we had both loved the house immensely when we first bought it, neither of us was particularly attached to the house at this point. We both now felt it was more than we needed and a lot of work and cost to maintain. We've both found that the whole "gay thing" has made each of us more focused on the people in our lives and less on material possessions.

Because I make more money as a full-time physician than Cathy makes part time as an artist, I would help her financially. It never crossed my mind to not want to help her; she is my best friend, and what was happening with our marriage was nobody's fault. I knew she would do the same if the situation were reversed. It's important to emphasize that there was never any hostility or anger between us, no tears or hurt feelings. Neither of us ever did anything to hurt the other. We didn't create this situation, it just happened. After this first conversation there was no reason to love each other any less than before, and we loved each other very much.

The sexual side of our relationship had really faltered over recent years, but we've always been strong friends, we've always loved and respected each other. We've always tried to take care of each other. Other than sexually, we had a really good marriage. There were no affairs, straight or gay. Cathy didn't even tell Judith she had feelings for her until after she told me. Although I had had an overwhelming number of fantasies, I had no experience with sex with men, I never cheated on Cathy with a woman or a man. Our conversation was marked by upbeat and positive emotions. I think the single emotion we both felt the strongest was relief. We knew that we could be free to pursue our new lives and interests without hard feelings. Not only is it now okay for me to pursue this major life change, but my partner is going through the same thing and we can do this together.

I have to admit that, in retrospect, knowing Cathy is a lesbian makes some sense. In our twenty-two years together, she had never once commented that a particular guy was attractive.

I attributed this to her superior manners and judgment, but now there was an alternative, and more pragmatic, explanation. But later she told me that even as a lesbian she doesn't scope out other women, so maybe it is superior manners after all. I sense that one of the differences between us, possibly relating to our gender difference, is that she doesn't think about sex that much. Sex is important to her, but she doesn't really think about it. Although I had many experiences that in retrospect showed my attraction to men, she found little evidence in her past for lesbian thoughts or feelings.

I had noticed that she had become more difficult to live with lately. Although I hadn't really come up with any explanation for her negativity, the thought of latent homosexuality wasn't on my list of potential reasons. Now I realized she had obviously been difficult to live with because of what she was going through and she was worrying about the ramifications, just as I had been experiencing a growing uneasiness regarding what the consequences of my pursuing a gay lifestyle would involve for Cathy and the rest of my family.

A few days later, when we had not discussed this topic at all since our first conversation, I was worried I was remembering it wrong. I was sure Cathy had said she was a lesbian and that she wanted to pursue it, but I had felt so much relief that I didn't recall some of the conversation.

I decided to bring the subject up. "So," I started out, "you're still thinking maybe you're a lesbian?"

"No," she said, "I'm *sure* I'm a lesbian. As I told you earlier, I've been feeling this way for some time and I even have someone in mind I'm interested in. I'm interested in Judith, from work."

"Oh!" I said. That's pretty conclusive. Whew! I felt relief all over again. She really is gay. "That's cool," I replied.

We discussed more details and began sketching out what we anticipated would change in our lives; separation, separate living arrangements, possibly divorce, who would have Andrew primarily.

There were many more conversations to come, of course,

and all were amicable. I sometimes wonder if any other married couple that has split up has gone through the entire process without ever fighting, being angry, or ever feeling hurt by the other. We approached the whole process joyfully, both of us very excited at the prospect of being able to pursue our incredible new identities and still remain fast friends.

Before our pivotal conversation, our marriage was in serious trouble. Our sex life had deteriorated greatly, going from pretty damn good many years ago to miserable; I was now trying very hard to avoid sex, and I, in retrospect, think she did, too. I went to bed earlier than she did, but would lay in bed reading. When I heard her coming up the steps, I quickly shut off the light, put the book down, and pretended to be asleep, saying over and over in my head, "Please don't want sex, please don't want sex, please don't want sex." I feel horribly guilty about it now, but I realize that she probably didn't want sex with me, either.

Our relationship on the surface had declined significantly, particularly recently. It seemed we were angry with each other constantly and we bickered openly quite often. I hadn't really thought about it beyond the idea that Cathy was becoming more and more difficult to live with. It never occurred to me that there was something deeper going on. Her small irritations probably had larger significance. One day she had asked me to help with the laundry (I've since learned what a big thing it is, to keep up with laundry). She wanted me to put her clean clothes from the washer into the dryer. Dutifully, I hauled them all out of the washer, pushed them in the dryer and hit the "casual" button.

After they were dry, Cathy pulled them out and found the $300 cashmere sweater that now might fit a petite toddler or possibly a miniature poodle.

"You can't just put stuff in the dryer!" she said, furious.

"You have to read the care tags to know how to handle each piece!" she said, angrily, showing me the little care tags on a few sweaters.

"Okay, okay, I'm really sorry," I apologized. I really was

sorry for the damage I'd caused and resolved to be more careful.

A few days later she again asked for help. Pulling a pair of dark slacks out of the washer I noticed the tag said dry clean only. I hung the wet pants up, not sure what to do next. Cathy walked past, noticed the pants, and asked what happened.

"They say dry clean only on the care tag," I explained

"What! You can't read the care tags, you just have to know how to take care of these things."

"So you don't want me to read the care tags?" I stammered, at this point totally confused.

"No, you have to ignore them," she said, really angrily.

Now I was getting angry. "Okay," I said, "That's it!" I resolved this would never happen again.

"From now on, I do my laundry and you do yours. I can't help with this if you can't decide what I'm supposed to do."

And so we had done our laundry separately ever since. Actually, this practice later served me well. After my coming out and transformation, I began wearing much fancier shirts that needed careful laundering and ironing. I'm pretty sure Cathy wouldn't have been willing to do that. She had said on many occasions, "I don't do ironing; if it needs ironing after washing, I'm not wearing it."

In hindsight, there was good evidence that we were both gay, but we had both unconsciously overlooked it. One of the most glaring pieces of evidence for both of us was our fantasies, where our true sexuality had subconsciously been revealing itself for some time.

I have pondered at length the idea that I was able to keep my feelings to myself for so long. Apparently, the human capacity for self-deception, or at least mine, is nearly boundless. But then I began to think of how other people deceive themselves, which was particularly gratifying because it involved other people's self-deception, not mine. Religious cults are full of people who deceive themselves that it all makes sense. My experience with the Mormon Church was like this.

Hitting close to home, I think many people who go along

with prejudice against any group are often deceiving themselves that it's okay in order to fit in with the group that's perpetuating the bias. At an extreme level, when whole groups of people participate in genocide, I think there is self-deception in their believing it was acceptable.

A very powerful concept I learned from social psychology classes in college is that people's beliefs are very malleable. We want to think that our beliefs are fixed and unchangeable, evidence of our superior intellect and moral competency. Unfortunately, the reality is much more prosaic. A multitude of psychology research supports the idea that people's ideas can be easily manipulated by a qualified person. This is the basis for brainwashing. Scary as this fact is, it makes me feel a little better about how I could have deceived myself for so long about something so important.

Comforting also are stories of other men who didn't realize they were gay until well into adulthood. Most of the gay men I've talked to about this knew they were gay at puberty, but a significant percentage did not. There are many gay men with ex-wives (or wives) and children. There is so much societal pressure to be straight that we all try to believe it to the very end.[6]

> I wasn't gay until 1983. I was thoroughly convinced that I wasn't a homosexual. I couldn't be a person like that. People wonder how I could have convinced myself of that, but from an early age it was a matter of building certain walls within my mind. Not only had the church told me about sin—and I assumed that anything like this was sinful—but I picked it up from my peers. A homosexual was less than a man. And a homosexual was something I was sure I wasn't, thank God!
>
> Somehow, over the years, I just did what was required of me as far as my emotions and sexual needs were concerned and, at the same time, I did what was required of me by my principles and the

church. There was no way I could reconcile it.
—*Robert Bauman, former U.S. representative*
from Maryland, 1st district

I know one gay man who just always knew he was gay. All the others I know went through some kind of coming-out-to-themselves process at some point in their life. Many did so at puberty when it became obvious to them that their interests were different from other boys'. Some didn't realize they were gay until later in life. The latter group includes men who are somewhat comfortable in romantic and sexual situations with women. The guys who knew they were gay right away at puberty were never comfortable with the idea of sex with a woman and were forced to acknowledge their preferences earlier.

In subsequent conversations with Cathy we often discussed how similar our experiences were. It's remarkable that not only did we go through this process together and at the same time, but that our thoughts and fantasies were so strikingly similar.

One afternoon, months after our initial conversations, Cathy brought up the idea of threesomes; I don't think she was suggesting we actually try it, but more as a general discussion. I offered that I had heard that, in reality, threesomes often don't work out very well; someone ends up feeling left out or hurt.

She said she had often had fantasies of a threesome with me. She'd invite a willing woman over for sex among the three of us, but admitted that in the fantasy, the sex ended up being between only her and the other woman.

Amazed again by how similar our experiences were, I recounted my version of threesome fantasies. Instinctively knowing I would like it, Cathy would invite a man over for sex with the two of us. In my fantasy, he would barely make it in the front door, whereupon I ripped his clothes and he and we would do it right there on the tile foyer floor.

Just this fantasy alone should have shown me I was gay, but as always, I suppressed that idea. Another threesome fantasy I often entertained was that of a young couple of childbearing age. It would seem that the man's sperm count was low and he and his wife thought that if they brought another man in for sex with them, when she inevitably got pregnant, they could pretend it was the husband's child. This fantasy also played on my virility and conveniently ignores the fact that I had a vasectomy years ago.

As the fantasy unfolded, though, it was always me and the guy, while his wife, wearing a sheer, lime-green top and a short black miniskirt without panties, watches with a bemused expression on her face (my fantasies can be very detailed!). But because there was a woman in the fantasy, I was always able to convince myself I was straight. Only after my epiphany did I recall that this fantasy included me performing oral sex on the man. I had, prior to that recollection, no idea that I fantasized about oral sex that way.

Amazingly, Cathy and I had both come to the same profound recognition about ourselves within a few weeks of each other, and without talking about it with each other. Our initial realizations were only the beginning of the process of understanding and accepting who we really are. The real work had just begun. Over the ensuing months, we both found that the reality is a little bleaker than our initial optimism would've suggested.

11

The Two of Us

We had been a fairly typical married couple; we owned a nice middle-class house in a good middle-class neighborhood and had a time-share at Disney World. We had a cat and a dog; we went to church (a very liberal Unitarian Universalist church, but church nonetheless). I was a respected physician in a local group practice; Cathy was involved with many charities and helped raise money for many worthwhile causes. We dressed like everyone else, ate what everyone else ate, and drove nondescript late-model cars.

Possibly in contrast to other couples, however, our relationship started off really more as a close friendship than raw blinding lust. We did have a really good sex life, at least at the beginning of our marriage, but that wasn't really what brought us together. When we both worked in the dark microforms area of the college library, we had a lot of great and deep conversations. She had become my best friend before we were romantically involved.

In what is probably a testimony to our maturity and commitment, we have survived as close friends despite having different personalities and having relatively little in common superficially. One of the consequences of our realizations is that now Cathy and I actually have something significant in common. We have many things we can talk about together. Previously, since our son was born, he was the one main thing we had in common. We also, by this time, had a significant shared history in common. I learned from my experience with Cathy that two people can truly love each other despite their differences.

In the turbulent aftermath of our first pivotal discussion, one fact clearly stood out; during the last twenty-two years, whatever our differences (and they weren't insignificant), we had learned to love each other very much. We now functioned as very good friends (without benefits, of course), a much better, much more mutually supportive relationship than we ever had when we were trying to be a married couple. We realized there was no appropriate label for our relationship. Husband and wife? Yes, technically, but that relationship generally involves sexual activity and we both adamantly wouldn't go there. Good friends? Well, not all that many friendships last this long, and, more importantly, most friends don't know each other as well as we know each other. I'm pretty sure that nobody on the planet knows me as well as Cathy knows me. Her intimate knowledge of me and who I am shows when I need romantic advice. Hers is always spot on.

Also, during our time as a married couple we've, naturally, had much more intimate knowledge of each other than friends typically have. We've seen each naked many, many times; we've had (but don't generally now) many conversations with one of us on the toilet; we know how each other sleeps, eats, poops, and vomits. I watched, and kind of helped, her deliver a baby (although she remembers me as being somewhat inattentive having been distracted by conversation with the ob-gyn resident).

Long-term living with a sexual partner is about as intimate as two people can be, short of somehow actually being inside of each other's head. Part of the struggle with a marriage is that the profoundly intimate knowledge of each after twenty years can result in either really knowing, loving, and respecting each other, or potentially despising each other. Long-term romantic relationships are about mutual trust, a great deal of compromise, and a good amount of give and take, mostly give.

Although Cathy and I have some differences in personality, and are interested in different types of things, we have done many things together. We have learned to respect our differences and respect each other a great deal. We have turned the differences in our temperaments into strengths; Cathy can outwardly be very strong in a way that's very difficult for me. This is a great benefit to our friendship.

So how else could our new relationship be described? We started off referring to ourselves as gay buddies, but the problems with that are it doesn't say much about the level of our friendship, and we may not want to discuss our gayness with some people.

When all this first transpired, we had several conversations about the fundamental aspects of our situation. We reaffirmed that we were gay and needed to pursue it. But later on as I began to feel how much pain the situation was inflicting on us as we struggled with heartbreak and failed relationships, there were times I wished it could all be undone. Of course, there was no way that was possible. Cathy and I both knew that when we accepted our new future, there would be pain. It became a sort of mantra. When things got difficult, we'd remind each other, "There will be pain."

We have always supported each other in this process. We both know that the other is there for us if needed. We've also found lighthearted ways of supporting each other. One day soon after our first conversation, Cathy said she was going to the bookstore to look for lesbian-interest material and asked if I wanted anything. Sure, I responded, find me something about gays. She returned with a copy of *The New Complete Joy of Gay Sex*. I got my first gay book from my wife!

Our lives up to that point had been so mundane by comparison, so ordinary and straight-married-couple typical, that we knew we were in for the ride of our lives. Our lives went from a boring kiddies merry-go-round to a giant upside-down roller coaster. We knew going in that it would be something like that. I recall both of us looking forward with anticipation to the excitement. At that time, we didn't realize how down the low parts would be and what it's like to cry so frequently. I actually remember a few years back thinking I hadn't cried about anything in years and wondering if I still could. Then, during one meltdown after my epiphany, I cried so hard for two hours that I became nauseous and dehydrated and had to drink extra water!

12

Immediate Reactions

Each of our immediate reactions to our personal revelations were very intense and largely positive. We both felt huge relief that we could pursue our newfound identities without inflicting additional pain on each other. We both also felt relief at having an out for the marriage. Gay or not, we had both known that our marriage was in bad shape. I doubt it would have been possible for one spouse to come out while the other is maintaining they're straight without inflicting a lot of hard feelings. The straight partner must inevitably feel betrayed by the gay partner. We were both immensely relieved that we could pursue our new lives without overtly hurting the other. I think we were also relieved to not have to pretend we wanted sex with each other anymore.

> Love for Cathy is due to lack of anger that covered
> my lack of interest in sex...
> —*Personal journal entry 8/17/09*

I realized a few weeks after our revelations that I had always been angry with Cathy. I was angry about different vague things, perceived slights, miscommunications, but always angry. Anger is a powerful emotion, one that can be stronger than the sex drive. If I was angry with her, I had an excuse not to have sex. If I love her (which I otherwise do), if I find her attractive (which I do), and I'm straight (oops), than I would want to have sex with her. Only after coming out to each other did my anger fade. The tragedy is that, only after all this anger dissipated could I fully appreciate how cool she is and how much I really love her.

It wasn't until much later that I understood the real reason I didn't want to have sex with Cathy. I thought my body didn't function right, that it was broken. But I later realized my body wasn't broken, it just doesn't function the same as a straight man's. I couldn't make my body do what a straight man's body ought to do. Now I understand, to my tremendous relief, that my body's perfectly normal and actually functions very well; it just wants sex with men.

I was constantly angry at Cathy pre-revelation because that was the only way to justify my lack of interest in sex. Post-revelation I know why and that leaves me free to feel about her the way I really feel.
—*Personal journal entry 8/16/09*

Long before I was ready to talk about my epiphany with people in general, especially straight people, I needed to talk about it with gay friends. I particularly needed to talk about it with Robert, who was a peer and a gay man, another one of the radiologists in my group. I had already been assigned as his official mentor, to help him acclimate to our practice and the Kaiser organization as a whole. Kaiser Permanente is an all-inclusive health care provider that incorporates hospitals, nurses, doctors, support staff, and equipment. Kaiser exists mostly in the western United States. Doctors at Kaiser are paid a salary to take care of a fixed number of patients and don't get paid for doing extra procedures, so, for example, there's no incentive to perform any surgery other than when the patient needs it. The mentoring process was instituted to help new physicians, particularly those who came from private practice, get used to the different environment and culture of Kaiser. The decision to mentor Robert was made because we seemed to hit it off right away after he joined us and we both have backgrounds in invasive radiology procedures. Robert has proven extraordinarily helpful in my process as a newly realized gay man. He has been my unofficial gay mentor. A few days after my first gay conversation with Cathy, I told him we needed to talk and we set up a dinner meeting at a local restaurant. Prior to my conversation with Robert, I had told no one else. I poured my heart out to him, told him I knew I was gay and how I felt. I didn't initially tell him about Cathy because she had asked me not to tell anyone about her yet. Robert's reaction was tempered, in keeping with his generally unflappable personality. Basically, what he said was "Take it easy, being gay's not the end of the world. You just need to take it slow and figure out where you really are with all this."

During the next few months, I only spoke to Cathy and Robert about it and Cathy only spoke to me and Judith, Cathy's coworker and the woman she had feelings for. We weren't even close to being ready to discuss it with any others. Gradually, though, there was a growing feeling of pressure to experience this. It affected me more slowly than Cathy because I was busy dealing with my neurologic problems. From my point of view, there was enormous relief at realizing that my gay sexual desires could be acknowledged. This relief was profound and talking to Cathy and Robert about it made it more real, more plausible. Particularly, talking to Robert made it seem normal; how could I tell him I thought it was crazy and wrong when he's gay, too? Talking to Cathy also gave a strong sense of camaraderie that bolstered my willingness to accept this as real and normal. Having been my life partner for so long, Cathy's support is very meaningful.

After my medical issues and coming out, I felt an intense interest in sex and romance with teenage enthusiasm and impatience. Cathy had beaten me to this, because I had been preoccupied with my illness. She was concerned about my illness, but realized that whatever happened to me, she still needed to get her life together. She asked me pointedly, and frequently, if I minded her dating while I was going through my illness. First of all, I didn't feel I had the right to tell her no, and secondly, I was getting some vicarious benefit from all of her exploits. If I was really that sick, there wasn't much point in initiating life as a gay man. I doubt a fifty-year-old newly realized gay crippled dying man is all that attractive as a romantic partner! It probably would have been pretty hard to find dates.

I was cautioned, over and over again, by Robert and the few other gay men I knew, to take it easy; that it will all fall into place. I was told that I was so new to this that I wouldn't realistically make a good partner for a man with an established gay history.

Robert cautioned me that I needed to find someone age-appropriate, with roughly similar careers. A large financial asymmetry would be problematic. I moaned that this would never happen; those guys are already coupled. He suggested that this would be hard, but not impossible. I chose to ignore that advice. Later on I would learn he was right: I did need someone fairly similar to me.

13

Initial Coming Out

Cathy and I both realized early after our initial discussion that we'd need to come out to a few people relatively soon.

I came out to my friend Robert a few days after my conversation with Cathy. This was far in advance of talking to anyone else, including other gay coworkers. After coming out to Cathy, it now seemed more real to me and this convinced me to discuss it with a gay friend and Robert was the natural choice. Since that time, Robert has been my main support, a parental figure of sorts.

> I'm in the middle of a shit storm (from a conversation with my mentor Robert).
> —*Personal journal entry 5/21/09*

Coming out to Robert was extremely beneficial to me in a direct way and necessary for my sanity. I didn't really come out to any other gay friends until I was ready to come out totally. From the beginning of the conversations with Robert it became apparent I could ask him anything. No sexual question was too explicit, no emotional issue was taboo. Do I need a condom for oral sex? Are the more-effeminate gays usually "bottoms"?

Eventually, after my medical issues, I started coming out to people around me, gay and straight. I didn't come out to my hair guy until later. (Later I was told that, because I'm gay, I should just call him my stylist!) He was sincerely the first openly gay man that I ever really had real conversations with. A close female friend had convinced me to have my hair colored to cover the gray. Amazingly effective, it took years off my apparent age. It also meant I'd spend about two hours with my stylist every six weeks. Although it seems bizarre now to realize I ever thought this way, I was totally caught off guard by how much a regular guy he is. He has a partner, with basically the same relationship issues married straight people have. They have an adopted son, and experience the same parental issues straight people with kids have. In short, he's a regular guy. Except he's gay.

I'm not sure I could have made my realization without knowing my stylist. I just had no understanding of what gay really was before I knew him. My limited contact with a few gays in one job in college didn't really help. I think it was too early in my life for me to face it all then. But after knowing my stylist for a while, I realized that gays are just like straight people! There may be additional issues gays face, like the fact that they have to move to Sonoma County so they could legally adopt a child, but gays are still just people facing the same emotional issues in relationships as straight people.

In coming out to people, I noticed general patterns of response. Gays and lesbians I had already known all had the same reaction:

"Congratulations!" they all said pretty much unanimously.

Straight women were almost universally very supportive. Some of my female coworkers can now allow themselves to be closer to me, as a friend, because they know I'm not a threat. I won't hit on them, fall in love with them, or grab some body part. I find this very rewarding because I've always been drawn to women for companionship.

The reaction from straight men has been mixed. I believe that relates to the extraordinary restrictions placed on men in our society to act a certain way, within certain constraints, even to think within certain constraints. I'm convinced that many, if not most, straight men would not even allow themselves to think about it if they felt attracted to another man. I didn't, and I always thought that I'm pretty open-minded and self-aware.

Some straight men seem genuinely accepting, but that doesn't mean they could handle seeing two men kissing,[7] or probably even holding hands. Other people have varying levels of discomfort, even though most will still say they're okay with my being gay. So far, no friend, family member, or coworker has said straight out that they don't like it. One coworker actually had the guts to admit he still wanted to be my friend, but was uncomfortable with the whole gay thing. That level of honesty has to be respected. The frequent response by straight men who aren't all that comfortable with it was, "Are you sure?" It became a sort of litmus test for acceptance. Anyone who said that, I needed to be careful around because they probably weren't all that comfortable with the idea.

Another comment that can come up with straight men with little experience with gays is the question, "Which one of you is the woman in bed?" The truth is that neither one of us is a woman in bed; if we wanted one of us to be a woman we'd be straight. Gay sex is, in part, a celebration of male sexuality.

So straight guys would ask, "Are you sure?" Really? If I said I was a Democrat would you say that? If I said I was a man would you say that? Why in hell would I make this up? Oh, sure, like I'd opt to be a member of a minority group where I can be murdered just for being who I am. And I'd really like to be in a group that can't get married because it's illegal. Yeah, I like being sneered at and made fun of. Doesn't everyone want to be gay? Why in hell would I say this if I wasn't sure? To come out in general, I waited five months with constant reflection and introspection as well as conversation with my mentor Robert. This is a pretty big deal, not something to be taken lightly. "I'm thinking about buying a motorcycle," is the sort of comment that, "Are you sure?" could be appropriate for. Why would I say it if I wasn't sure? That's like what parents say when their daughter says she's pregnant, "Are you sure?"

During the initial time of my coming out, I felt a strong desire not only to have a boyfriend, but also specifically to have sex, to hook up. I probably felt this for a number of reasons. Prior to my realization, my libido was so poor I was considering asking my primary care doctor to look into it, order some labs or something. Both Cathy and I have found that realizing we're gay supercharged our interest in sex; even our interest in life. We became like teenagers again, eagerly taking in everything new, eager to experience more new things. The wonder at finding our sexuality suddenly more fulfilling than we ever dreamed possible gave both of us tremendous energy. We approached our sexuality and life itself with newfound vigor. We both suddenly found sex, or at least just the idea of it, incredibly powerful; being with the gender our brains were wired for is extraordinarily powerful after a lifetime of misunderstanding. We both found our initial experiences with kissing and tentative sex with same-sex partners very, very powerful.

Cathy was the first to kiss a same-sex date romantically. I asked her how it went and she said it was great. I walked out of the house, got in my car to go to work, and was crying before I left the driveway.

Really in the middle of a shit storm.
—*Personal journal entry 7/17/09*

I realized that I wasn't jealous that my wife was kissing someone else, but jealous that my gay buddy was ahead of me. I felt left out. I pushed Robert to help me with this. He managed to find a friend of a friend who was willing to kiss me. That first kiss, the feeling of his mouth full on mine, his beard stubble scratching my face, was so powerful, so intoxicating, I got weak in the knees and had to sit down. Another kiss, with tongue, was even more powerful; this was way more exciting than pretty much any attempt I had ever made toward passionate kissing. I asked if we could do more. Cathy had only kissed a woman; they had done nothing more. But my impromptu date/ sex partner agreed and unzipped my pants and then his. We briefly exchanged favors. I found both giving and receiving normal, natural, and thoroughly erotic. This was my first sexual experience with a man and it was incredible. After having been told by my culture and my peers that giving sexual gratification to a man was wrong, well, I did it and it felt wonderful, totally normal and natural, totally acceptable. It felt like giving sexual gratification to a woman, only better. I had not had any sexual contact with a man until this point.

If I had experienced sex with a man sooner, I think I would have realized that there wasn't anything weird about it and how much better it was for me than straight sex. In most of the stories I've heard of men not figuring out they were gay until adulthood, they had had some sexual experience with guys earlier. I had no prior experience and just assumed automatically that it would feel weird and that I wouldn't like it. I was wrong.

I was in a very unusual giddy mood that afternoon. I was willing to cast all careful reasoning aside, to completely ignore any suggestion that I take it easy and wait for things to develop naturally. I would not normally get involved in any way with someone who is already spoken for. I have strong feelings about monogamy and normally respect that with others. I just felt such wild abandon that I had to experience everything I could no matter what the consequences. I felt in every proverbial fiber of my being the need to reach out, to go beyond, to try something new.

I've thought about this experience a lot since then. It was, in real terms, a very brief encounter, but it had profound impact on my life. I learned that I can fulfill these sexual fantasies and not only is it okay, it's fantastic. It felt so right, so normal, so appropriate.

In truth, kissing a man was like kissing a woman except for a couple of things. I could feel his beard stubble on my face. That's pretty universal. Also, a man's body is usually larger than a typical woman's, so my arms don't go as far around. I've also found that to be pretty universal. The biggest difference, though, is in how it felt emotionally; it was incredibly good and satisfying. I had expected kissing a man to feel weird, but it didn't at all. I actually expected everything to feel weird, but none of it did or does. Kissing a man, dating a man, having sex with a man, it all feels totally normal, totally right, like I was meant to do this all along.

When I informed Cathy of my recent experience she was a little put off; she wanted to experience lesbian sex beyond kissing, but had to find the right person and get the relationship to that point. It took her a couple of weeks to have sex with a woman. I ultimately waited for months for any more sexual experience, or even anymore kissing.

After my initial experience, the opportunities for such contact pretty much dried up. Robert took on the responsibility of helping me with this, calling it the "Get Dave Laid" project. The GDL project was mentioned, probably far more often than necessary, among the few coworkers I could be candid with. Ultimately, as I grew more impatient, the GDL project turned into, "I need someone to fuck my brains out." I never came up with a good acronym for this, though.

When I started weight lifting, my initial goal was that I would make my body more and more buff until some guy would have serious ongoing sex with me. Ultimately, I kept going with the weights because it's fun to watch myself get buff. Of course, being able to see myself in a mirror without wincing probably helps, too.

Some months after my revelation, I opened my laptop computer for some mundane task. I have a habit of doing computer things and surfing the web while lying in bed with my laptop on my chest. The display is a weak mirror for a few seconds before the system lights it up. For a brief instant, I caught my face in that mirror and my immediate gut reaction was profound, revolutionary. For the first time in my life, I saw my face in a mirror and thought, "Yeah, you're okay. You're a good guy." Wiping away tears, I realized I had never, ever, as far back as I could remember, been able to stand simply seeing the reflection of my face. I had despised myself so thoroughly that I had to look away. Any representation of me was hideous; no doubt this led to my reputation for being unkempt. If I can't stand to look in a mirror, I can't see that my hair is messy.

Come to think of it, I probably now look in mirrors more often than is truly necessary. Before all this I never could have imagined myself primping in front of a mirror. My dramatically increased interest in looking good obviously comes in part from actually being able to stand seeing myself in a mirror.

Unfortunately for me, Cathy's progress and experience having sex with women blossomed, while my opportunities dried up. I found this disturbing, less out of jealousy probably and more like simply missing what I knew could be really good. Dwelling on my loneliness only increased it. My goals increased with time, too. What I really wanted, I thought, was a boyfriend. Then I'd have a relationship, someone to fill the gaping hole in my psyche caused by losing Cathy as my special someone. And, of course, I could get sex, too.

Later on I learned that the whole "special someone" thing isn't as cut and dried as I had thought. In a way, Cathy still has been my special someone; we've both declared that we will not allow a romantic partner to get between the special friendship we have; a twenty-two-year relationship doesn't just vanish, it tends to hold on, at least as a friendship. Truthfully, she probably hadn't been considering me that much of a special someone before our gay realizations; our life together was in pretty rough shape as a marriage (but not so bad as a friendship) and she probably wouldn't have felt romantic feelings for someone else if she had still considered me, "her one and only." Letting go of her as my special someone was very hard on me, even though it happened under the friendliest of circumstances. I can't imagine a more benign marital breakup, yet it was still painful. There was no hostility between us, but losing my special someone and being alone was extremely difficult.

14

Pondering Sexuality

Following my big awakening, I spent a lot of time pondering my sexuality and what I'd already experienced as fantasy and desire. Now that I was really thinking about it openly, it was quite obvious that I'm very different from a typical straight man. From what I observed of straight men, it seemed to me that they localize their sexuality in their penises. That's what real men like to do, right? Stick their big erect penis into some woman. I had never really felt that desire. I never really wanted to stick my penis in anybody all that badly. I localized my sexuality to my ano-rectal tract. My penis was helpful for some things, like peeing standing up, but it didn't seem the center of my sexuality.

Recognizing my homosexuality was, in hindsight, unavoidable. But while I was still on a path to accepting this, some of my coworkers and larger circle of friends were not at all surprised. At one point, after coming out to the mother of one of my son's friends, she said, laughing, "Oh, I knew that!"

At a charity art event, one of the artists who's married to one of my coworkers chatted briefly with his wife and me. As I walked away, he turned to his wife and said, "That man's gay."

"Impossible" his wife insisted, "He has a wife and a child."

"No, I'm telling you, he's gay," he said again.

A year later at the same event, the same thing happened. This was a few years before my realization and yet, clearly, some people could tell. I later asked him how he knew and all he could say was my mannerisms, my patterns of speech, my eloquence.

Accepting my attraction to men was much harder for me to acknowledge. In the first few days after my epiphany, I would have given anything to be straight. I specifically even thought that I would give my life to be straight. I can die, as long as I can die straight.

Although it doesn't fit with my current religious beliefs, the thought crossed my mind that this could be some kind of punishment or divine retribution. My neurologic problems could be punishment for being or for accepting that I was gay. Perhaps, out of bad karma or something, I somehow deserved this horrible evil fate. I don't think I ever seriously believed this rationally, but it did occur to me, and I think I believed on an emotional level.

Part of me at times, in the first few months, would think that the acknowledgment that I was gay was a big mistake, yet another part of me would think this is the greatest thing that ever happened to me. Over time, my feelings have shifted strongly toward the latter assumption. Now, almost three years after I admitted my sexuality, I still feel incredibly grateful for having been able to acknowledge this about myself. The relief I feel in knowing there's nothing inherently wrong with me is overwhelming and worth all the agony I've been through. The joy of gay dating and gay sex is just icing on the cake.

I was probably gay from the moment of conception when the content of my genome was fixed. It is obviously deeply ingrained in who I am. To have survived this long living as a straight man probably indicates some hint of bisexuality. The Kinsey research suggests that most of us are not completely gay or completely straight.[8] The seminal Kinsey research on human sexuality established the concept that gay and straight are not black and white; there is, rather, a continuum, with gay at one end, straight at the other, and bisexuality in the middle. We each fall somewhere on that line, most of us toward one end or the other, but many fall somewhere in the middle.

For several weeks after my revelation, as I continued to think about my sexual orientation, reflecting on my past, I was nowhere near ready to talk to anyone other than Cathy and my mentor Robert about it. I also was thinking about what it was I wanted now; did I really want a gay relationship? My choices other than another man are a woman or no one, no romantic or sexual relationship. The latter was out of the question. I could, and ultimately did, enter a holding pattern to focus on who I am. But in the long run, I knew I was going to need someone. I still felt somewhat drawn to women, probably because it was what I was familiar with and there was a lot going on in my life that was unfamiliar. But I had tried for thirty-five years to have romantic and sexual relationships with women and they never worked. I now knew that a heterosexual relationship was not sustainable.

But a relationship with a man? I knew not only that I could, but I wanted to, kiss men and have sex with them. The idea of me having a boyfriend surely sounded odd, though. I just wasn't sure how it would work and what it would be like.

As time went on, my belief in and acceptance of my homosexuality solidified, although I was not always happy about it at first.

15

Worsening Illness

At this time I was also dealing with some serious medical issues. My orthostasis worsened as weeks went by. It became less responsive to any preventative measures. I was getting used to what to say to store personnel when I collapsed at a place like Best Buy. Then, one night out with Cathy, she said, "You're walking like an old man; quit it." Being a typical husband (at least in this sense), I immediately responded, "I am not!" The next day I realized what she meant by the remark and I broke out in a cold sweat at the thought. She meant "old" as in shuffling when I walk. She meant "old" as in Parkinson's disease. As a physician, but not a neurologist, I had some understanding of Parkinson's disease, but not a lot. I spent hours online, researching it, trying unsuccessfully to fit orthostasis with Parkinson's.

Over time, more symptoms emerged. Eventually I learned if I walked downhill, I couldn't stop walking; the only way to stop was to turn around and head back uphill. Because my driveway slopes strongly, someone else had to get the mail. Although I couldn't detect any difference in how I drove, my car had an unsettling tendency to wander into adjacent lanes. My ability to use my hands diminished, but I never demonstrated the classic Parkinson's tremor.

Finally, one Thursday, on the Internet, I discovered that Parkinson's basically never starts out like this, Parkinson's virtually always starts as that characteristic tremor in the hands which I did not have. A little more research revealed "Parkinson's plus" syndromes, a group of thankfully rare disorders related in some ways, but with different presentations. It turned out that multiple system atrophy, a Parkinson's plus syndrome, presents very typically with orthostasis symptoms followed by gait disturbance. It fit the description of my symptom progression really well. It's also untreatable and inevitably fatal.

On the following Sunday, I ran into the chief of neurology in the hospital while I was working. I had spoken with him by phone a few days earlier; his main comment when I listed my symptoms was, "Oh, my God!"

He hadn't said anything else or offered a diagnosis. Now he was startled to see me there working, surprised I was still functioning well enough to come to work.

I said, "I don't think this is Parkinson's."

He nodded, "What do you think it is?" he asked

"It fits with Parkinson's plus," I stammered.

"Yes, it fits very well with multiple system atrophy," he said glumly.

Then softly and with compassion, he added, "I'm sorry."

"Are you a partner?" he asked, referring to my status as a physician within the Kaiser organization. I had joined as an employee a few years back and, liking it, stayed long enough to have been made a partner.

"Yeah," I said, "I made partner several months ago."

His face brightened a little. "Then you have excellent benefits. We'll start the paperwork for disability payments now."

All I could do was nod, biting my lip to hold back tears.

"You'll need to stop working and driving in a matter of months," he continued. "You'll probably be confined to a wheelchair in several months."

I nodded again.

"I'm sorry," he said again.

I knew I was really, really sick. My doctor thought I was dying and I was pretty sure he was right. I had been willing to sacrifice my life to be straight; incredibly, now, I actually was dying, but that still didn't make me straight. I was not only going to die, I was going to die gay. Nothing could make me straight, but at that point the immediacy of my symptoms and the prognosis took precedence over my sexual issues. I discussed this all with Cathy, in a difficult and tearful conversation. Although obviously aware of the ramifications to our marriage that both our newfound sexuality had, she promised, through tears, to stay with me until this was over, one way or the other. That was probably one of the most intense conversations we've ever had.

While I probably didn't really want to die, I really didn't want to be sick. I felt it was acceptable to be dying, but I wanted some more time to feel healthy first. I realized what a tragedy this would be for my family. I had some medical problems for most of my life; there have been many times I was convinced I had some new problem and it would turn out to be all in my head. Now there was really something serious wrong with me. As time passed after my epiphany and I could see the benefits of being attracted to men and truly knowing who I was, I became less concerned about not wanting to be gay. As the benefits of knowing who I really am became more and more obvious, I became proud of who I am.

When things started to look bleak and my death seemed reasonably assured, Cathy and I discussed the situation. We both knew we were gay. Cathy was more eager to pursue this actively both because she had a specific someone in mind, and, realistically, I was dying and she wasn't. I was distracted from the whole gay thing by the whole dying thing. I told her not to make her romantic life wait for me. Between us we had clearly moved from attempting a romantic relationship to being good friends.

I scheduled a formal appointment to see a neurologist for a physical exam; the clinical exam was essentially normal with minor findings, neither proving nor disproving the disease. An MRI of my brain was ordered, to exclude anything else that might possibly be causing my symptoms but there was no expectation for any other cause. A tumor might be responsible, but that didn't fit that well, either.

The MRI clearly showed that the normally fluid-filled cavities inside the center of the brain, the ventricles, were very large. The large ventricles could be caused by a buildup of fluid, which might possibly cause my symptoms, but the ventricular size could also just be secondary to atrophy of the brain for any of a number of other benign reasons that are far more common. There are no significant findings on an MRI for multiple system atrophy, so while this imaging was suggestive of a treatable cause, it was not definitive. My neurologists were still worried that I had MSA. The MRI findings suggested normal pressure hydrocephalus. This is an imbalance of cerebrospinal fluid that could cause symptoms similar to mine, but this usually presented with a different clinical picture. Orthostasis, my first and possibly most significant symptom, was not commonly associated with normal pressure hydrocephalus.

I was started on medication to attempt to decrease the fluid pressure and asked a good neuroradiologist I knew to look at my scan. He agreed it was worrisome and I was ultimately referred to the chief of neurosurgery. The neurosurgeon felt that a relatively minor procedure to insert a shunt—a tube to drain the fluid—was worth doing, but there were no guarantees that it would have any positive effect. He felt that my ventricles might be large from atrophy and I could have MSA or something else, but the ventricles could possibly be large from blockage and a drainage procedure might be helpful, at least to some extent. If I had a blockage or normal pressure hydrocephalus, the shunt could help.

The surgery was scheduled, and the symptoms progressed. Gradually I became too weak to stand for more than a few minutes. I had previously been a runner, completing a 5K race in the middle of the pack; now I couldn't even walk from the parking lot into the grocery store. I could drive short distances, a few miles, although I probably shouldn't have been doing even that. I applied for a handicapped-parking placard for my car. I couldn't really use my hands because my fingers felt an inch thick and I fumbled and dropped things. I was too weak to stand up from sitting without using my arms and a lot of exertion.

David Kaufman, July 19, 7:40 pm
    Pretty rough—I've been off work for a week or so waiting for surgery (I can't work like this). The surgery is this Tuesday, the 21st. My legs are very weak and sore. It's hard to even stand up! It's been a pretty wild ride. I've never been this sick or this scared before. I'm not so much scared of the surgery, but the possibility that it won't work, and I'll be stuck like this.
                                        I'll let you know....
                              —*Facebook post, 7/19/09*

As my hands got worse, I ultimately had to give up hobbies or anything that required manual dexterity. Attempting to solder electronics, a favorite hobby since very early childhood, now resulting in burns to my hands and fingers. Things were looking very bleak. The newfound realization that I'm gay gradually slipped to the back of my mind as the realization sank in that I was truly dying. I was distraught over the prospect of going down this way; I wished I could just be okay for a little while before it got worse. Had my symptoms been from Parkinson's disease, medications would probably alleviate them and I could be relatively symptom free, at least for a period of time.

Up to the day of surgery, the neurologists still thought it could be MSA and the neurosurgeon couldn't say the procedure would help. He even said it could make things worse and I might need more surgery to tie off the tube that had just been placed.

I think, in retrospect, that I was more upset over my actual suffering from the illness, rather than worried about the prospect of dying.

I woke up from the forty-five-minute procedure in the recovery room and instantly knew I felt better. Something that had been wrong before was now fixed. When I mentioned it to the surgeon he smirked a little and said he thought it was the powerful narcotics they were giving me for pain.

The drainage tube had to be passed under the skin from the back of my head down my neck and down the front of my chest to be inserted into the abdomen where the excess fluid can be harmlessly reabsorbed. This is a fair amount of manipulation and meant a belly scar. Plus there was a hole the width of my thumb in the back of my skull. The following day I was sent home for an approximately two-week recovery.

Twenty-four hours after the surgery, on my way home, I was seriously drugged up but still felt better. The following day, the pain was much less and I was clearly virtually 100 percent better. All the prior symptoms appeared to be gone. It seems that my symptoms were due to a condition called aquaductal stenosis, a benign narrowing of a passage in the brain that carries cerebrospinal fluid. The treatment is to drain away the excess fluid by having a neurosurgeon surgically place a drainage tube, called a shunt, in the brain.

I was cured!

16

I'm Going to Live, and I'm Gay!

Maybe the shunt miracle is to show me that I was meant to be gay [that my illness is not a punishment] and come out.

—Personal journal entry about 11/1/09

Lying in bed, at home, recovering from successful surgery, something that had been at the back of my mind suddenly jumped to the front. I'm gay. And I'm going to live. It's time to do something about this.

Some thoughts about my neurologic illness being coincident with my awakening were starting to form. It seemed to me, from the moment I knew I was better, that this was some kind of cosmic sign. Although I'm not sure what about God I believe, this was like a sign from God that I'm gay and it's okay. I'm meant to be this; this is good, I'm supposed to do this. I was prepared to die and now I'm going to live, and live as a gay man.

By the time I returned to work, I was ready to come out. The process of facing one's own mortality can be a powerful experience. It's something that cannot be perceived or imagined; what it feels like has to be experienced to be understood. It turns out that dying can have a very profound effect on values and opinions. Things that used to seem important, like material possessions, become meaningless, and things that used to get pushed aside become obviously very important, like family. Suddenly the people in my life took center stage.

I'm even more impatient now than I used to be because I have a sense of purpose about what my life is meant for now. It's like the original me died and I was reborn during the shunt surgery with a different personality and a different outlook on my life.

I felt different about life, and about my life. It felt like I was given another, so now I'm willing to take more chances with it, to be bold. I need to do what I want now with this life because it's a bonus. It's like I lost my main life and this is a freebie, a do-over. Where I had been socially cautious and careful, now I'm not only willing to stand out, to be wild, but I feel I have to live life a little on the edge. This was, at this time, a huge adolescent-like rush. I just had to do it all, to see it all, to experience everything possible.

Never a particularly patient man, I find myself with no tolerance whatsoever for bullshit. What's important is usually really obvious; the rest can go in the trash. I have a new sense of urgency regarding the things that are important.

> I'm OK, I really am :-)… …Is the newfound calm and self-confidence related to the now lack of sexual insecurity?
>
> —*Personal journal entry 7/23/09*

The combination of almost dying and suddenly knowing I'm gay has had a profound effect on me. I feel very compelled to be me, whatever it is I really am. I don't have time not to; I don't know when my time is coming. This illness came out of nowhere and suddenly became very significant; all of a sudden I was crippled and dying. I have heard from friends and coworkers who have had to face their own mortality and they recount similar transformations.

> Transformation partly from facing mortality and realizing I have to be me. I'm giving myself the gift of living the rest of my life the way I should (this is very important). From a conversation with a friend.
>
> —*Personal journal entry 10/29/09*

My earlier midlife crisis had prepared me somewhat for this feeling that life is too short to not live it fully, but many of my issues remained unaddressed. The sudden realization that people really mattered stood out strongly. Money and what it can buy are pointless by comparison.

I had been willing to die to be straight, and then actually was dying, but still gay. Now I'm fine, and still gay. It's hard to see this in any other light than—Wow!—I need to do this gay thing!

At about this time, some other issues gelled. I began to feel an immense sense of personal strength and power. The relief of not having to pretend, not only to myself but also to others, and being able to consciously be who I am is incredibly empowering. It makes it hard to be bashful. Over the years I had expended a great deal of emotional energy keeping this fundamental truth from myself and coping with the feelings of being different and, therefore, by inference, bad. To know I'm not an aberration of nature is transformative in and of itself. I don't walk hunched over, trying to hide in my own body anymore. I walk tall and proud because I know who I am and I don't have to pretend.

Suddenly the combination of dying and realizing I'm gay synergized into a powerful feeling of urgency. This isn't someone on the news somewhere or in a magazine, this is me. I did have the time while I was sick to get more used to my new gay identity. It represents the most fundamental aspect of who I am. For someone who assumed he was straight for 49½ years, it was a lot to get used to. I also realized that being gay is a very important aspect of who I am with regard to others. If a new female employee thinks that I'm really nice, if she knows I'm gay, then she can realize I seem nice because I'm a nice guy and not because I want to try to hit on her. And if that hot guy from down the hall thinks I'm hot, well, if he thinks I'm straight, it probably won't go anywhere. But if he knows I'm gay, he might ask me out. This is personal knowledge about myself that's up to me to tell as I choose. My personality transformation may be obvious, but the reason for it is not. One reason to come out is so people will know why I'm suddenly so different. For me personally, I want everyone to know. I was dying, I don't have time to waste. Do I want to come out to my coworkers? Does it matter to me whether my friends can accept me? Should I even waste my time trying to be friends with someone who can't accept me as I really am? It's all my choice.

> Clearly, the shunt miracle made me conscious of my mortality and left me utterly convinced that I need to be who I am, without compromise. I'm doing it, but it's sometimes hard.
> —*Personal journal entry, 11/15/09*

The path from not even knowing at all who I am to being closeted and sick to being out and healthy has not been an easy one. There were many things to consider: a marriage, a teenage son, two adult kids in college, and an extended family. Most of my day is spent at work; I have about seventy-five coworkers, most of whom can deal with my news, but a few who can't. But as time passes, those who initially had trouble with it are coming around.

Essentially, if I were not out, I was holding a secret inside. I wouldn't know how people around me would react if they knew. This makes it my problem. But once I came out, they can deal with it or not, and if they can't, it's their problem, not mine. Being out is very empowering. The mental energy it took to constantly hide who I am was very draining and so I got rid of an emotional black hole that sucked up my personal energy.

Unfortunately, gays and lesbians are still very much on the periphery of our society, so much so that we can't even marry in many states. Where are our civil rights? In being out I have had to experience rejection for who I am. Usually this occurs in the context of my being out in public with another man because people can see that we're a gay couple, if they care to know, just by looking at us, by the way we look at each other or just stand next each other. It's hard to hide romantic interest, even without doing anything obvious like holding hands. Two men kissing in public could risk serious repercussions, even in a liberal place like Sonoma County. I can't imagine how hard it would be in less-accepting places, like in the Deep South. I have friends who have lived in Missouri and felt this threat frequently. They would overhear comments like, "Look at the two fags."

Throughout this period, with all its difficulties, I have struggled to cope. Besides the outward changes, there are very powerful inner adjustments. For months, I would find myself doing an internal double take multiple times throughout the day, every day.

"Who am I again?"

"What! I like men not women?"

Most of the time, although I know it's true and I'm okay with it, I sometimes find it very hard to get used to. I have constant reassurance by observing my own responses that I'm really much more attracted to men than to women. With the old defenses down, it's very easy to see. It is still, however, very different. Even though this is technically just my sexual orientation that appears different, it feels like my identity is changing in a very fundamental way. It feels really good to know I'm not a singular freak; however, it feels really bad to realize that everything in my life and about me now seems altogether different. This has been extremely hard to get used to.

Many times I've said through choking tears, "My whole world is upside down and on fire." Why is nothing familiar? Where is there something unchanged?

How do I make sense of all of this? Mere human speech can mean something different. What did he mean by that comment? Was it yet another, more modern insult; a more refined and up-to-date version of "faggot?" It often feels like I've just started the fight of my life.

I thought of the passengers on the *Titanic*. Were they upper class from England? I could picture them, in one of the dining rooms, commenting on how the steak was a little overcooked and how the trumpet player in the band was wonderful. Was it the first trip for many of them? Were they looking forward to coming to America. Who were they with on this voyage, family? Then, suddenly, only moments later, they're all in a lifeboat or the icy water. They can see the ship is sinking, taking all that's familiar with it. They're looking for something to cling to, something to save them. What will become of them? That's me.

Well, what can I find that's familiar? This has been a central struggle for months, even alongside the profoundly positive aspects of all this. I am often amazed at how one intense thing can be so good and so hard at the same time. It's hard to believe that habits and patterns built up over years have ended.

I often found myself looking for the familiar in the strangest places. Feeling attracted to women is much more familiar than feeling attracted to men; it was a long time before this even started to change. An attachment to Cathy, even though she's always been there as a true friend, feels familiar. I find it hard to let go of what can no longer be with her just because it's familiar. The only thing I really lost with her is what I hadn't wanted and tried very hard to get out of: sex. Still, I found myself longing for the old relationship. I'd give everything to have my old relationship with Cathy work, but that isn't enough.

I had abandoned the blues music I had liked before for more-modern cutting-edge pop music, particularly Lady Gaga. I couldn't turn back to the old music for familiarity; it just wouldn't work. I need edgy and upbeat now. I also tried numerous times to go back to my old style of dress, even setting out more-conservative clothing the night before. But the next morning I'd go to the closet and pick out something different, more youthful and urban-fashionable. I found my new choices in music and clothing comforting even though they represent change. I had, for all my life up until now, wanted to just be ordinary, just to blend in. I was the drab brown field mouse scurrying from cover to cover, trying to blend in and not show. Now I want to be a peacock! I can't pretend I'm an ordinary guy anymore, but, more importantly, I don't want to be ordinary.

This represents an additional source of conflict: I want to be the new me, but it represents yet more change.

Reflecting on my relationship with Cathy, both before and after these issues arose, something powerful emerges. After more than twenty years together, we had the most amiable separation imaginable, but there was, and still is, pain because of it. Ultimately, neither of us could pursue our new lives while we lived together. Cathy moved out about three months after I came out. In some ways, this was the most painful of everything that happened in 2009. For more than twenty years, through all my medical training, living in three different states, and countless apartments and houses, at the end of the day, I came home to her. There was obviously something lacking in our marriage, but we have always been friends who have always loved and respected each other. Even now, we can still finish each other's sentences. And while all I've really lost with her is the part I didn't want anyway, I have found myself sad, upset, and crying frequently. On introspection, it's basically grief for what's lost, and what can no longer be. Losing my live-in friend is extraordinarily painful. The loneliness really hurts.

I know couples that are struggling and, after many years together, can't really know the pain of separation unless and until it actually happens. There were many times near the end of our marital relationship that I contemplated leaving. I had absolutely no idea then what pain I would have been in for. There's no doubt, had I left under any other circumstances, I would have wanted to come back, and soon.

Cathy and I have significantly different personalities. We were initially drawn to each other by a particular bond of friendship; we seemed to work well together. Emotionally, she's that mountain by the ocean, unfazed by practically anything. Emotionally, I'm a flag in a hurricane. This led to many, many instances of misunderstandings throughout our entire time together. Ultimately I didn't completely understand this fundamental difference until after our marital relationship was over (this observation was a profound gift from my mentor

Robert). Even so, we still learned over the years how to get around that, how to make up after a fight and stay together. Our differences have led to much consternation, but we have also been in many ways complementary. In some ways, we could make up for what each other wasn't as good at. I know I needed to explore the sudden realization of my true sexuality, but if Cathy had not turned out to be a lesbian, I'm pretty certain that I would have been willing to try to swallow the whole idea of being gay and tried to make our marriage work.

We now have a relationship that defies definition. We are much more than friends, but absolutely not lovers. We are very supportive of each other, frequently turning to each other for advice, even romantic advice. Some of the best romantic advice I've received during this time has come from Cathy.

Throughout this entire process we have both been very open with each other about what's going on in our lives, particularly romantically. We can, and very often do, have extended conversations about whom we're seeing and/or sleeping with without the slightest trace of jealousy or animosity. But we do have an understanding that started right from the very beginning of our sexual awakening that we don't discuss the intimate details of how we have sex with our respective partners. We know each other probably better than anyone else does and we have the added benefit of objectivity with the other's relationships. What's not at all obvious to me about my relationship is clearly defined to Cathy. Truthfully, I think we're much better friends now than we ever were before.

17

Coming Out

What does "coming out" mean? Why is it such a big deal?

Coming out, simply put, means informing those around you that you're gay. It marks a milestone in personal development. Although strictly just an outward sign of being gay, it really is an inward commitment to live out, to no longer hide, a part of you that might be unattractive to others. This is what it really hinges on; I know who I am, but others might not like me if they knew. Coming out lays it on the line. This is who I am; one way or the other you just have to deal with it. It's not my problem anymore, it's no longer my secret; it's up to you to decide how you feel about it.

Why is that such a big deal? Well, I didn't have to come out as left-handed or blue-eyed. Why not? Because nobody cares about those things. When society no longer makes such a big distinction between gay and straight, when society can accept that we're humans with civil rights, too, then there won't be a need to "come out" for gays and lesbians. Just consider the civil rights issues: gays and lesbians can't legally marry in most states. If my partner of thirty years is dying in the hospital, I have no more right to see him than if I were somebody he just met at a new job. There are no marital rights for gay partners. Most employers will not consider a same-sex partner equivalent to a spouse in terms of benefits. If my wife needs medical coverage, she can be covered by my policy at no charge. If my same-sex partner needs coverage, he has to apply and pay for a separate policy. What is going on here? Are gays and lesbians subhuman? Why don't we have civil rights? Why is it such a big deal that we're even gay or lesbian?

What I've seen in the gay male community is that coming-out stories become a sort of identity for us. Coming out is part of the process of making it real. If no one knows you're gay, it's in the realm of fantasy, not quite real. The first person I came out to was Cathy, of course, but in my head that still made it that much more valid. I don't think it even occurred to me to talk to my mentor Robert about it until I'd spoken to Cathy; my conversation with Robert was a few days later. My journal entry wondering what/who I am was made the day I came out to Cathy, not the day a few weeks earlier when I'd figured it out. Telling people that's who you are makes it real. The inverse of this is that when a straight man experiences homosexual urges, fantasies, or dreams, if he never tells anyone, then they don't really count. After all, it really is literally, all in his head.

I'm somewhat rare in that I didn't even realize that I was gay until well into middle age, although I came out within a few months after my epiphany. I've met other gay men who didn't completely realize they were gay until their thirties, or even until they were in their sixties. I've met a surprising number of gay men with ex-wives and children. I've even met a gay man whose ex-wife is a lesbian, but it apparently took her quite awhile after his coming out for her to figure it out. Cathy and I were lucky in the sense that we were both able to figure it out without knowing about the other. If I had my epiphany after she came out to me, I'd always wonder if I was really gay, or just felt that way because she was.

Many gay people have great difficulty coming out. Probably most of the gay men I know realized they were gay around the time of puberty, but didn't come out until much later. I have a friend who knew when he was ten years old. I have one gay friend, in his eighties, who always knew he was gay; he insists there was never a time in his life when he suddenly realized he was attracted to men, he just always knew it. I have spoken with many gays who find it exceedingly difficult to tell their loved ones they're gay. The number of gay men who knew in their teens but didn't come out until later teens or twenties is a testimony to the difficulty. The fear in coming out to your parents when you're still a dependent living at home is strong; many young gays and lesbians find themselves out on the street, thrown out by parents who can't accept who they are. For me, I didn't find it all that difficult. I was at a different point in my life; I just said, "I think you should know I'm gay."

I feel that anyone who would really care should know. If it matters to a given person, than I have an obligation to be out to them or I'm being dishonest. It's like a lie of omission.

> Long talk with my mom, re: only that Cathy and
> I are separating...
> —*Personal journal entry 8/23/09*

The hardest person for me to tell was my mother. I know that she had always been fairly liberal, particularly about social issues. When they were together, my mother and father were pacifists. As we were growing up, my mother brought us to United Methodist churches where a liberal social agenda was taught to the kids. I remember Sunday-school lessons about the need for population and birth control as well as support for those in poverty. I was taught strongly the need to respect others who are different. I remember one song from my early Sunday-school days,

> "Red or yellow, black or white;
> they are precious in his sight;
> Jesus loves the little children of the world."[9]

I was also aware, however, that my mother was or had become more conservative politically, definitely more right wing than me.

When I decided to come out to her, I called her on the phone and said I had to talk to her about something.

"Cathy and I are separating," I said.

"Well," my mother said, "you've had your differences, that's not a total shock."

I continued, "Part of the reason is because I'm gay. I'm not sure how you're going to take this, but I feel I need to tell you."

"Oh," she definitely sounded surprised, "that isn't something I ever expected to hear you say."

"Yeah," I said, "I kinda figured that."

"Well, dad [my stepfather] and I can accept it; we have many friends at church with gay or lesbian children."

The conversation continued and she said she wished that I could be happy, whoever or whatever I am. This was touching and I was relieved she wasn't upset.

"Be careful," she also added.

This is an unnecessary comment as gays are acutely aware of the HIV/AIDS risks. Unprotected sex is generally viewed as suicidal behavior, like Russian roulette.

I told my father earlier that I was gay, but given both his background as a therapist and my knowledge of how liberal he is, I was sure it wouldn't be a problem with him. When I told my father, he was a little surprised but advised me not to box myself into categories like "gay" or "straight" and just be me. It turns out that he is one of the few straight men I can be completely open with, even explicit with about the gay experience.

Cathy and I knew we needed to tell Andrew, our thirteen-year-old son. The two of us together approached him and said we needed to talk. We all sat down at the dining room table.

"You talk," said Cathy

"Okay," I said, "Andrew, you need to know that your mother and I are separating. The reason is because we're both gay." I just laid it all out there.

"Okay," he said simply, and pretty much left it at that. He didn't seem all that impressed by anything I had said. Perhaps he wasn't surprised to hear of our separation having seen how on edge we were around each other. Gay is apparently not as big a deal with his generation as it was with mine when I was his age.

I continued, explaining that of course we both still love him the same, that we actually still love each other the same, it's just that a romantic relationship between the two of us obviously won't work anymore. I explained that one of us would be moving out of the house, probably in a few months, but we would stay close together and he would have contact with both of us.

We ultimately found a therapist for him, to make sure he was really as okay with everything as he appeared to be. After several sessions the therapist reported to Cathy and me that Andrew was truly okay with his parents being gay.

I came out to my older daughter, a medical student at the time, and she was fine with the news, too.

"Whatever makes you happy, Dad," was her response.

When I came out to my older son, also a medical student at the time, he asked, "Are you sure?"

"Of course I'm sure," I replied, fearing that he was having trouble with it. Later in the conversation he mentioned he liked the movie *Milk* so much he bought a copy. Later, when I had a chance to see the movie myself, I realized that no one who likes that movie could be a homophobe. He readily accepted my being gay; however, he warned me to be careful, knowing my tendency to throw myself into things. I reassured him that I was trying to take it easy and get used to everything slowly.

I had actually had the few months between my realization and coming out to pace myself and get used to things. Unfortunately, it turned out that the hardest adjustment came after I started coming out. My life really started changing then. Initially, it was basically just something in my head. After coming out and living as a gay person, it became much more real.

I've found that while going through this process, I really need people to talk to. Gay friends are ideal, but I have a limited number of them and sometimes it's helpful to have a straight person's perspective. The more support and the more friends I have the better.

Cathy has more difficulty telling people she's gay than I do. I think a lot of the difference for me comes from my concurrent medical issues, and the need to live my life my way now, like *immediately* right now. A lot of my strength probably comes from the feeling that my miraculous neurologic recovery is a compelling sign that it's okay for me to be gay.

I have known gays who, like Cathy, will say that they're willing to tell anyone who asks, but don't think it's anyone's business and therefore they don't need to tell anyone who's not asking. Although strictly probably true, I and the out gay friends I've discussed it with agree that with people we're closest to, it's in a way dishonest to hide something that important. Ultimately, if it feels like I'm hiding it from someone close to me, they probably should be told. At one point later on, Cathy said that she doesn't want to come out, that it's nobody's business who she has sex with. I think those are two very different things. Gay is about fundamentally who I am; and it's true that who I have sex with isn't anybody's business.

I basically came out to my little brother the same way I came out to my mom; I was reasonably sure he'd be okay with it and he was. He volunteered to tell my sister, fearing that with her Islamic beliefs it would be difficult for her. Apparently, it wasn't, and I've received very supportive emails from her and her daughters.

I've heard of gays coming out to loved ones by writing letters to them, after struggling for years to tell people. When I discussed coming out to one gay friend he had profound advice.

"How do I know who I need to come out to?" I had asked.

"You should tell the people you spend the most mental energy thinking about," he said.

I felt my peers, my colleagues, the other radiologists I practice with need to know; we discuss our personal lives somewhat and the separation from Cathy would surely come up at some point. I felt then, and still do now, that an explanation of why we separated is reasonable information for friends to know; it helps explain the unusual relationship we have now. We've found quite a few people who don't seem to be able to understand that we're not fighting, that there's no hostility, and that we cooperate with each other very well. Occasionally, acquaintances who see the two of us together at a social function will be surprised. Well, we still do things together, as good friends.

Diametrically opposed to Cathy, I came out with exuberance. I came out so strongly and to so many people I felt embarrassed afterward. But, looking back, I don't regret it; I'm glad to have as many people know as do. I realize now that I came out to some people so I'd have someone to talk to about it. If I had to do it over again, I'd probably do it differently, but I'd still come out to about as many people. I just feel it's something people should know. I realized in a flash of inspiration a year after coming out that part of the reason I wanted to come out to everybody is because I'm finally proud of who I am. I've been very embarrassed to be me my whole life, always apologetic, always deferential. I didn't think highly of myself at all and saw no reason anyone else should.

I'm not embarrassed about who I am anymore. I'm proud. I feel profound strength in understanding that I'm not broken, not some mutant freak, I'm just gay. I appreciate that I'm leery in situations where strong homophobia could emerge; I have the brutality of my childhood burned into my memory and I'm at times reluctant to face a potentially angry mob. But I think I could if I had to. It just feels so good to know that there's nothing wrong with me, it's just that I'm attracted to men. It feels good, but it's hard to get used to.

Coming out to Cathy's parents was difficult; she had wanted to not tell them even though she realized that at some point she'd have to. The four of us had been close; I've been as close to my in-laws as to much of my own family. I ended up being the one to tell them because I had an opportunity to meet with them in person before Cathy did. Cathy's mother said she had already figured out that Cathy was a lesbian by things she'd said. The shocking part is that Cathy's mother heard confirmation of this from family members who had promised not to tell. Outing someone against his or her will is a grievous wrong. I would hope that people can understand what a sensitive issue this is, but apparently there's something about playing "guess who's gay" that some people can't resist. It's been much more difficult for Cathy's mom than for my parents, but she loves her daughter very much and is really trying to understand.

One illustration of how coming out can be beneficial is the time one of my female colleagues asked if I been to a different part of the department. It seems there was a new guy working there who's gay and cute. I found an excuse to venture over and she was right; it was a bright spot in my day. This wouldn't have happened if I hadn't come out to her.

No one has the right to out someone else, but those of us who are not out are contributing to the suffering of those that bear the brunt of homophobia. The more of us that come out, the better off we'll all be; when society sees that so many of us exist and are just normal people, gay rights will naturally follow. This is an incredibly important concept. The more ordinary, normal queer people everyone knows, the harder it will be to persecute us. My observation of the many gay men I now know is that the large majority of them don't come off as particularly gay. Most seem like ordinary straight men. Those of us that are particularly effeminate are often forced out because we can't hide it. Too many of us who can hide it do.

I am so lucky (medically and probably otherwise).
—Personal journal entry 8/11/09

Part III
Later

For a brief moment I felt shot from the ground
into liberation and freedom...

—*Personal journal entry 1/22/10*

18

Who Am I Now?

It's now some four decades since elementary school and, well, it turns out the accusation from my peers is, in a sense, correct. The assaults from bullies still hurt deeply, but the power of self-knowledge now reigns supreme. Self-determination lends enormous strength and power. I have conquered those feelings of insecurity with the sure knowledge of who I really am. I'm no longer trying to pretend I'm something I'm not, I'm no longer having to live a lie. I know I'm not some weird freak, I'm just a normal gay man. I can now stand up straight and walk tall with my head up, with a poise and confidence I had never had before.

Months passed from my initial epiphany; my transformation had began, likely from both my miraculous medical recovery and my coming out. A few things started becoming clearer to me.

It became evident that my attraction to women, which had seemed so incongruous, was just a habit I'd learned from my peers back during puberty. It was impossible then to admit being attracted to men; peer pressure forced all behaviors, thoughts, and feelings into the framework of a straight male personality. So I conformed; I simply copied what other boys did and said. I had no idea what I was hiding; self-deception can be amazingly powerful and efficient. As bad as I've felt that I did this, embarrassed by how I could have concealed this from myself for so long, I've thought of other acts of self-deception.

> Still thinking about [his] comment—I also feel that
> I am totally a real man, even if I also realize that I'm
> more femininely passive... ... (this doesn't feel like a
> conflict).
>
> *—Personal journal entry 8/29/09*

During the three-year period that I questioned myself if I was gay, I was still convinced of my masculinity. I didn't see masculinity as incompatible with being gay. I had the utmost respect for people born male who believe they're supposed to be female. Transgender is another human variant. I was pretty sure I wasn't a transgender, though. I didn't wear women's clothing or makeup. Yet, there are situations where I can see I'm a total girl. And I like it. Often, when with a date, I see myself as acting like a girl. For example, my date would sit straight up in the movie theater seat while I leaned against him in a traditionally feminine way.

I think I always felt feminine this way, but was very uncomfortable about admitting any tendency toward femininity, especially to myself.

> I'm so different I don't even recognize myself
> anymore.
>
> *—Personal journal entry 9/24/09*

After I recovered from the shunt surgery and starting coming out, I began to notice changes in my behavior. Although I had previously, on occasion, enjoyed dressing nicely from time to time, suddenly I wanted to dress nice *all* the time. No longer limited to special occasions, now I always want to be stylish, much more stylish. The old standard dress shirts gave way to a hip, younger, and a more-urban style; usually shirts with embroidery or appliqués. I would have never been willing or even able to wear a shirt with "stuff" on it before. So I realized that I couldn't put on something fancy and just hope I could pull it off. Fancy clothes have to be worn with conviction. Yes, it is stylish, because I'm wearing it. Robert, my gay mentor, is very fashionable, although he usually dresses more conservatively than I. He realized long before I did that I needed more-stylish pants. This means much more form-fitting. Every pair of pants I bought on a mutual shopping trip was carefully evaluated by Robert to make sure they adequately showcase my assets.

One day, in a discussion with Robert about my clothes, we remarked that, while still very fashionable, he dresses more conservatively than I do. He responded that my style of dress is more "sparkly" than his. It had never been any form of conscious decision, and I have no recollection of ever thinking about how I wanted to change my style, it just happened spontaneously.

Virtually everyone around me noticed the changes in my demeanor and dress. I had also stopped buttoning the second top button on my fancy shirts. A few of my older coworkers expressed having difficulty with my new attire.

One older close friend, at dinner over wine, said to me, "What's with the clothes? Button your fucking shirt, you look like a sleazy woman."

That was a painful way to see a friendship end; it's hard to be friends with someone who can't accept something this fundamental about me. There was little other resistance to my change in style.

The youngest coworkers were very impressed. One highly respected and wonderfully warm file clerk approached me early in this process one day and said something to me in Spanish. Seeing the blank look on my face, she said slowly and clearly in English;

"Young. Handsome. Happy."

Much more recently, the same coworker, on a day when I was dressed only somewhat sparkly, implored, "You've been looking so good, please don't change, please, please don't go back."

Another area that blossomed is a desire, and possibly a little talent, in arranging flowers, especially silk arrangements. Actually, going to Michael's crafts store and shopping for different decorative items like vases and colored stones, felt more feminine than almost anything else I had ever done. It felt weird to be buying fake flowers; I don't know why. I wondered if the cashier knew I was gay. I mean, first of all, I'm there in that store alone, without a wife or girlfriend. That should probably be a sign. And of course, I was wearing one of my favorite shirts with a big swirly appliqué on it.

I realized early on that I don't do anything just *because* it's gay; I only do what I specifically want to do. It is highly likely, however, that I do a lot of things that are stereotypically gay, but I don't do it to be gay, I just do it because I want to.

I had always had a problem with dancing. I have some musical experience, starting from an early age, and I always thought dancing should be enjoyable, but I could never get into it. I just couldn't get my body to move right. My fingers can play notes on an instrument, but I could never get my body dancing.

Cathy loved to dance and went out frequently while in college before we met. Like many straight men, I was unable to dance without a lot of beer. And by then I was so drunk I made a fool of myself. This was always a conflict with Cathy when we went to some function or party that included dancing.

Sometimes at work I listen to music through headphones so as not to disturb others or impair my work. One day, after my transformation, while doing so, I realized I was moving around in my chair to the music. Kind of like dancing, but while sitting down. Given my music background—I play a little piano and guitar—I've always imagined myself as someone who belonged in the band, not on the dance floor. My hands know how to create music on a few instruments, but my body never before knew how to move with the music. And here I was doing a fair imitation of something like dancing while sitting in my chair.

I decided to explore this somehow. I realized that I didn't know any moves; I didn't know exactly what to do with my arms and legs, only that know they seemed willing to move in time with the beat.

Finally, I did something I had never done before in all fifty years of my life. In the garage, with a loud stereo on, I moved stuff out of the way, and danced by myself until I was sweaty and exhausted. That was really fun! Why didn't I know how to do that before? I suspect I *did* know how, but felt too inhibited to be able to do it. Many of my old inhibitions were falling away—there seemed no need to continue with most of them. At a recent work party, I danced until my glasses fogged up.

I also discovered I like taking better care of my skin now, particularly my face. I never thought before that I would be shopping at the Clinique counter at Macy's, but there I was getting a run-through on the different Clinique for Men products. I suppose I could have been really feminine and bought Clinique for women. I think in the end I don't really care. I really like having my face so soft and smooth. The closest I have come to just flat out wearing makeup is using the concealer I bought to cover blemishes on my forehead. It works really well; I feel somehow rebellious using it.

What I'm willing to do or like has changed; I kind
of like washing dishes by hand and am less driven to
do what I want for me (like milling machine stuff).
—*Personal journal entry 10/5/09*

I thoroughly enjoy kitchen work, and not just cooking, but cleaning up and keeping the kitchen tidy. I washed the good china myself by hand after Christmas and enjoyed it. I understand the term for me in this context is, "kitchen queen." For Christmas a gay friend got me a professional chef's double-breasted uniform shirt. It's embroidered with, "Chef David, *kitchen queen*" and I find great satisfaction in it.

I've always enjoyed cooking, but was never before fond of cleaning up after it. One factor limiting my "queenliness" in the kitchen is that, since I started learning to cook when I was about ten years old, I've cooked predominately basic, inexpensive food. I'm much better with ground beef than lobster (I've never been all that fond of lobster—eating them is a lot of work and I consider them something of an underwater cockroach).

Yet, the moments of satisfaction in activities I've always liked and now feel more comfortable doing, go hand in hand with the moments of unease.

The feeling of being lost is constant. I am never sure who I am anymore, frequently feeling that I'm no longer even the same person. At times this was intensely frustrating, although occasionally it was fun and exciting. I'm racing down this winding road, I don't know where it's going, but it can be thrilling to watch the scenery go by and see it all happen. Yet, at times, everything still seemed like the aftermath of a big natural disaster; everything's torn up.

> I don't know who at all who I'm becoming, but it's fun to watch. The loss of what was familiar is unsettling at times though.
>
> *—Personal journal entry 10/5/09*

Finally, after months of figurative wandering, things started to come together a little. I began to get the feeling I could, at least a little bit, see what I was becoming. For months, I was observing changes in my behavior, changes in what I like and don't like, and wondering when it would end. Who will I be in two years? Will I have taken dancing lessons? Will I still wear fancy shirts? During the earlier phases, it was hard to see that all that was new in my personality and behavior was really me and had always been there. I felt frequently like I'd gotten a brain transplant with the shunt.

As the future started seeming clearer, it was evident that all this new stuff going on with me had always been there. It doesn't seem related to the men-who-like-men part of gay. It seems more related to the larger issue of who I really am as a person and an understanding of what was going on while I was feeling so different from other men all my life.

I think I can actually see where this road I'm on is going, and where/what I'll be when it's done. [Happened] while at Safeway.
　　　　　　—Personal journal entry 10/8/09 2pm

The actual man-attracted-to-men part of the whole package stopped being a big deal after a few boyfriends. I saw that gay relationships are really the same as straight ones, and gay sex is really pretty much the same thing as straight sex. It's just that in both cases a few of the details are different.

What makes the gay experience so enormous for me is that it is the defining crisis of my life. For virtually my entire life I have struggled with feeling odd, different, left out, abnormal. I've known my sexual idiosyncrasies since puberty and, truthfully, they seemed pretty strange for a straight man. The underlying and overwhelming sense was that there was something wrong with me and therefore I'm a bad person.

What makes my coming out not just enormous, but enormously positive, is that this means I'm okay. There's nothing wrong with me and I'm not a bad person. I'm just gay.

I'm gay. That means I'm a member of this marginalized minority group with limited civil rights and could possibly, in the wrong circumstances, even be murdered just for being who I am. This is still much better than feeling like a solitary isolated freak. But now I realize I'm not abnormal, I'm not weird, and I've got a lot of company, an awful lot of company. For as hard as this lifestyle can be, there is a sense of community.

It's wonderful to have a straight family member, friend, or coworker who is supportive of me. It's a whole other universe of emotion when that person is gay or lesbian. They know what I'm dealing with; they know what we all go through. I've had straight people, in an attempt to be supportive, say they know what it's like to be gay because they have friends who are gay. Right. I don't think that counts. Can you know what it's like to be married just because you know someone who is? Can you possibly know what it feels like to be a parent just because you know someone who is? Parenthood and gayness are very hard to describe to someone who has not been there. Imagine that you've never had kids and your friend's child is gravely ill; can you possibly really understand how they feel?

Still, gay beats freak by a huge margin; I wouldn't go back to not knowing who I truly am for any amount of money. So would I be straight now if I could? I don't think so. Being gay is fun and I'd miss that. Being gay is also hard, but life is hard. A year after coming out, I realized one day that I was pretty happy with who I am now. I feel really strong, much stronger than ever before. It occurs to me that, honestly and truthfully, if I woke up tomorrow straight I'd be disappointed. It would feel like, "Well, damn, that was fun. And now it's over?"

An obvious question for people when faced for the first time with my announcement of being gay is, "So, for how long have you been gay?" There is no how long; my history in the vast cosmos as a human coincides with my history as a gay human. I believe, based on recent research, that it's genetically determined.[10] A million sperm battled to conquer that one ovum in my mother's reproductive tract way back when. When one solitary sperm made it in, and its genetic material fused with that of the ovum's, I was made, and I was made gay. That's just the way it is.

Like all gays and lesbians, I can choose my behavior. I don't have to do what my feelings tell me to. I could act straight, but I'd just be acting. Who I am as a person is gay. No amount of pretending can change that. I know this because I did pretend for thirty-five years. I did such a good job of pretending that I didn't even know I was pretending. And though the pretense was subconscious, it took a big toll on me. How much better I feel now, acknowledging that I'm gay. I was made this way.

There have been public examples of individuals who "were gay" and then were "cured" and "became straight." This is very deceptive. The ground-breaking work by Kinsey in the 1940s is still considered valid today.[11] We humans, apparently like all animals,[12] are innately basically bisexual. There is the famous continuum initially promoted by Kinsey, with straight at one end, gay at the other, and bisexual in the middle. We are all of us somewhere on that continuum, but most of us are not exactly at one end or the other. Someone who is actually somewhere near the middle could live their life either way. This person, for circumstantial reasons, might have ended up living homosexual, but then be faced with internal dissonance over this. Converting to a conservative version of Christianity might do this to someone. Feeling bad about being gay or lesbian, this person undergoes a "cure" to make them straight. They successfully transition to a straight life, and seem functional and happy.

So were they cured? No, of course not; they're bisexual; they can live as either. There are gays and lesbians so far toward the homosexual end of the continuum that they can't possibly live straight. I know a gay man who tried to have sex with a woman once, but became so nauseated that he had to stop. This is not an insult to women, it just means this man is way toward the gay end of the spectrum.

One of the issues that occurs in the lesbian and gay community is the idea of bisexuality. Gays, and apparently lesbians, are discouraged from being openly bisexual. The cultural standard in the gay community is that you have to pick one sex and stick to it. This doesn't sound entirely fair, but imagine being the partner of a bisexual individual who, after awhile, decides they want the other sex now and the heterosexual partner becomes disposable? Bisexuality could be better tolerated, but it is problematic, at least depending on how it's interpreted. Someone who's bisexual could settle down with either a man or a woman, whoever strikes their fancy first. If they then stay with that person for an extended period of time, there's no violation of community standards there.

Ultimately, we all need to be true to ourselves and who we are as people. The following quote was given to me by a friend from work during some of my darkest days and is written on the inside of the folder I carry around at work with my important papers:

To be yourself in a world that is constantly trying to make you something else is the greatest accomplishment.[13]

—*Attributed to Ralph Waldo Emerson*

19

The "Jewish Thing"

I have, at times, encountered objections to my venting. Surely, some people think, I'm making this a bigger deal than is necessary. Anyone who thinks this is really not all that important has absolutely no idea what they're talking about. Many times the comment was made, "I have friends who are gay, I understand what it's like." Really? Do you ever, in the course of the day, stop to think about the fact that you're straight? I think about being gay constantly. Although there is great power in the knowledge, this is not an easy thing to be. Stereotypes, opinions, and values abound, both in society at large and even in our own minds as gay men. I had previously witnessed minorities express outrage that they were being discriminated against when I was sure they weren't. Now I understand. Of course I don't see bias against blacks, I'm not black. I've attended schools that were around 50 percent black kids, I've lived on the edge of the black inner city, and I've attended medical school in downtown, inner-city Detroit. I feel familiar with blacks and have learned to respect the difficulties they can face. But do I know what it feels like to be black? Not a chance. Can I judge the degree of bias against blacks in our society? Of course not, I'm not black. I can imagine what it might feel like, but I can never know.

Prejudice is rampant and often subtle. One tends to get hypersensitive out of necessity, however, and this can lead to overreaction.

Even in such a liberal part of the country as Sonoma County, California, I've encountered homophobic prejudice frequently. At one point at work, after officially separating from Cathy, I was criticized for talking about being gay and dating too much. I had only mentioned it was happening; there weren't any explicit details to tell, even had I been willing to share them. If I was straight and was talking about meeting women, it would have seemed natural and I doubt anyone would have even noticed or thought about it.

Probably only gender and race are bigger deals than sexual orientation. I was born a male, white, Anglo-Saxon Protestant. Now, this single blinding flash of insight has pushed me off the deep end as a persecuted, controversial minority. All those faint feelings that I knew I belonged to some minority have now come back full force; they've been vindicated.

Now that I know this is the minority I'm a part of, I can seek out others of my kind. This is an incredibly powerful thing. What if I was black, Muslim, or Jewish, but couldn't hang out with other blacks, Muslims, or Jews? What if I didn't even know there were any more like me?

Is ethnic background a bigger deal than being gay?

I had always been told growing up that my family is German. All my ancestors came from Germany (except my father's mother who was French). That my last name is distinctly Jewish was not made apparent to me until adulthood. My family's response to the idea that our name is Jewish was always that it was a mistake. In the past, Kaufman was spelled with two "n"s, which is not a Jewish spelling of the name. Or so I was told.

My first experience with Jews I actually knew were Jewish was in medical school. For the first time in my life I knew quite a few, and I knew they were Jewish. I had an uncanny sense of familiarity with many of these guys when it seemed that their being Jewish and from far away (at that point the other side of the state seemed really far away), I should actually feel distant from them.

On moving to Sonoma County, I began to know, associate with, and work with many Jews. I had noticed an odd sense of camaraderie with those I knew without knowing why, particularly the men. This was similar to, but stronger than the feeling toward my male Jewish classmates in medical school.

A few years back, I developed vague but persistent abdominal pain without a definable cause and was referred to the chief of gastroenterology, who happened to be Jewish. On meeting me and reviewing my records, he commented,

"So, David, you're Jewish."

"No, I'm not," I responded immediately.

"I'm not asking," He said, "I'm telling you you're Jewish."

"No," I said quickly, "My family is German, it's just an accident that we have a Jewish name."

"Well I'm telling you you're Jewish," he continued, "I'm looking at the list of your diagnoses and medications and listening to you now and I'm telling you you're Jewish."

"Probably what happened generations ago," he said, "was that your family got tired of the negative aspects of being Jewish and decided that they'd had enough, and just dropped it. They chose to try to blend in instead."

"Huh?" I was dumbfounded. This was a real paradigm shift. My department chief at the time was very much in touch with his Jewish heritage and I asked him about it.

He smiled and said, "It's possible the spelling of your name doesn't actually mean anything. Spellings got changed back and forth quite a bit generations ago."

"How could I find out?" I asked.

He explained briefly that if I could find a German birth certificate for an ancestor, it would give the religion and if it was Jewish, it would say so.

I worked very hard on this but am still stuck at my paternal great grandfather in Canada. I then learned of genetic testing, which can be done with the Y chromosome. This is equivalent to patrilineal descent, which would be the same as the heritage of my last name, which was a main clue.

I sent in a swab of the inside of my cheek as a DNA sample and a few weeks later was rewarded with information on the testing company's Website. Most of the handful of people with my Y-chromosome type consider themselves Ashkenazi Jew. Well that explains a lot. It explains why I feel a certain bond or kinship to the Jewish people I've known. My ancestors could drop the religious observance and identification of being Jewish, but they couldn't change their culture or their DNA. If my ancestors were German Protestants all the way back, I probably wouldn't have felt I have that much in common with Jewish men. So, after most of life thinking my people are German-descent Protestants I learned that we're (at least on my father's side) Jewish, which is significantly different. There is a world of culture associated with Judaism and the Jewish ethnic group that I now seem to own or at least be on the periphery of.

When I mentioned the genetic test to my Jewish chief, he asked how I felt about it.

"Actually," I said, "it feels pretty good."

"I now know that I'm a part of this group." I continued. "I can have a lot to be proud of."

The thing is that since then I've found another group with an even deeper association—the gay culture, one that speaks of who I am on a profound and fundamental level, and a group that I've actually been part of for my entire life. I may be of Jewish ancestry, but I'm also gay, and gay men are clearly my people.

So is my feeling that I'm part of a minority related to my also being Jewish? The Jewish connection certainly has a strong pull, but the minority I feel an even bigger deal to me than Judaism is the gay community.

20

The Dinners

As time after my awakening passed, mostly before I had surgery and came out, I began longing to feel a part of the group, to feel a sense of community, not just a desire for sex, although that was still strong. I felt very lonely and insecure, lost as to who I was; I needed more people to talk to, a group to feel camaraderie with. I found myself preoccupied with feeling bad about some aspects of my situation. I came to realize that when I felt down in general, I would tend to feel like I missed my old relationship with Cathy. It was very rare that I felt I missed my old life; the power of self-knowledge was too great. I would discuss this desire for community, to some extent, with the few gay coworkers I had.

Robert already knew of my desire, of course, but the two gay technologists had not had near as much contact or discussion with me. Robert was not particularly involved in the gay community and didn't know of any specific activities. One of the gay techs mentioned one day that he knew a gay man, James, who organized monthly dinner groups at different local restaurants, just as informal get-togethers. Coincidentally, the next one was in two days.

I quickly emailed James and his partner who organize the dinners and received confirmation that I could come. The two days went by slowly. It seemed to both Cathy and me that our sense of time had changed. Something that happened yesterday seemed to have been at least a month ago. So much

113

was happening so quickly at times, yet it all felt agonizingly slow for me. During this time, Cathy's involvement with women grew considerably. She had regular dates with the same women, and had reasonably frequent sex. This drove me crazy. Again, I don't recall feeling typical husband jealousy that my wife was getting it with someone else, only that my gay buddy was ahead of me again. The first initial truth of my epiphany was that I wanted sex with a man, not a woman. I really wanted more than my first tiny experience I had earlier when I learned that kissing a man was not only okay, but insanely good.

I arrived at the specified restaurant for dinner very anxious. I wasn't sure what I was getting into; I would not know anyone at the dinner. I walked into the restaurant alone and the hostess looked up and asked, "Party of twenty-five?" That was us.

I said, "Yes" and she gestured to the back deck.

How did she know I'm gay? I wondered, or did she just assume that because I was a man and alone that I was with that group. I realized much later that she may not have even known it was a gay event, just a bunch of men having dinner. Gay men, of course, demonstrate varying degrees of effeminacy. I've been told a few times, in different settings, including at this dinner, that I'm pretty butch for a gay man. I doubt that I seem gay just by my demeanor. I'm probably faintly effeminate but I don't think most people would assume I'm gay, except possibly based on the clothes I wear. Regardless, she didn't seem all that interested. This observation about what strangers think of me has turned into a recurring theme. Just as blacks in America are wary of prejudice, I, too, am wary of bias. Most of the time I don't think it's actually present and am not overly conscious of this, but sometimes I am very sensitive about it. The brutal treatment from schoolmates, in the guise of homophobia, left very deep scars.

Walking into a small crowd of gay men for the first time was telling. First of all, they were very nice and polite. I was asked who I was, was I from around here, the usual introductory questions. I mentioned that I was new to all this and someone asked, "Oh, how long have you lived in Sonoma County?"

I said, "I don't mean that, I've lived here 4½ years, I mean the gay thing." I explained that I had just recently realized I was gay.

"How long have you been out?" Someone asked

"About two weeks," I replied.

"What?" There were looks of astonishment on their faces.

"You just came out two weeks ago and you're already coming here?" They were amazed I had the guts to come to something like that so soon. One of the guys admitted it was hard at first to walk into a restaurant alone to a group of obviously gay men. It had honestly never occurred to me to feel that way. I don't think I cared. I don't generally feel that self-conscious. In fact, sometimes when I'm feeling devious, I enjoy watching people get uncomfortable. It's a game I like to play on rare occasions, I call it, "fuck with 'phobes."

"Well, I needed to find my community," I stated.

They were unfailingly gracious and gentle, a few were flirtatious, and quite a few were cute. I noticed this right away. When I first came out, in public situations I hadn't generally noticed men I was attracted to , but I began to later. I realized that night that I definitely noticed hot-looking men in a group of gay men. Over time I've realized that I'm generally less attracted to straight men, only gay men.

The men in that group were amazingly supportive, warm, and compassionate about my situation. I received a lot of advice about my situation with my wife (I didn't mention my wife was also gay because she had asked me at that point not to say anything unless she gave me specific permission).

Some of the comments were unanticipated and much more compassionate than I would have thought. I was told not to regret or bemoan my "lost years" when I thought I was straight. I was told that clearly a lot of good came out of it. One older man poignantly observed that I had children to comfort and support me in my later years and that most gay men did not. Two men swapped email addresses with me and we've kept in touch to some extent. I had really expected that they would be more critical about how I could go so long without knowing. I guess I actually expected that classically straight homophobic man response, "Are you sure you're gay?" Or that they wouldn't accept me as a member of their community because I might be someone sent by the religious right to infiltrate the evil gay empire and help find devious new ways to cure and deprogram us.

I also noticed at this dinner, and have seen at every gay event I've been to since, that these men are obviously my people. I could definitely observe, in this first time with a group of gay men, that, yes, many clearly set off my "gaydar." The attitudes and even topics of conversation fit me totally. I recall discussions of gardening and botany and camping (as recreation). There were no discussions of cars, guns, or professional sports. Of course, there were no discussions of women.

I'm not saying that some gay men are not drawn to some sports. After all, think of the football uniforms; there is padding in all the spots that accent a brawny, buff, and masculine man. And they wear tight pants. There's even a guy on the field called a tight end. We gay men must really find the game boring, considering how much fun it could be to watch for nongame reasons.

I also realized that gay men must obviously come in all different forms, shapes, and sizes. Some men at the dinner were stereotypically effeminate, and some were very butch, appearing for all purposes as straight men. I have never felt all that comfortable in the company of straight men, and I had never before in my life ever felt this comfortable with a group of men.

I left feeling much, much better. For the first time, I hung out with a whole bunch of gay men I didn't know. Previously my entire contact with gays was my mentor Robert (and his partner), my stylist, and the two gay technologists. I had never been in a group of more than three or four gay men.

I didn't know it at the time, of course, but most of my subsequent gay contacts and experiences would come from these dinners or connections I made through these people.

21

Bobby

Within a few weeks of coming out I was getting restless about wanting to date. Of course, I had been told to be patient and that I wasn't ready yet. I still lived in the same house with my wife, although we had been functionally romantically separated for months. Cathy's dating activities, including sex, were driving me crazy—not out of jealousy that my wife is getting it on with someone else, but frustration that she was ahead of me. My gay buddy was out there having the time of her life.

Actually, she wasn't exactly having the time of her life. Dating is hard. I think this is one reason why people get married, so they don't have to date. Also, while Cathy was pretty stable in her process as far as who she was, life-as-a-lesbian thing was also new for her. And although she was meeting some really nice (and attractive) women, her dream partner didn't seem to be interested in her. Cathy had joined a lesbian dating Website and was getting a lot of responses. I tried the same on two different gay sites with no response at all. Well, actually I got several responses from very young gay men in the Philippines. That's a little too much of a commute for dating, and I suspect what they really wanted was a plane ticket to the United States.

Ultimately, for reasons neither of us can fathom, Cathy has found many women to date but little in the way of a lesbian community. I've found multiple, extensive, gay communities, but very few men to date. Some of this could be due to differences in our personalities.

Initially, I was attracted to a coworker; he seemed really hot, although I couldn't tell if he was gay or not, and my gaydar didn't really seem to help. Shortly afterward, I noticed his wedding ring. Very likely he's straight, but at the least he's gay and spoken for. The bottom line is, when there's a wedding ring, forget it. I fantasized about a few other men at work, but ultimately realized that they were all straight.

All through this process, Cathy and I have been very open about what's going on as far as who we like and who we don't think is going to work out. As close friends embarking on a very new and exciting journey, somewhat together, we were both eager to share our successes and occasionally needed a shoulder to cry on for our disappointments. We both have a great deal of relationship experience, and through this process we have always freely asked each other for romantic advice. At one point Cathy thought I wanted to know exactly what she was doing sexually with her lesbian girlfriends. But I didn't. I'm a physician and took a human sexuality course in medical school. I know what lesbians do when they have sex.

We have had a few explicit conversations regarding safe sex. A condom is necessary for safe gay sex for men and apparently saran wrap can serve a similar purpose for women. We discussed this sort of thing, a kind of, "I've read that I need plastic wrap for oral sex, what do you think?" On a few occasions, I've been blunt and explicit because I'm not sure what's going on and I need her opinion specifically. Probably no one in the world knows me as well as Cathy. She knows me sexually and intimately. Even though neither of us has sexual interest in the other anymore, and probably hadn't for some time even before our individual awakenings, we know each other's sexuality well.

Cathy and her closest lesbian friend, Judith, felt bad about my loneliness. Judith had a neighbor who's a single gay man about my age so she suggested I should meet him. This was after the first monthly dinner group.

This was the first blind date I'd ever gone on in my life. Bobby and I set up a place to meet, a juice bar called Jamba Juice. This was his suggestion; I was going to suggest a restaurant, but I think he wanted something that involved less commitment so that if it was obviously not going to work, it would be easier to part company. That experience could be a metaphor for the whole dating experience: protect yourself for the inevitable. He described himself so I would know who he was, although he wasn't hard to pick out when I got there, given there were only a few other customers at the time.

We talked for a while and ultimately seemed to hit it off. I sensed he was being a bit standoffish at first, probably reluctant to go wholeheartedly into this too quickly. I asked if he knew my situation and, although he said yes, I emphasized a few things like newly realized gay, newly out, never had a gay relationship before. He said he wasn't looking for someone, but if the universe offered him a partner, he wouldn't say no.

We moved to a nearby Thai restaurant, ate dinner, and talked. It felt totally normal and natural. As we got up to leave, I was very startled to remember that we were two men out on a date. It felt so natural, just talking to someone and trying to see if there was any connection for a deeper relationship, that I had completely forgotten it was a "gay thing." Except that, it wasn't a gay thing, it was a romantic thing. That we were two men was irrelevant. We agreed to see each other again and went our separate ways. It felt really good, a positive reinforcement for the whole process.

This first date for the first time with a man showed me a powerful truth about gay existence: Gay relationships are the same as straight relationships. Gay dating is the same as straight dating. Although it was a while before I found out, gay sex is really the same as straight sex, just that some of the technical details are different, the parts fit together a little differently. Gay men aren't doing anything sexually that straight couples haven't done; straight women have been known to give oral sex to straight men and straight men have been known to give anal sex to straight women.

Sex, both gay and straight, is about close physical intimacy, usually with orgasm. Exactly what activities are performed to produce these results is very much secondary.

There is the perception in the straight community, I think, that somehow gays and lesbians are really weird, really different (I know I did when I was trying to be straight), like we're extraterrestrials or something. We're not; there may be some extra stresses like the need to limit public displays of affection because straight people have trouble seeing us do that, but basically we really aren't all that different.

Being gay is totally normal. When interacting with gays and lesbians and unsure how to act or what to say, just treat us like we're straight; say what you'd say if I was straight. The only correction that would need to be applied would be referring to romantic partners as "he" instead of "she."

One of my more outspoken coworkers, a particularly liberal and open-minded straight man, asked me, when hearing about how I'd had my first gay date, if it seemed weird or different. In total honesty I said it was so normal and natural I had completely forgotten we were a gay couple instead of straight.

Things progressed slowly with Bobby. We had a few more dates, a few times going to concerts at a local theater. We liked similar music, which is interesting given how hard it is to find a romantic partner with similar taste. Cathy and I had not liked similar music when we were trying to be a married couple, but our interests had somewhat merged into cutting-edge adult pop after our awakening and first conversations about ourselves.

Bobby and I planned to go to a men's retreat (mixed, gay, and straight), but I couldn't go because of a complication of the shunt surgery that could have catastrophic consequences. My shunt was allowing too much fluid to drain from my brain and a part of my brain collapsed in on itself. This pulled on the draining veins at the brain surface and I bled into my head. I was experiencing minimal symptoms from it, some alteration in speech, but if this bleeding, a subdural hemorrhage, increased it could potentially be fatal. I needed to stay close to medical care in case it got worse. Ultimately, it did increase a little and I needed repeat surgery to drain the blood. This was a five-minute procedure under local anesthesia and sedation. The shunt has a valve to regulate the pressure and if I had continued to have problems, this could be changed. After the subdural hemorrhage drainage procedure, I did fine and no additional surgery was needed.

I had a recurring fantasy of walking with Bobby down the rocky and dramatic northern California beach holding hands. I finally convinced him to go to the beach, but there was no holding hands.

> I asked Bobby what our relationship was and he said, "friends." He said it shouldn't be more than that because I'm such a newbie (and because of his issues). That was excruciatingly painful. I'm still like a teenager in some ways—enthusiasm for relationships...
> —*Personal journal entry*

Being referred to as newbie, a baby gay, a kindergartner by established gays happened again and again. Many gay acquaintances told me that my lack of gay relationship experience was a stumbling block for me at this early point. If only they knew how much that hurt. It wasn't my fault I was a newbie, and, personally, I probably have more experience in romantic relationships than many of them. My most recent romantic relationship, marriage to Cathy, had been stable for more than twenty years. Experience in how to maintain a positive and stable long-term relationship is something not all that common in the gay world.

Bobby insinuated that I was too teenage, too exuberant in my newfound self-knowledge and freedom.

> If I was straight and a 20 yr relationship was ending (happily), I'd be like this—excited and teenage.
> —*Personal journal entry*

So although Bobby obviously wasn't going to work out as a boyfriend, we could still be friends, but we didn't really do anything together after this, just a few phone calls. I do miss him, though.

I suspect he had other significant issues with me he didn't say, like he just wasn't attracted to me that way. There's not much I can do about that. I did realize with him that I can fall in love with a man because I know I was falling in love with him.

22

HIV and Drugs

One of the other comments I frequently hear from straight people (particularly close friends and family) upon hearing my news is, "Be careful!" I realize that they mean well by this response, as it usually comes from those closest to me, but they don't understand what a significant and emotional issue this is in the gay community. Interestingly, none of the gay men I know have given me that advice. Would anyone boarding a commercial jet poke their head in the cockpit and say to the captain, "Be careful"? No one has to tell gay men to be careful regarding safe sex. Most of the gay bars I've been to, although admittedly not a tremendously large sample, have containers of free condoms just inside the door. The Billys, a local group that serves as a combination club and support group, always have free condoms and lube (which, besides being generally necessary for anal sex, also decreases disruption of the rectal mucosa) prominently displayed by the main door of their lodge.

Within a few months of coming out, I already knew men who were HIV positive and men who had lost partners to AIDS. I also know men who are hepatitis C positive. This is an incredibly powerful and emotional issue within the gay community and has brought profound changes to gay culture and how gays meet and hook up. Casual sex could be fatal; that requires some thought. It has occurred to me that had I known I was gay at puberty and started having sex with guys shortly thereafter—in the era before effective treatment was available—I might have contracted HIV and died of AIDS.

So what is HIV and AIDS? HIV is a virus that can infect humans. When it does, and remains untreated by drugs to decrease its numbers, it will, in virtually all cases, become AIDS. AIDS is a disease caused by a weakened immune system that includes many otherwise unusual infections (like pneumocystis carinii pneumonia) and an otherwise very rare form of cancer (Kaposi's sarcoma). Untreated, AIDS is always, sooner or later, fatal. Far too many gay men, but also IV drug addicts, have died of this disease. The virus, and therefore the disease, has been communicated to infants from HIV-positive mothers (during pregnancy or during delivery), and communicated via blood transfusions to patients requiring frequent transfusions. HIV and AIDS, as well as hepatits C, can be acquired through needle-stick injuries with used needles. These two infections remain an occupational hazard for health care workers.

I went to medical school in downtown, inner-city Detroit, during the peak of the AIDS hysteria. The number of cases was growing rapidly, and at that time there was no effective treatment. Detroit, at least in that era, had the largest heroin addict population in the United States outside of New York City. I saw, and helped take care of, a very large number of not just HIV-positive, but all-out AIDS patients. Virtually all of the patients I took care of were IV drug addicts, usually heroin addicts. One thing became obvious quickly. Gay men and IV drug addicts were the main populations HIV/AIDS was first seen in. Although there is no difference with AIDS as a disease whether in an IV drug addict or a gay man, there is a dramatic difference between the two populations.

Heroin addicts will steal from stores and people's homes for money to buy the drug from someone they don't know on a street corner. They heat this drug up in a dirty spoon and inject it into their veins using, quite often, a borrowed and used syringe. An addict's drug habit borders on suicidal. Getting them to understand that they shouldn't share syringes is a near-hopeless task. Gay men are normal people. Many are educated and very few are overtly suicidal. It didn't take long for the gay community to catch on to the dangers of AIDS and change its collective behavior. Many aspects of gay culture changed dramatically with HIV/AIDS. The bathhouses where gay sex was not only readily available, but blatant, diminished dramatically. So while IV drug addicts may act in a suicidal manner, gay men aren't stupid and catch on pretty quickly as to how to minimize their exposure to HIV. The searing pain of watching loved ones die of AIDS only made our resolve to fight this and win all that much stronger. From outside the gay community it's hard to understand the incredible emotional power this issue has on the gay community.

Another potential fatal sexually transmitted infection is hepatitis C. It's not uniformly fatal even if left untreated, but can be fatal even with treatment. Unlike HIV, which will virtually always progress to AIDS if untreated, hepatitis C has a variable course even when left alone. Like HIV infection, there is no completely reliable cure for hepatitis C infection, only treatment to help stave off the natural course of the disease. A new drug regimen has the potential to eliminate the infection in some people.

Both HIV and hepatitis C are blood-borne viruses, transferred by body fluids through broken skin. In gay sex this generally only happens with anal intercourse. Anal sex without a condom, known as barebacking, is a very high-risk behavior. These viruses can be transmitted from semen to the mucosa of the rectum, which can be disturbed or broken by mechanical irritation. Most gay men consider barebacking to be a form of Russian roulette, but a small percentage are either willing to accept the risk or are just crazy. Although most of us don't feel this way, self-destructive behavior can occur in gays who harbor guilt over their orientation.

Note that, although the straight community probably doesn't refer to this practice as barebacking, a straight woman receiving unprotected anal intercourse is at equal risk and there are HIV positive women who got the disease this way.

Transmission of HIV or hepatitis C from giving oral sex to a virally positive man is of lower risk than anal sex because the oral mucosa is generally not disturbed in the same way. How much contact is made with semen also affects the risk. Women engaging in vaginal sex with an HIV or hepatitis C positive man are also at risk, but probably less so than receivers of anal sex because the vaginal lining is more resilient than the rectum. However, this still represents a significant risk and many women have been infected with HIV this way. The risk is much higher where, for cultural reasons, vaginal secretions are removed prior to sex. This supposedly increases the man's pleasure but dramatically increases the risk of trauma to the vaginal mucosa and therefore increases the risk of being infected by HIV with a virally positive partner.

HIV can now be treated with a regimen of drugs. This will generally prevent the otherwise inevitable progression to AIDS, but it is a difficult and very expensive treatment and insurance will only sometimes cover it.

Gays are susceptible to many of the other sexually transmitted infections (STIs), like syphilis. These are considered to be of somewhat lesser importance because, once diagnosed, they readily respond to antibiotics. Other concurrent STIs may make transmission of HIV more likely, however, and these infections should be taken seriously. The medical challenge with these diseases is to make sure the patient will take all the medication as prescribed. Promiscuity among gays certainly exists, but in general this may be less prevalent than believed from the hype. Segments of the straight population can also be promiscuous and all STIs are common in the straight community as well.

To add a bit of history here, AIDS was first recognized in 1981, ultimately being seen first in homosexual men, then intravenous drug users, female partners of HIV-positive men, hemophiliacs who had received blood transfusions, and infants born of HIV-positive women. The human immunodeficiency virus was subsequently isolated from these patients and shown to be the causative agent. Virtually all physicians and scientists in related fields believe that HIV is the causative agent of AIDS.

A subset of lymphocytes, infection-fighting white blood cells, CD4+ T lymphocytes are reduced in HIV infection and monitoring of the levels is used to help assess patient's overall health and response to treatment. A multitude of opportunistic disease processes are associated with low CD4+ T lymphocyte blood counts.

HIV-1 is responsible for the majority of HIV infections. It originated with chimpanzees and/or gorillas. HIV- 2 is responsible for more-focal outbreaks. Like many viruses, HIV ultimately results in viral-associated DNA incorporated in the host's cellular DNA. DNA is the root material of our genes, providing cells with a template for creating the necessary proteins that form the building blocks of life and enzymes that catalyze cellular biochemistry.

HIV is transmitted primarily by sexual contact, male to male, as well as heterosexual contact. HIV can also be transmitted by receiving infected blood or blood products and by sharing used syringes and needles. There is no scientific evidence that HIV can be spread by casual interpersonal contact or mosquito bites. In developed countries the rate of heterosexual transmission is 0.04 percent for female-to-male transmission and 0.08 percent for male-to-female transmission for each sexual act.

HIV is present in seminal fluid and a man's penis discharges some seminal fluid early in intercourse, even before ejaculation. HIV is present in vaginal fluid in infected females. The rate of transmission for unprotected anal intercourse is 1.4 percent for both receiving men and women. Through heterosexual vaginal intercourse the virus can be transmitted male to female or female to male. The risk of transmission is significantly higher with the presence of other STDs (sexually transmitted diseases). Circumcision may provide relative protection for a man from acquiring HIV through vaginal intercourse. Transmission of HIV from receiving oral sex is very low, even though seminal fluid contains the virus. Nevertheless, HIV transmission has been reported from oral sex between two men and between two women.

The transmission rate from receiving infected blood products is very high. Blood and blood products in the United States and other developed countries are now screened for HIV. The risk of transmission of HIV from infected blood products in the United States is estimated now at 1 in 1.5 million blood units. Four cases of blood-product-related infection have been reported in the United States from 2000 to 2008 despite the blood products testing negative. Blood can test negative early in infection but can still transmit the infection. Feces, nasal secretions, saliva, sputum, sweat, tears, urine, and vomit are extremely unlikely to transmit infection.

HIV can be transmitted to the fetus in utero, during delivery, and probably also to the infant from breast feeding. There is no convincing evidence that HIV can be transmitted by saliva. Any body fluid contaminated by blood could be infectious, of course.

In the United States, it is estimated that 56,000 individuals are infected with HIV yearly, mostly from male-to-male sexual contact. The rate of new HIV infection in the United States is disproportionally higher in blacks.

One barrier to eradicating the virus in any given individual is reservoirs of virus in some body cell types, including CD4+ T cells. The virus is remarkably adept at evading the normal immune response and, so far, an effective vaccine has not been found. HIV infection can be treated by a cocktail of anti-retroviral drugs. This generally prevents the progression of HIV infection to AIDS. Once again, HIV is the infectious agent, a virus, and AIDS is the disease it causes.

Thirteen percent of homosexual men remained free of clinical AIDS for greater than twenty years even before effective anti-retroviral therapy. With modern anti-retroviral therapy, long-term survival is generally expected. Less than 1 percent of HIV-infected individuals appear genuinely to halt the progress of HIV infection to AIDS without medical therapy. There is probably a genetic predisposition to being able to fight HIV innately. Genetic factors probably also underlie some individuals' rapid progression to AIDS and ultimately death.

HIV infection can cause encephalopathy as a direct result of infection. This produces symptoms of intellectual incapacitation and difficulty with motor movements. Kaposi's sarcoma, an otherwise very rare form of cancer, is much more common in AIDS patients. Acute HIV infection in some individuals is associated with a flu-like illness. Accumulation of fat in unusual locations has been associated with HIV infection (lipodystrophy).

Gay men are also susceptible to sexually transmitted diseases such as syphilis, gonorrhea, and chlamydia. These generally respond to medical treatment and can usually be cured. Herpes can infect gay men, and, as in straight men and women, is treatable medically, but is incurable. These non-HIV sexually transmitted diseases are more serious in the presence of HIV infection or AIDS.[14]

I have to admit I don't have a lot of experience with drugs, other than alcohol, but they can be a big part of the gay experience for some of us.

I've had my share of alcohol and found it generally enjoyable; I've smoked pot a couple of times and thought it was okay. I've never wanted to try anything else. I've pretty much given up alcohol—it doesn't mix well with my antidepressants and I don't feel I need it. I like myself now and am generally happy without it, so there's no need.

Within the gay community, alcohol, pot, cocaine, and crystal meth are used by some. The first two are relatively harmless in the context they're normally used, but crystal meth is, in my opinion, very dangerous. Any time you're buying something illegally there is risk, and the risk of being caught and punished is only the beginning. There is risk that the substance actually purchased is not what was expected is a very real danger. Many illegal drugs have potentially very dangerous effects. Cocaine, both powder and crack, as well as crystal meth present significant cardiac and other health risks.

The fact that risky sex may be engaged in when one is high is another serious issue. When drunk and or high, sexual participants may allow more-dangerous practices and may be less sensitive to pain and therefore risk injury. Finally, both meth and cocaine are highly addictive and this can lead to a vicious downward spiral in those who use them.

If you need drugs to have sex I think you need to reevaluate your sexuality and your feelings about it. Guilt and/ or homophobia could drive the need to be numb emotionally in order to have gay sex. If gay sex is really better for us than straight sex, we should be able to practice it without chemical enhancement.

23

Cathy's Moving Out

> ...I'm scared to death. I'm back in the master
> bedroom because Cathy moved out...I'm depressed.
> Does Cathy's moving out bother me more than I
> realize? Just minutes later I find Cathy's wedding dress
> in the closet...
>
> —*Personal journal entry 10/23/09*

It was inevitable that one of us would move out at
some point; we needed to have separate residences.
It's difficult for one of us to bring someone home when the
other is there. We had lived together for about six months after
our revelations, considering ourselves separated but sharing
the house.

Cathy felt, and I understood completely, that she and I
both needed the opportunity to live alone, truly alone. Neither
of us had ever really lived alone and she wanted the experience.
She felt at the time, and I felt later, that we needed to be able
to be alone first to really understand ourselves before starting
a new relationship.

Cathy's ultimate decision to move out, then, was not to get
away from me, but to take advantage of the opportunity to live
alone, to learn to be self-sufficient materially and emotionally.

I was thoroughly convinced that I was ready for this. It
was an obvious development given all that had happened
and it would have positive benefits for me. After Cathy moved

out, I could sleep in the master bedroom and park my car in the garage. We had decided that Andrew would stay with me because he and I have many interests in common, specifically, we have many geeky interests in common. Anyway, one of us would have to continue to live in the house we owned together at least for now. The house would not sell for anything close to a reasonable amount given the economy and the fall of real estate prices. Because Andrew would stay with me, the two of us would stay in the house. This meant that Cathy was free to find a place near the arts district in town where her friends were.

Rationally, I was ready for her departure. In my heart, the center of my feelings, I was totally unprepared and when it happened I was devastated. For twenty-two years; including more apartments and houses than I can remember, all of my medical training, multiple jobs, and living in three states, when I came home at the end of the day, Cathy was there. Andrew joined us about halfway through, but Cathy had always been there. Now she wouldn't be; we'd still at least be as good friends as we were when we were trying to be a straight married couple, but we have to live separately. No matter how much we love and care about each other, we're not as close functionally as we were when we lived together.

Unfortunately, this was one of those times when there's a disparity between my rational thoughts and emotional feelings, and I was not consciously aware of it. I have learned, in part through this particular instance, that when there's a gap between thoughts and emotions that I'm not aware of, I get depressed. This time I got really, really depressed.

>...Cathy called this morning to say she wouldn't be by today, had other things (hiking with friends) to do. It really hurt. How do I stop being this attached?
>—*Personal journal entry 10/25/09*

My coworkers could see how down and lethargic I was. Normally prone to conversation, I became very closed-mouthed.

I was also having difficulty working and my colleagues were advised by my boss, the chief of medical imaging, that I was having medical problems, and would be in and out for awhile. That left me a convenient out to call in sick when I didn't feel I could work. Nevertheless, one day while working, I made a critical mistake; fortunately for the patient, it was caught quickly and no long-term harm was done.

My psychiatrist doubled the doses on two of my three antidepressants; the third was discontinued because of side effects. My therapist and I explored what was going on with me and, gradually, I began to realize that I was suppressing a great deal of pain. This pain was not at all Cathy's fault; rationally I still now believe her moving out was necessary and overall a good thing. She was a little hurt to realize my pain was somehow related to her. I made sure she understood it wasn't in anyway her fault.

> Left work around 10am—couldn't talk w/o crying. Talked to Cathy by phone and she just found out her moving out is related to it; she felt bad...
> —*Personal journal entry 10/26/09*

Usually feeling bad about one thing carries over into my feeling bad about a lot of things; actually, pretty much everything. I tend to have more doubts about who I am and what I want.

> Left work around noon. Feeling a little better. My future still feels bleak. Flirting with pretty woman at coffee shop—is that what I want? I just don't know. Can a relationship with a man be as good as with a woman? It seemed like it with Bobby, but in the end it didn't turn out well. Maybe I just need to be patient (which is what everyone tells me)...
> —*Personal journal entry 10/27/09*

I was told over and over to be patient, it would happen. I just couldn't accept that; my teenage exuberance was pushing me madly toward sex; the emptiness I felt losing Cathy as a special someone pushed me very strongly to find another relationship, to somehow replace what I perceived as lost. Her moving out made it much more acute.

I also discovered, now a newly single custodial parent, how hard single parenthood is. With no other parent to diffuse the responsibility, it's all me, all the time. With schoolwork, housework, and a job, there's no time for anything, no breaks. Andrew doesn't need to go to bed as early as I do, but he does sleep in, so there's a little break then. Just because he's a teenager doesn't make it any easier. He needs constant attention like when he was five—getting him to do his homework, go to bed, get up in the morning, clean up after himself, and take showers. I now have great empathy for single women raising children by themselves, like my mom did. It's really hard. Cathy calls to recommend a movie; I'm too busy to go to movies. I can only watch movies at home if I'm able to do something else that needs to be done at the same time. It's getting comical; I'm now so busy I have to make an appointment with myself to cut my fingernails, and I'm booked a week out.

24

Halloween Billy Gathering

I continued to feel a need to be a part of the larger gay community. A prime opportunity for this arose when James, who helped sponsor the dinner group, was a coordinator for a gay men's retreat.

The Billy Club was founded years ago to provide support to a young man dying of AIDS without family or even friends. The basic goal of the organization is to be, "a heart-centered brotherhood." The majority of the group's official activities are oriented toward advancing personal development, community, and compassionate support for gay men in need. Just like similar groups for straight men, some of the people it helps are prominent, successful men with a stable long-term relationship and solid family ties. Some of us are not those things. Initially oriented to the more-rural gays, as opposed to the younger downtown gay men, the Billys are a diverse and eclectic lot.

The retreat was over Halloween weekend, traditionally a major holiday in the gay community; the gathering lasted five days. It was held at a rustic resort very isolated in the woods with no neighbors. The resort is an older place, with simple accommodations. Most of the sleeping is multiple bunk beds packed into rooms.

During this retreat, we were very isolated. Everyone present was gay. The manager of the resort was gay, and the cook, the only other paid staff, was gay and a Billy. Being surrounded by only gay men is remarkably supportive. The rest of the work that needed to be done, mostly kitchen work, was done on a volunteer basis by any of us at the gathering.

I arrived anxious and frightened, but as I walked through the main door of the lodge I realized I was surrounded by brothers. Every one of these men instantly became a brother. Some of the older men became like fathers, watching over me, helping me to not get too carried away, coaching me. The older men helped me keep my perspective and not get talked into doing anything sexual that I might regret later.

Specific planned activities were mostly oriented toward personal growth and development. There were meditation groups, a session on the history of the Billys, and the main daily event, the Heart Circle. This was a meeting with carefully defined dynamics, something like group therapy, but without a specific theme. We sat comfortably in a big circle, stretched out on yoga mats and cushions. We took turns speaking, but there are specific rules. We are to speak from the heart rather than the mind. There can be no interrupting and no criticism of anything anyone says. What's said in the Heart Circle cannot be discussed outside the circle.

> The first evening at the Billy Halloween event. I think this is going to be less about romance and sex and more about community. I've never spent more than a couple hours immersed in a group of gay men, and that only infrequently.
>
> —*Personal journal entry 10/29/09*

A group of men, alone and isolated, whether gay or straight, can get a little wild. There was frequent nudity; the weather was quite warm and one guy just went around completely nude for two days. There was obvious sexual activity going on, although closer to PG-13 than R rated. There was a big hot tub; we all wore bathing suits *to* the hot tub, but not *in* the hot tub.

Although I'm generally shy and easily embarrassed, I wasn't put off by any of this at all. I was even an active participant in some ways.

At a retreat spending five days with as many as ninety gay men, I realized what was missing: not a single conversation about team sports, professional athletics, guns, hunting, fishing, trucks, or cars. What did we talk about? Relationships, romance, sex, and coming-out stories. That this latter subject is so important to us is a sad commentary on our society and culture. We need a culture in which there is no such thing as "coming out" as gay, just as no one has to "come out" as blue-eyed or left-handed.

Undoubtedly, a bunch of gay men together are obviously different from a group of straight men. Although we're similar to straight men in many respects—we all feel happiness and joy, sadness and pain, and hope and despair the same—that's innately the human condition and we are fundamentally the same in those emotions. But what we like and what we value can be really different from straight men.

It's confusing to say we're just the same as straight people and yet very different from them, but let me explain what I mean. Living in California I encounter a large number of Latinos. I feel that they have a very colorful culture and generally a positive attitude. California would not be the same without them, and I thoroughly enjoy their presence.

And although some aspects of Latino culture can seem different to white Americans, Latinos are really exactly like white Americans: they laugh, love, cry, and experience relationships just like the rest of us. Gays are like that; gay men may have different cultural preferences from typical straight men, we may like and dislike different things, but fundamentally we are exactly the same. We laugh and cry the same. Our relationships are the same. It's the same, "Honey, do these pants make my butt look fat?" And it's the same, "Why did you say that to him?" It's the same give and take, the same effort to maintain a relationship.

Of course, we have some superficial differences in our interest from straight men. When in a group of gay men, I've now gotten completely used to seeing someone crocheting or knitting. I've become so accustomed to effeminate behavior among gay men that I don't even see it anymore. It still does surprise me that gay men generally want to talk about what I want to talk about. What a huge relief! Much of what I've

137

always found uncomfortable about being in the company of straight men is that they want to talk about things I don't have any interest in or know anything about. It's a relief to be with a bunch of men and not have to fake my way through a conversation about professional sports!

Being gay gives me carte blanche to ignore pro sports, which I really did anyway, but always felt guilty about. There are a lot of things I don't have to feel guilty about anymore.

Some difference between gay and straight men in our culture can be overwhelming, difficult to overstate. It's the difference between rooting for a football team and shopping for fine china. Straight men fight, hunt, shoot guns, and support competitive sports—dominate, conquer, compete, and win. Gay men dance, explore their feelings, and shop for clothes and crystal stemware—create, cooperate, and collaborate. Gay men would generally rather create than compete. Creativity is, of course, not universal in the gay population, but our lack of competitiveness seems quite widespread. Of course, to apply these blanket stereotypes to gay and straight men seems ill advised and probably rightly so; these are just general trends. I do know some gay men with some interest in sports. And in California, I find straight men in general much less driven to fit that typical macho-man stereotype. So maybe our differences aren't that universal after all.

On our five-day retreat there wasn't a single activity that was competitive and involved winners and losers. I think this is a fundamental difference between gay and straight men. Gays, in general, just don't want to be involved in anything that involves separating people into winners and losers. People being good or bad at something is more subtle in the gay community, it's more about who's a good artist, a good musician, a good dancer.

So we may be less competitive and more collaborative. But would gays accept defeat? Never. Allow ourselves to be walked on? Again, never. We have learned to stick up for ourselves and demand to be treated equally. This is part of the "gay pride" movement. We're not quite there yet, but we keep trying.

I noticed seemingly new personality traits in myself. These profound, yet sometimes subtle, differences don't change overnight. Where did my new "feminine" attributes come from? I realized, after some introspection, that these feminine characteristics were always there; I just hadn't allowed them to show very much. Whatever "masculine" traits I had, I didn't feel compelled to eliminate or downplay all of them. I like to read tool catalogs. I definitely still enjoy riding my big Harley wearing full riding leathers. For the first time in my life I'm now free to be who I really am. but it took my realizing I'm gay to achieve this. It's tragic that I couldn't accept myself before.

Everyone should feel free to be who they are without restrictions. There's no reason I should have felt bad recognizing my feminine traits. Some normal straight man also have feminine qualities. It's wonderful that I can feel so free now. Observing the behavior of a large group of gay men at the five-day retreat was fun and interesting. A fun example of how our group was not like a group of straight men was the meal line. Food was good, but not overly fancy; it was served in a buffet line for every meal. The resort's dishes for eating off of are about twenty different patterns, all mixed in. We would form a line, at times maybe seventy-five guys. The line often moved slowly because the guys in the front of the line had to pick out an acceptable plate.

"I'm not eating off that," one would say, "that's god-awful ugly."

"Can you imagine people actually eating off this?" another would comment.

"Okay," I'd say, "now here's a plate I can use; I can stand to eat off of this plate."

In general, the sense of aesthetics was heightened compared to most groups of straight men. We looked at, and talked about, each other's clothes, too.

"Nice shoes!" someone would say.

"Great shirt!" someone else would offer. I got that a lot, now being partial to fancier shirts.

For the Halloween party we were told to prepare costumes

before the event and I understood that there would be some good ones. The only remotely cool costume I could come up with that didn't entail a lot of work and/or money on my part was my motorcycle riding gear. I wasn't even sure I wanted to attend this so I wasn't about to invest a lot of time or money in a fancy costume.

I wear full black leather riding gear when riding my Harley. I purchased and use the outfit because it's very practical and very necessary. Leather is extremely durable, particularly in an accident, to protect my skin. Black is needed because the road a biker is exposed to contains a large amount of dirt and bugs.

I knew that in my gear I was a perfect caricature of masculinity. I wear leather chaps over pants because they can be put on and taken off in front of other people. Chaps are really only the legs of pants and a belt to hold them up. The parts of pants that cover the groin and buttocks aren't there. This proved to be interesting at the party.

My motorcycle hobby was and is quite disconcerting to my work colleagues. No doubt they picture themselves in a bind at work without me after I've been smeared down the highway by a big semi truck. Of course, they might be genuinely concerned about me, too. My masculine caricature in leathers sometimes disturbed me because it made me look like either I'm a big-time biker dude, or I'm *trying* to be one. Back when I bought this gear, long before my awakening, if asked about that I probably would have said that I'm not an outlaw biker; the motorcycle leather thing for me is closer to the Village People than to the Hell's Angels. I still feel that way, but find it even more amusing. I must confess that I like playing with people's heads; I have so many more opportunities now with the whole gay thing, it's part of the fun of being gay.

I threw my leathers in the trunk of my car before leaving. My mentor Robert heard of my costume plans and made me promise to wear jeans under the chaps. On Halloween night, the Billys twisted my arm and convinced me to go to the party without my pants. I arrived with just underwear and a shirt under my leather jacket and chaps. Within a few minutes of arriving, however, my arm was again twisted and the underwear and shirt came off. I recall standing up after putting the chaps back on and wincing, but only briefly. I had a wonderful time at the party. Incidentally, the strongest beverage served was lemonade; the Billy events are substance free.

> The party was wild—I didn't make it to the door with pants, only underwear—took underwear off shortly after party started—I'm really glad I took it off—it was rebellious and wild and felt good.
>
> —*Personal journal entry 11/1/09*

The substance-free environment of the Billy gatherings is due to many reasons. Some subsegments of gay culture are heavily into drugs; meth, in particular. This is very destructive and totally opposed to the mission of the Billy organization. Additionally, there was a very tragic occurrence at a past gathering where a young man arrived high, left for more drugs, and was murdered. The older Billy who told the story became quite emotional as he told it. This tragedy made a very deep and sad impression on the organization. During the five-day Halloween gathering, I might have smelled pot smoke a couple of times but I never saw any alcohol being brought in, never heard anyone talk about it, nor smelled it on anyone's breath.

Although this seems amazing in a way, alcohol just isn't necessary at an event like this. The intensity of the atmosphere is so great, all we really need is one another. The DJ for the event wore only shoes as his costume. The DJ's entire costume was a pair of athletic shoes and a short piece of red yarn tied in a bow around the base of his penis. One thing I learned from this gathering that I had never figured out before is that basically all men have a really small penis when it's not erect. Because my un-erect penis isn't smaller than the other men's, I felt I had nothing to be ashamed of, I was comfortable being essentially nude in front of a group of people. Granted, it was entirely a group of gay men and I had already realized that I felt very comfortable with them.

One thing I observed over and over that totally blew my doors off was how I was complimented on my looks. I'm pretty sure I'm not ugly or really fat, but I've been aware of only a few times in my entire life when a girl or women has found me particularly attractive. Truthfully, women probably don't readily admit that as compared to gay men, but even Cathy and I always knew that what drew us together was less hot physical lust but more a sense of a sort of kinship, a friendship that quickly became very deep, which is interesting, because this is where we are now, in a friendship.

At this Halloween gathering, guys were coming out of the woodwork telling me how hot I was. Guys would be talking to me about something totally unrelated, then out of the blue say, "You're really hot, you know." My butt was being grabbed frequently.

Standing on the front porch of the main lodge in the cool evening I would usually be in bare feet, as that's how I roll. Invariably, standing around in a group of guys, someone would say, "Aren't you cold like that?"

My stock answer, something I came up with a long time ago and used without thinking about possible implications in this environment was, "Naw, I'm okay, I'm always hot."

Every time I gave this response the four or five guys standing closest to me would nod vigorously and say, "Uh-huh, Yeah, uh-huh."

I arrived frightened and lonely and left having to push people away. "Okay, Okay, I get it. I'm hot, now let go of me." I felt like the homecoming queen at the prom and turned down multiple offers of companionship and/or sex. I arrived alone and left with a boyfriend and boys on the side.

Probably in order to spare me the big ego trip, it was commented later that some of that was just because I was new, fresh meat. I like the explanation that I really am hot, though, so that's what I'm going with!

There were many comments about my "hot ass," many grabs…being essentially nude at the party felt very safe and secure—I'm with my brothers.
—*Personal journal entry 11/1/09*

25

Jason

At that point in my life I was still having some trouble accepting that ultimately my romantic interest/partner would be male. Somehow it feels less worthy than female; like I'm accepting a lesser option, so I'm a lesser being. I think I'm still okay with being a man attracted to men, but on some level in the back of my mind, it just feels inferior. This is yet another example of persistent stereotypes, another way to feel like a bad person. Over time this feeling faded, and a year later I didn't feel inferior anymore; it's just me, just who I am.

When I attended the Billy Club Halloween gathering I had considerable anxiety and apprehension. I didn't know what was going to happen. I'd gotten the feeling ahead of time that I could get sex there if I was open to it and that sounded good to me at the time. I was very new to the whole gay idea and wondered what sex with a man would really be like. The possibility of finding a boyfriend never crossed my mind. Truthfully, I didn't really know what a boyfriend would feel like; would it feel different from a girlfriend? I'd had many of those, even two wives. Mostly I went to the gathering to find community, to be with my people. The dinners I had gone to, the first only a few months prior, had given me community, but only for a few hours. The Halloween gathering would give me community for five days. When I arrived on Thursday night, after dark, scared and lonely, I recall thinking that at least it was only a couple of hours' drive from home and I had my car. Worst-case scenario: I could say I was sick and leave early.

I remember walking in the main door of the lodge on my arrival and being greeted warmly. I was introduced to Jason, the coordinator of housing arrangements. My immediate reaction was, "Oooh, housing guy is cute." We had communicated a few times prior to the event, as there was initially insufficient indoor housing for me. That meant on Saturday, the busiest night, I would have to sleep outside in a tent. Not my ideal sleeping arrangement. I'd had enough of that kind of camping as a child, because that was all we could afford for summer vacations. At the last minute something opened up and I could stay in a bunk for the whole gathering.

My second night there, the Friday before Halloween night, the retreat organizers planned a special entertainment event. They called it "The Journey." It was something like a cross between a haunted house (but not very scary) and a stage show. Those of us attending were spread out in a big circle, similar to and in the same space as the Heart Circle. There were yoga mats and cushions in a big circle and we all sacked out to watch the show.

I was reclining on a mat near the main door next to Manuel, a new friend I'd made. The two of us were moving toward a more serious relationship and I anticipated sex with him before the gathering was over.

Suddenly, Jason, the cute housing coordinator, walked in and laid back on the floor between Manuel and me.

"What's going on here," I wondered, a little miffed that he'd come between Manuel and me. Soon, however, Jason was gently caressing my arm and I couldn't believe how good it felt. He made faint gestures with his hand toward my chest and groin and my breath began coming out in gasps. I'd really never felt anything like this before and this was the mildest of physical intimacy, much too minimal to be considered sex.

This went on for several minutes; I still have no recollection of what The Journey was about. After some time with Jason, I was ready for more than this.

"Can we go somewhere?" I questioned Jason.

"I have a semiprivate room, and my roommate is probably here at The Journey," he responded.

"Can we go there?" I pleaded, still breathing in gasps.

The clothes flew off, just like I'd been told would happen when the chemistry was right, just like what I knew from steamy straight sex, only better. It was pretty amazing. It felt like coming home. I was worried it would feel weird. It did not. It felt totally normal, totally natural. All the proscriptions against same-sex contact from my adolescent peers went out the window. This was glorious. This was fantastic!

> 10/31/09 (paper journal) Lost my gay virginity last night - Wow! OMFG! The (mild) foreplay during the "journey" was the most intense I've ever experienced. Jason is sweet and attractive…
> *—Personal journal entry 10/31/09*

This was my first complete sexual contact with a man, including foreplay and cuddling afterward. When I was with the man I had been set up with months ago, we did just enough for me to know I liked it and my behavior wasn't a mistake. I liked and wanted sex with men.

What struck me as interesting later on, when I thought about our first contact and, ultimately, all our contact from just being together to holding hands, French kissing, and sex, was that it never occurred to me that being with a man was weird, wrong, different, or odd at all. It felt absolutely normal and natural, in a way definitely better than the experiences I'd had with women. Even though I had stereotypes and reservations about some aspects of being gay still in my head, being with Jason, and the fact that he's a man, was absolutely exhilarating. Sometimes realizing what I'm thinking about feels weird, but never when I'm actually doing it. It took almost three years to get used to what I find myself thinking about now, namely sex with men instead of women.

11/1/09 (paper journal) I wanted my loss of virginity to be special and it was! I feel like the Billys really are my brothers; they (the older more senior anyway) watch over me with protection and support...
—Personal journal entry 11/1/09

I realized that my relationship with Jason was facing really long odds. It had been incubated in a very artificial environment very different from either of our real daily lives. There was a large age difference; he's the age of my oldest child, my daughter. I felt particularly guilty about that because my daughter had been seeing a man about my age and she knew I didn't think it was a good idea.

Interestingly, the reactions Jason and I both got from people we talked to about us were very consistent. If the person was straight, they'd caution that the age difference is a big thing. If the person was gay or lesbian, they'd invariable shrug their shoulders and say, "So what." Statistically, gay relationships don't last as long as straight relationships, maybe because the odds against us were big either way. But, because many gay couples don't even try to raise a family, a big age difference isn't as important. In a straight relationship with an expectation of children later, having one partner much older can cause trouble as the children age. Daddy could be retired using a walker by the time the youngest child graduates from high school.

Ultimately, when I spoke to my older children about Jason, my daughter thought it was no big deal and didn't hold a grudge for my position on her relationship with a much older man. My older son, who's two years younger than his sister, was unhappy about it. He couldn't see how it could be okay. I suppose that in the end he was right; the relationship didn't last all that long. But it was fun while it lasted.

...[Jason] left [the gathering] after lunch and I think I really miss him. I'm not sure what he sees

in me. "David" (older general contractor) says it's highly unlikely this relationship will last, because of age difference. I'm very, very tired, but feel very comfortable in this group, more than I've ever felt in any group. Some of the behavior seems extreme (nudity, public sex), but not that uncomfortable...
—*Personal journal entry 11/1/09*

I noticed that during my time with Jason, at least at the beginning, my discomfort over the changes in my relationship to Cathy, my mourning for what can no longer be, felt much less acute. But I knew the whole time that if anything happened to pit Cathy against Jason, Cathy would win, without even a fight. I can't turn my back on twenty-two years of real friendship; I think the feeling that our relationship is changing is what I'm mourning. Even though our marriage was in trouble near the end and before my epiphany, I could still pretend everything was okay, and I did. I can't pretend anymore; the marriage part of our relationship is over.

...David said the old relationship is gone, I think referring to Cathy. May [sic] pain about Cathy seems very far way right now; only minimally felt...
—*Personal journal entry 11/1/09*

My feelings with Jason were so intense it was hard to believe. It felt like I had waited all my life to experience this. Nevertheless, would the age difference be a problem?

My relationship with Jason in [sic] incredible; I'm scared that something will go wrong and it will be over, but I know that a good relationship with a man is better than women. My relationship with Jason is better, stronger, more intense, more romantic, better sex, than any relationship I've ever had with a woman.
—*Personal journal entry 11/15/09*

147

Struck by how intense and real my feelings were, I realized I am capable of having these feelings for a man; I am capable of having an emotionally powerful and fulfilling relationship. It was so good, and such a relief.

> I can love! 11/7/09
> —*Personal journal entry 11/7/09*

Jason and I continued to see each other after the gathering was over. Amazingly, given how far away some of the guys live who came to the gathering, Jason and I lived only a few miles apart and both work daytime jobs. There would be many opportunities for us to see each other after the retreat, and we took advantage of that as much as possible, at least at first.

> [Had] 3 lunch dates with Jason this week on call, met him briefly after my work for a bit at Applebee's. It feels really good; warm, not just sexual. It's almost midnight—I'm tired.
> —*Personal journal entry 11/6/09*

We were with each other constantly, sometimes twice a day. We texted each other ten to fifteen times a day; it was always going back and forth. I actually got used to texting while with Jason. I was never in that much contact with Bobby, possibly because he knew it would accelerate my feelings in a relationship he didn't believe he wanted or even existed.

Because we were dating we needed things to do together. We went to a lot of shows. We bought each other flowers so often the girl in the Safeway florist shop began to know us by name.

One day early on as I was buying extra-special flowers for a particularly special occasion, the young woman was chatting, happy and bubbly.

"These are really nice," she said, "These are really special."

"She'll really like these," she continued.

I looked up from the flowers to her face and said slowly,

"His name is Jason."

She barely missed a beat, "Oh, I'm sorry, well, *he* will really like them."

A few weeks later, Jason was buying me flowers with the same girl waiting on him.

"I'm Jason," he said.

"What?" She looked puzzled.

"David's boyfriend," he explained.

Her face brightened, "Oh, you guys are so cute!"

We enjoyed playing those games with people; it was fun, and we felt we were raising awareness to gay rights. We took to drinking "Go Girl" energy drink because it was packaged so femininely. But later on I had to reject, or at least put on hold, much of this.

> Saw "Santa-Land Diaries" at Spreckels Theater with Jason; everyone there, even the actor, knows him. I'm totally overwhelmed; I've never felt so absolutely totally and deeply in love. This is incredible, actually really hard to believe, so soon after the entry of 10/26/09 when I wrote the future looks unalterably bleak and missed Cathy so much...
> —*Personal journal entry 12/10/09*

I had wanted a boyfriend so badly, I realized later, partly because I wanted to prove to myself I was really gay, that it would really work. This motivation could only be seen in retrospect. On the one hand, I'm really sure I'm attracted to men. All those years of fantasies, cravings, dreams can't be denied. On the other hand, there was a faint sense that I hadn't actually done the relationship and sex thing, as some of my gay acquaintances have suggested: I'm not really gay if I haven't done it yet; maybe it's just all in my head (this is the type of comment from a gay that's equivalent to the "Are you sure?" comment from straight men). There's no doubt now. Jason's broad manly chest under the touch of my hand, his beard stubble on my face, was totally intoxicating.

For the issues that surrounded our time together, particularly my ultimate difficulty with that level of immersion in the gay community, I never had the slightest reservation about my relationship with Jason because he is a man. From holding hands to kissing to sex, it all felt absolutely natural, even better than natural, like what I was meant to be all along. It felt like finally coming home.

> Still seeing Jason frequently—last night he fell asleep in my arms with his head in my lap. I bent down to rest my head on his and it was so beautiful in the face of all my struggles that I started crying. I told him about it today and he said it was also a very powerful experience for him too…
>
> *—Personal journal entry 11/12/09*

I had felt an emotional hole in my life; Jason filled that gap. Through this whole process, Cathy had one specific person whom she looked forward to as a romantic partner. And although that relationship may never materialize, her degree of aloneness was less than mine. In Cathy's mind, she had gone more or less from her being my significant other to her having the distinct possibility of having a specific other person fill that gap.

> Things with Jason still good—I'm crazy about him, but I've been spending too much time with him (instead of sleeping at night) and am totally exhausted…
>
> *—Personal journal entry 11/22/09*

I began to have doubts about my relationship with Jason after several weeks, but I felt it was salvageable. Many friends, curiously only the straight ones, had warned that the age difference was too much for this to work out. I was also beginning to have nagging feelings that the sex wasn't really all that great. It was cool at first to finally be having sex with a man, but questioned myself whether it was really all that better than sex with a woman.

> I really need to love and be loved; to make love, not have sex…
> —*Personal journal entry 10/12/09, before Jason*

I felt at the beginning of our relationship that I had learned something new about romance and sex. My experiences with Jason taught me what romance is about—the simple acts of touching, hand holding, the brush against the cheek. These are very powerful feelings in the context of a loving, romantic relationship with a person of the correct gender. I also felt I had learned the difference between having sex and making love. If it only takes ten minutes, it's probably just sex. While sex with the right person can still be gratifying, making love is a whole other thing. If it takes two hours, it might be making love. The actual sex act is only a small portion of the lovemaking experience, which is about romance, like the small gestures and holding hands.

Jason and I lasted almost exactly two months. We were inseparable during that time, together any time both of us were free from work. If we weren't together we were texting or talking on the phone. At the time, he lived with his parents and I lived with my son Andrew, so there was no place we could go to be truly alone to have sex. Cathy and I had decided it was good for Andrew to see us with same-gender partners, but no overnights or sex while he was around. So Jason and I had precious few opportunities, but made the most of them. Being with him felt really good; being physically affectionate with him felt so right, so normal, so natural, that it became hard to even remember being with a woman like that. But after awhile I began to think that we just didn't have the right chemistry between us. I didn't have anywhere near enough experience with multiple different sexual partners to be able to know this in my own life, but I understand that some couples just have the right chemistry and some don't.

151

The two months we spent together were very intense. Perhaps because of how much contact we had, in communication or together constantly, it seemed a very different period of time in my life compared to the lonely time before our relationship and the depressed time after it. During my two months with Jason, I thoroughly enjoyed all the contact, in every form, with him. When the loneliness resurfaced later, I realized I missed all of that.

Through this entire process, save a couple of months, I had no idea who I might end up with, or even if I'd end up with anyone at all. Outside of the time spent with Jason, it seemed a daunting task for me to find someone. I had originally been advised by my mentor Robert to find someone age-appropriate and at a similar career level. I completely disregarded that advice in my mad rush to have a boyfriend, any boyfriend. Obviously, I can now see Robert was right. But this appropriate person is going to be a hard person to find.

26

The Interview

Jason has friends in the radio business and a local
station has a weekly program featuring LGBT (lesbian-
gay-bisexual-transgender) issues. A wonderfully charming
lesbian couple also does a show through this program. They
particularly feature coming-out stories and part of the idea
behind the show is to help others who haven't come out yet.
When they heard my story they were eager to interview me.
They really wanted to interview both Cathy and me, but she
wasn't ready for "prime time," not ready to be that out. I agreed
without a complete understanding of what it was about.

We all met at the studio an hour ahead of time to go
over what we'd talk about, with me needing to be particularly
clear to them what was off-limits (pretty much anything about
Cathy), and them needing to be clear to me what I can't say on
the radio, which is a lot of what I'd normally say.

We spent some time discussing how I could tell the story
of my revelation. In particular, I shouldn't say "tranny" because
that can be construed as derogatory. I can't talk at all about
the male "G" spot. And of course I can't use any profanity.
We discussed the difference between who the show's regular
listeners *would* be (probably LGBT), and who the listeners
might be (grandma and grandpa accidentally tuning into the
station). Because I didn't know anyone who'd be listening,
I wasn't sure how important this was, but I didn't want my
interviewers to be in trouble with their superiors.

The interview was streamed live over the Internet, but I don't know anyone personally who heard it this way. Actually, I don't know anyone who heard it over the radio when it originally aired. It's been saved, along with everything else the radio station does, in the archives and has been available over the web. My family and friends who've heard it got it this way.

Overall, I thought it went pretty well; my interviewers were impressively warm and compassionate, there was no bloodthirsty, go-for-the-jugular, tabloid approach. We discussed my own realization and my reflecting on it, then coming out. I emphasized that I believe my strength in this process comes in part from my near-death experience.

My interviewers brought up that not every gay man feels this much strength in this process. My interviewers asked where my strength came from and how could I pass it on? I had observed that Cathy had less conviction than I did about coming out. But this is a difficult subject for me to address because I'm not entirely sure where my strength comes from. I think it's a combination of the relief in knowing I'm not a freak and the relief in knowing I'm not dying. Somehow the two are related, even though they shouldn't necessarily be. I think, in retrospect much later, that on a semiconscious emotional level I had associated my dying as a sign from God, fate, the stars, whatever, that dying was a punishment and that gay is bad. After my original thoughts that I would sacrifice my life to be straight, then being very sick and told I was dying, then being miraculously cured, I felt that my recovery was a sign that it was fine to be gay. The only meaning I can construe from my miraculous save from the jaws of death while remaining gay is that I was meant to be gay and not to hide it. And, for the most part, it felt really good to be gay. After thirty-five years of post-pubertal life trying to be straight, I had finally found the group of people my mind and body are tuned in to. It felt like I had a mission. I find being gay both fun and amusing at times. When homophobes get bent out of shape, it's fun for me to play with their heads. I know that's rude, but I consider it consciousness raising. I think playing with racist people's heads and misogynist people's heads is probably equally gratifying and justifiable.

I felt we in the LGBT community should be proud, both proud and strong. There's nothing wrong with us, we're normal interesting people. This became a driving force in my life, my own special reason for existence.

The interview itself went pretty well. I explained briefly, in a sanitized-for-radio version, how I recognized I was gay. As agreed, we didn't talk at all about Cathy's sexuality. I don't think they ever really know how many people actually listened in on the show. In theory, a very large number of people could have been listening. When the issue of how my family, and in particular, my wife felt about my coming out, I said my family is fine with it and my wife is very understanding. We avoided mention of my older children to keep them from being pulled into something they might not want. .

My relationship with Jason was discussed as we were still seeing each other at that time and Jason works at the radio station. We discussed how beautiful it was, even though gay relationships face extra challenges.

The interview concluded with what was probably the most important thing to communicate: what we can offer gays and lesbians to cope with the difficulty in coming out.

I said that realizing I'm not a freak gives me strength. I am proud of who I am.

Our final words of advice to struggling gays and lesbians were to know you have company and community. Believe in yourself and be strong.

27

Feeling Down

Ultimately, in between the up times, there are a lot of down times associated with this whole process. There is also occasional self-doubt, with both Cathy and I wondering if we're pointed in the right direction.

After the initial excitement of self-discovery fades, reality sets in. My life seemed to have fallen apart; I felt estranged from my sons, two of my three children. Obviously, even after two decades, there's no marriage left in the traditional sense. Even though our relationship, now based on an honest appraisal of who we really are, is much better than it ever was, there's still a feeling of profound loss. I felt the loss much more than Cathy did and it took two years for me to recover. There was an empty hole in my life, a huge gaping hole. I notice I feel much worse in the evening. "Cry in the night if it helps."[15] It does help, somehow. I had heard so many song lyrics about people who are lonely or sad who cry in the night. I never understood before what they meant; now I know. On a reasonably good day, I can be fine at work, but still cry myself to sleep at night. Through my psychiatrist I get pills to help me fall asleep.

The future feels inevitably/unalteringly [sic] bleak—a partner? Someone who'll sleep in the same bed? (Tigger the cat on the bed—looking for Cathy?)

—*Personal journal entry 10/26/09*

156

For me much more than for Cathy, the changes in our relationship feel like loss. We were a couple for so long, almost half of my life up to that point, that it is taking me a long time to get over it. Over time I can see I'm doing better, though. I think Cathy's relative ease with this process is due mostly to her much greater emotional resilience. She's also had romantic companionship for most of the time since our awakening.

> I always tear up when I see photos and things related to Cathy on Facebook. I don't think it's related to her specifically, but part of mourning for what I've lost; the old me, the old life.
> —*Personal journal entry 12/6/09*

At one point, I realized I was angry, furious at having been rejected by Cathy. Is this idiotic, or what? Why should I feel rejected by my wife's realization that she needs a woman, not a man, when I'm going through the same thing? Still, somehow, ego dislikes rejection, and that's what it feels like. This feeling of anger only lasted a few days. I think it was a phase I had to go through. Even though I was relieved when I heard she's a lesbian and she wanted to be out of our marriage, just as I'm gay and want out of the sexual part of the marriage commitment, it still felt like she left me, at least a little bit. We never fought over it and she was very sorry that I was going through this. But it still hurt.

> It hurts that Cathy wanted out 1st, dated 1st, & moved out of my house because of ego—I want to call the shots [in conversation with a friend at work]
> —*Personal journal entry 10/29/09*

The sense of loss with my wife is part of an even bigger loss in the sense that I've irrevocably lost my innocence, my naiveté about life. Life's not going to be easy anymore; it's vastly more complicated now. I can't pretend I'm ordinary.

Just feel like I don't care about anything and I just want to die. Nothing is really resolved... ...except I know Cathy does seem to care about me.
—Personal journal entry 10/15/09 8:45am

Many times during this process I was depressed and Cathy and my large support network of friends have always been there to help. I've been very fortunate to have them.

The bleeding will stop...in conversation with a friend
—Personal journal entry 9/2/09

Yet there are still times when my support group seems to fail, and I'm left feeling alone. Although the group is very helpful and really necessary, it's also necessary to have the strength to do this on my own so that I'm not dependent on others. It's just a lot easier when I have friends.

I have to figure out how to be OK when no one cares about me (except me). This is really important.
—Personal journal entry 10/15/09

What has become evident is that throughout most of this, I have missed Cathy in a way that she hasn't really missed me. Besides physical intimacy, we had been emotionally intimate for a long time, and in some ways, that has continued, even improved. For most of this process, I have not had anyone else I could be emotionally intimate with like that; I've relied on her in that way.

What hurts now is the loss of a "special someone."
—Personal journal entry 10/15/09 2:15pm

Although the level of emotional intimacy between us has stayed the same or even increased, the degree of direct intimacy in our lives has obviously decreased dramatically since she moved out. Although it bothered me during our marriage, having conversations with her while I'm seated on the toilet doesn't happen anymore. We're still occasionally together while one of us is naked or dressing and it feels like no big deal. We're used to seeing each other naked and it doesn't really mean anything.

When she moved out, Cathy had expressed that she wasn't moving out necessarily to get away from me, she was moving out for the opportunity to live by herself and learn a form of self-sufficiency she had never experienced before.

> Cathy's moving out also allows me to be/live by myself (Andrew doesn't count since he's a dependent). I think I prefer that now that she clearly isn't my special someone, it's actually hard to live with her in this situation.
>
> —*Personal journal entry 10/17/09*

There were a few times after my revelation when it was hard to be around her, particularly early on. Being with her intensified my feelings of loss; ultimately I needed to learn to be alone and be okay with it as much as she did. When I was around her it was hard to let go. It took almost three years, but ultimately I was able to let go.

Over the years, Cathy and I had gotten in the habit of quick smooch kisses with hellos and goodbyes. This continued after our first conversations, as did the habit of calling each other "Hon." The kisses were clearly nonsexual and the term of endearment was such a long-ingrained habit it seemed pointless to try to eliminate. Also, of course, while trying to be a straight married couple we smooch-kissed and called each other "Hon" and we weren't having sex then either. Because, in a sense, nothing had overtly changed, we couldn't see why we should change these little habits. The woman Cathy was dating most consistently at this time had known both of us for some time prior to our awakening, and found our kisses amusing.

> Rough night—can't smooch kiss Cathy anymore; really bothers me—why? [it feels like she doesn't want to be my friend] She thinks because I'm grasping at anything familiar; that's the best explanation so far.
>
> —*Personal journal entry 9/25/09*

One night I came home from getting my hair done and bent down to kiss Cathy. She immediately put her hand up to block me, saying, "I don't feel comfortable doing that anymore."

"That really hurts," I said

"I'm sorry," she replied, "I didn't mean to hurt you. It's just that it seems like a big deal to me now, and anyway, you want to do it all the time. Lesbians are real careful about who they kiss."

"Oh," was all I could come up with at that point. This happened during a time when she was dating and I was not. I realized later that I enjoyed the feeling of closeness kisses brought, even if it wasn't sexual. I had noticed that smooch-kissing was common among gay male acquaintances.

Over time, the smooch kisses returned, the only difference being that I rarely initiated them. We always greeted each other with hugs; I imagine that people who've known us for some time would see little difference in how we act toward each other, but then, why should there be any difference? We still love and care about each other.

> ...light will come again.
>
> —*Ingrid Michaelson*[16]

28

New Year's Gathering

[New Years with old friends] party last night with Cathy. Went well and felt good to be just me, not gay man me. Cathy joked that I was a Jewish KP doc, referring to my employer Kaiser Permanente, and that's how I fit in. Learned that when nothing is familiar, it's easier to be back to things that are familiar (leave gay behind for a little while), than force the new stuff to be familiar (this doesn't work). It will take a long time for these new things to feel familiar. The New Years Billy gathering still feels like too much, but I'm tired and need some sleep.

—Personal journal entry 1/1/10

Initially, I accepted everything that I found with whatever gay community I found—the dinners, the Billys. Nothing was too weird or too odd. The very idea that I was gay was by far the strangest thing that ever happened to me; after that nothing seems too different. I just tried to take in everything my new culture had to offer, or at least the portion of gay culture that came my way.

During my time with Jason, I had became more and more stressed out, to the point of not sleeping at night, tossing and turning. I wasn't sure which part of my life was messed up, but something surely was.

A very difficult night—so many changes since last Christmas…X-rays show still have curved spine, looks worse. How can I accept all my flaws? I just want to be right, the way I'm supposed to be. But what is that? Straight? Straight spine?…Last night went to S.F. with Jason for a show and went to bars in Castro. I don't think I want to be this anymore… …I don't even want to be alive anymore.

—Personal journal entry 12/24/09

I had been diagnosed with scoliosis of the thoracic (chest) spine as a teenager. It generally doesn't cause trouble, it just gives me a sense of being flawed. I had a whole bunch of bureaucratic hassles when I started my residency because the radiologist who read my chest X-ray said my spine was curved and that technically meant I was disabled.

Cathy offered her point of view and suggested that I was trying too hard to be gay, trying too hard to be involved in everything gay I could find. At first I couldn't see the wisdom in this, at first I felt I was supposed to just experience everything I could find. Out of my transformation those few months back came the sense that I just had to do the whole gay thing, now. And now Cathy is suggesting I had gone overboard.

"You don't have to do any of this, you know," she said the night before New Year's Eve.

"I think you're overwhelmed by everything you've found," she continued, "and it's too much for you."

"Why don't you just stop for awhile," she said.

It's funny that she said that. I had been feeling that on and off for some time, but it had felt like too radical a solution. Now that she suggested it, it seemed easier to decide.

I think I'm done with the whole "gay community" thing…

—Personal journal entry 10/12/09

Cathy had a suggestion: Why didn't I go with her to the New Year's Eve party she'd been invited to by some longtime friends. One of them, Bonnie, was very open-minded and very supportive, knowing the full story of what was going on with us. Furthermore, Cathy herself represents the familiar to me, and is not personally a symbol of all that's happened. Going with her could be comforting to me in my overwhelmed state.

"I can't." I answered, "I have New Year's plans with Jason."

"Then tell him you can't go," she pushed, "you need to do what's right for you."

I called Jason and told him I couldn't do our original plans and that I would be going to a party with Cathy. He was very disappointed. What had been planned for us was to visit some gay bars in nearby Guerneville, a gay haven of sorts in the woods just east of the coast. He was to be in drag as one of the Sisters of Perpetual Indulgence, a very philanthropic organization of men who mostly dress in drag as nuns; they are a bit on the wild side. Some of the other sisters would also be there. The Sisters of Perpetual Indulgence are a wonderfully charitable, compassionate, and philanthropic organization with fascinating people who want to serve the community. It is a worldwide organization; the local chapter is mostly men, mostly gay, but not necessarily. They are a magnet at night in Guerneville: following them around is like being a rock band groupie. People recognize them and want pictures with them; it's all quite amazing.

At the time, only a few months after coming out, I didn't feel I understood drag at all. Although I liked all the individual sisters I'd met, and some are very admirable, I just wasn't sure that I got the whole drag thing. When a member of the order (usually a gay man, but could be a straight man, lesbian, or straight woman) wants to pick a persona, they can choose to be a nun or a priest/monk. Most select to be nuns. I don't know why. Jason explained that for him and many others, it's not a sexual thing, it's just a form of theater. But I thought, if that's the case, then why do essentially all men in drag dress as women? The Village People was theater and they weren't in drag as women. They were in a form of drag as caricatures of macho stereotypes. I didn't understand why men who do drag don't dress up as cowboys or pirates or policemen. I realize that they are not trying to look so exactly like women that no one can tell they're men. Men who really want to be women are transgender, not transvestite or even necessarily gay. Drag is not about trying to really look like a woman, but more looking like a totally outrageous over-the-top, trashy, campy woman. I know some men who do drag who have grown beards just to look more outrageous. Similarly, some men will occasionally wear spaghetti-strap dresses, clearly showing their chest hair. At the Halloween gathering party, there was a man with a full beard wearing a wedding dress. In any case, I felt then that drag as women was harmless enough, for whatever reason they did it. Much later I began to understand the drag thing a little better.

For the first few years after I came out, I felt that I had no interest in wearing women's clothing. I had never considered wearing women's clothing after my sexually charged experiments as a teenager. But later, when I felt I was finally open to all possibilities and liberated enough in my thinking as a gay man, I could accept my doing drag as a woman if I wanted to. I have entertained, at some point or another, the idea of my exploring pretty much every aspect of gay culture and community I'm aware of. I know, for example, that I can be quite a bit of a girl in some settings, particularly romantic settings. I have thought seriously about whether or not I want, in addition to acting like a woman, to *look* like a woman with women's clothing and makeup. I had seriously entertained the thought that maybe I really am a woman in a man's body. But I was quite sure at the time that I didn't want to look like or truly be a woman. I felt I'm a man, and I'm happy to be a man. I believed I'd actually found my masculinity by realizing I'm gay.

I've found my masculinity
—*Personal journal entry 10/2/09, with therapist*

164

I don't think it's my place to judge what other people think they are. I believe it's a fundamental human right to be able to define our own sexuality. Right or wrong, if I say I'm straight, everyone has to respect that. And if I say I'm gay or a woman in a man's body, everyone has to respect that, too. It's not for someone else to say what my sexuality or gender identity is.

I have observed that different segments of gay culture and different gay men have varying levels of wildness. Most of the gays I know lead very conventional lives. Other than the fact that they are men who have male partners, they are pretty much stereotypical American men in stereotypical American families. None of them run around in bars dressed as nuns! I've also observed the variability in comfort level with open sexuality. The Billys as a group both tolerate and demonstrate a lot of open sexuality. My gay coworkers, although probably not overly offended by such talk and behavior, seem to feel no need to participate in such behavior. I think this shows the variability in the gay culture, just like some straight couples are very conventional and some are swingers or nudists or like to frequent prostitutes. Probably very few straight married women own a strap-on dildo, but that doesn't make doing so wrong. We all fit in somewhere.

Early in my gay life, I found that some behavior in gay communities was wilder than I wanted to be, but not truly objectionable or reprehensible. It's just people having fun with who they are and that's the hallmark of the human spirit. I was just not comfortable with the wilder side of being gay. I figured then that at least in the immediate future, I'll more likely turn up at the Zen Center in meditation robes rather than running around bars dressed like a nun. To each his or her own.

I'm not sure I really know how to do this...I just don't want to do this anymore. I can't think, my mind keeps going blank. I'm tired of being paraded around to Jason's friends; I'm just really tired overall. I really care about him and I think he cares about me, but the relationship is really hurting me...Will it be better tomorrow...I'm pretty sure I'm still gay, but where did proud and strong go? I don't want to talk to anyone about it (or anything else).

—Personal journal entry 12/13/09

Cathy and I went to the New Year's party together. We were introduced as Cathy Kaufman and her husband David. That's it. There were Kaiser people there, non-radiology physicians and psychologists. It was quickly established that I was a physician and a radiologist. Many in the group were Jewish, so my being of Jewish descent came up. Other than that, I was just David and it was wonderful. No more fighting for truth, justice, and the gay way. If anyone had been watching carefully, they might have noticed that Cathy and I weren't as affectionate toward each other as most of the other married couples, but then, we might not have been very affectionate years ago, either.

It was a pivotal event, and I realized that Cathy was right: I was trying too hard to do something that wasn't really me to begin with. I am gay, but I don't have to participate in every single aspect of every gay community.

Feel like I don't know who I am. A gay man? A man? The changes are affecting me on a deeper level. Probably with Jason, it's sinking in more, and I'm feeling it deeper, I still think I'm proud and strong, but I'm less defiant in being out. I'm [not] sure I always want to be "a gay man"; can I just be a man? I'm feeling profound feelings of sadness? Or grief? Knowing in some ways I can never be the same...

—Personal journal entry 12/14/09

The day after the party, Jason and I left for the Billy Club New Year's gathering. We were to be there two nights. This was held at a different resort from the Halloween gathering but was at a similarly rustic place that had been used as a youth camp.

166

Jason had mentioned to a friend who knew me and also volunteered at the public radio station what had happened regarding our New Year's Eve plans and how I didn't feel I could go. His friend Greg handed Jason a book and said, "Have David read this." It was *The Velvet Rage*, by Alan Downs. The book is about the emotional repercussions of being and knowing you're gay.

We arrived at the gathering and found, as Jason suspected would happen, we were both put together in one semiprivate room with two beds. This would afford some privacy that the majority of the participants who were in bunks would not have. He was more excited about this than I was.

The tone of the gathering overall probably wasn't much different from the Halloween event; many of the same people were in attendance. But the difference to me was like night and day. For one thing the atmosphere was different. This resort was set on a hillside under big redwood trees and it was cold and rainy the whole time. At the Halloween gathering in late October, the weather was like summertime.

Also, this time the Billys seemed to be trying to outdo each other in outrageousness. The drag, the hypersexual talk, the kinkiness seemed like some kind of contest to see who could be the most extreme.

We arrived in the drizzly rain; the other guests seemed disappointed about this, although to me it matched my mood and was welcome. In what seemed to me like an omen, the first night we were there a tree slid down the hill in a mudslide and crushed two parked cars (thankfully, it happened in slow motion and no one was injured).

Billy accommodations are rustic at best; indoors, but with minimal comfort. Of course, the humility of the accommodations keeps the cost down and gives men who couldn't otherwise afford it the opportunity to participate. It was chilly, but our room was heated. The main rooms of the resort were heated by woodstoves, giving a cozy atmosphere. I was disappointed to see that this resort's dishes were all the same pattern. It had been fun at Halloween watching us all pick out dishes we felt were attractive enough to eat off.

Our room was near the communal bathrooms. With the door open I could hear the sound of men peeing in a toilet, standing up. It felt somehow, to me, that it's a joyful sound, a celebration of our maleness and masculinity.

Jason and I arrived for the end of the Heart Circle that day; we both professed our love for, and gratitude for finding, each other. Of course, the fact that we found each other at the last gathering had a special meaning for us.

During the event I essentially avoided all activities. I spent most of the time in our room reading. Jason didn't seem to mind, but was a little concerned, I think.

At this gathering, there was one guy I hadn't met or seen before. He was from southern California—a long way from home. He was stunningly attractive; never before had I been so entranced by a man. Not only that, he was educated, intelligent, and incredibly articulate. I sat listening to him speak in rapt attention. Wow, this guy hit me like no other ever had. This is what serious attraction feels like. That settled the question of whether I could ever be overwhelmingly attracted to a man.

Finally, I realized I needed to leave, and soon. I just couldn't take any more of it. I informed Jason; hopefully someone would be headed back to town toward my house that evening. Jason offered to take me home himself, saying that the following day was the last day anyway and not much would be going on.

We drove home in silence; it was rainy, foggy, and dark. Although preoccupied with the difficult driving conditions, in the forty-five-minute drive he never noticed I was crying.

Ultimately, after that weekend, I'd had enough. I started mentally and emotionally retching, as if my mind had ingested poison. Everything now had to go; I couldn't handle any of it. All I could think was take your makeup, your dresses, your bondage ropes, and your constant hypersexual talk and go away. I needed all of it to leave me alone. Let me be with my thoughts to try to make sense of it. I needed time to think, time to be alone and sort this out.

Looking back on this experience much later on, I realized

that at the time of the New Year's event, I was still forming my identity as a gay man, still getting used to the fact that I'm gay. Nowadays, after taking stock of who I am, and who I want to be as a gay man, some of that wild stuff appeals to me. I'm not put off by drag at all, I think it's interesting and entertaining. I also realized in retrospect that some of my problems with the gathering were probably my feeling smothered by my relationship with Jason. Not smothered by Jason as a person, he didn't do that, just my being overwhelmed by the relationship itself and what I was putting into it.

Months later I realized that part of what was wrong during my time with Jason was that I wasn't yet completely comfortable with who I was as a gay man, and having a boyfriend made it worse—it really emphasized that feature of my new life. Having a boyfriend made being gay seem much more real and pressing. It just took me a long time to get used to.

I found after this gathering that for a while I needed to be alone as much as possible. On the one hand I was lonely for human contact in a specific form, yet I was overwhelmed when around other people in general. Can I just be a normal everyday guy who happens to have a male partner? Could this ever happen or work?

The following day I broke up with Jason, explaining I wasn't ready for a relationship. He was upset, but took it rather well. He asked if we could have any contact, and I said I didn't think so. After it was done, I cried for a while (the crying gene must be very close to the gay gene). Finally, it was time to get on with life.

On a short excursion to a supermarket later that day, I realized something strange was happening. For the first time in my life, the women were all transparent to me and all I could see were the men. This guy is kinda cute, but probably straight. That guy is cuter, but probably also straight. Who cares if they're straight, some are hot! Suddenly I just looked past the women to see the men, the ones I really wanted romantically.

Recently, my stylist commented that the ideal guy for me may be hard to find, and he probably wouldn't even be interested in me now because he'll know I'm not ready yet.

> Talking to one of the older surgeons; when I'm finally comfortable with being alone is when I'll meet the right person.
> —*Personal journal entry 01/23/10*

I realized then I needed to learn to be alone, without any romantic partner, for the time being. Since meeting my first wife in high school, over thirty years ago, I have only been romantically alone for a grand total of about three months. I needed to learn how to do this. I needed to learn how to be okay just being by myself.

Much later in the process I realized that I've had a romantic partner in my head continuously since puberty. It's true that the large majority of the time the girls didn't like me back or want me, but I had someone in my head I was bonded to all the time. When it become obvious that a specific girl was out of reach (usually because she'd say so on knowing of my interest!), I simply replaced her with another in my head. I did this continuously in between actual relationships, which were few and far between in middle and high school.

> I feel like this is the first time, ever in my life, I was comfortable with the idea of being alone. I think I need to get used to the idea of (for example, with friends and family) being just "David," instead of "David and _____." I've felt lost through this process not knowing who my ultimate partner will be; what name will fill in that blank some day? I'm realizing it doesn't matter; who I am is "David," not "David and [someone else]." My family and friends can identify me as just me, not me and a partner or spouse.
> —*Personal journal entry 01/23/10*

Dave and Cathy, Dave and Barbara, David and Jason; I've always been defined by who I'm with. Now I'm not with anyone and have no one in my head; I have to define myself as myself, alone. It's a frightening prospect.

I worry about the stability of relationships. I've heard that gay relationships statistically don't last as long as straight ones. This is probably related to the extra public pressure on gay relationships, having to keep any display of affection private. I wonder if it also isn't the relative scarcity of available gay men. Perhaps we settle for companions and partners who are intrinsically just less compatible.

Given that gay relationships are not as stable as straight ones, this is another reason for me to get used to being alone. The model in the straight world of being married to one person for better or worse for a long time may not hold in the gay world and I need to be prepared for a life with a series of partners and long periods of aloneness.

29

Ending My Relationship with Jason

There were two serious issues with my relationship with Jason. The first was the vast difference in relationship experience. The two months with Jason was the first big relationship he's had (at least that's what he said). My first romance happened when I was twelve years old. By the time I was his age, I'd had almost a dozen serious girlfriends (where the interest was actually reciprocated), slept with a few of them, and was already divorced from a woman I'd been married to for eight years and had two kids with. And all of this doesn't even count the twenty-two years with Cathy.

Gay relationships are basically the same as straight relationships, with a few extra stresses thrown in, like being aware that public displays of affection can be dangerous. But it's the same basic dynamics, the same interpersonal give and take (usually give) and learning how to be romantic with another person. It's about learning to live with and be accommodating toward another person, who may be quite different from you, with different likes and dislikes. In reality, a good romantic relationship is about compromise, something someone with little experience in it would naturally have a hard time understanding.

I never realized, in a relationship, some things that were always there until they weren't. It was hard for Jason to think of me, what I wanted or needed, my interests. I learned so long ago that it's a subconscious process to constantly think of the other person. Even now, at a party with Cathy next to me while I'm conversing with someone else, I'm subconsciously thinking about how what I say will impact her. I know without thinking about it not to say something that makes her look bad or puts her on the spot.

The night Jason and I left the Billy gathering, Jason, with me in tow, went around to pretty much everyone he could find, saying in a stern tone, "We're leaving tonight."

The response was the same every time; the other person would then look at me and ask, "What's wrong?"

This really put me on the spot; I was very upset and doing my damnedest not to cry in front of these people, and now I not only had to talk, I had to come up with the excuse why we're leaving.

"I'm not feeling well," was the best I could come up with.

After repeating this experience several times, I was about to tell Jason to shut the fuck up. It didn't seem to occur to him at all that he was putting me in an uncomfortable situation, only that he felt put out to have to leave early and wanted to share this with everyone present. I had presented him with other options earlier but he had earlier assured me he didn't mind.

I think I would have handled this differently if I had been in his position. Approaching the few key people that really needed to know, I would have said something like, "I'm sorry, but we need to leave tonight; Jason's not feeling well." Then all he'd have to do is stand there and look sick.

After the drive back to my house, I managed to stop crying long enough to bring my bags into the house. Jason left and I immediately started crying again. Cathy was in the family room watching TV, having come over to watch Andrew for the duration of the gathering. She said later that when she heard the noise of someone at the back door, she knew right away what happened.

Crying, but otherwise silent, I walked past her and up to my bedroom, where I sat on the floor in the dark and cried. After about a half an hour, there was a light tap on the door,

David L. Kaufman, M.D.

"Do you want to talk?"

Cathy came in and I tearfully spilled my guts. She listened patiently and then offered, "You've really thrown yourself into the whole gay thing; you probably need to back off. If the relationship with Jason is as bad as you're saying, you need to break up."

"It would crush him," I said.

"He'll have to deal with that; you have to do what's right for you," she countered.

I think Jason's view of relationships was very idealistic, drawn from the media and observations of friends, both gay and straight. He didn't have a lot of pragmatic experience. Observing other couples won't teach how much give and take, how much self-sacrifice is required in a relationship. To keep a relationship going requires each party to subjugate themselves for the sake of the other and for the sake of the relationship. He'll learn in time though; he's not a bad guy, and he's really very sweet. He's just inexpert in the ways of romance.

The second issue I had with Jason is another naiveté thing, but now flipped around. Jason has known he is gay since he was twelve and had been out for a few years. I had only known I was gay for several months before I met him and had only been out for three months. I threw myself wholeheartedly into the whole experience, but I was very naive; I actually knew nothing of the culture of gays, drag queens, and other variants of gay. I never even stood next to, let alone talked to, a man in drag until the Halloween gathering. Just like Jason's knowledge of romance was only theoretical, my knowledge of all things gay pretty much all came from a few sections of *The New Complete Joy of Gay Sex* (which is about a lot besides sex). Jason pulled me into a world I didn't know much about and wasn't ready to enter. Experiential knowledge is generally preferable to book knowledge.

It feels like 2010 is starting out a lie, but its probably more like confusion. Part of me doesn't want this relationship, but I think part of me does. If it

174

ended I would feel hurt, but free. I just don't want to do the gay thing right now. We just had lunch and I'm still hungry, but my friend Ana won't let me eat.

—Personal journal entry 1/2/10

Most people afflicted with anorexia nervosa are woman and most are very thin. Anorexics often try to justify their extreme dieting with the idea that being very thin is good. Of course, there is a lot of societal pressure on women to be thin. My friend "Ana" is the figurative voice in my head that tells me that I can't eat because I already ate too much, or that I'm going to have to work out on the treadmill for two hours today because I ate an apple yesterday.

Part of what was wrong with my time with Jason was that I wasn't completely comfortable with who I was as a gay man, and having a boyfriend made it worse, it really emphasized that I was gay, but what did that really mean?

I didn't really know who I am in the sense of my being gay. Was I was trying to be "Gay Man," in a tight pink leotard with a big purple "G" on my chest when what I really want to be, at least for a time, is just "David," who incidentally happens to be gay. I also didn't really know what I wanted from the gay community. Discussing this issue with my gay friends and associates from work, I've discovered that most of them have very little involvement with the gay community at large. They have some friends who are gay and that's pretty much it. Probably the best example is my mentor Robert. He is a typical, ordinary, straightforward physician with a practice and coworkers and friends, who just happens to have a male partner. That's it. No drag, no bondage, no constant hypersexual talk. I mentioned to him that all anyone seemed to talk about at the last Billy gathering was sex.

"Thank you," he said emphatically. He went on to say, as Cathy had, that I don't have to do any of that gay community stuff, I don't have to be "Gay Man." I am gay, but I can be gay without participating in the gay community.

David L. Kaufman, M.D.

I had, in those last two months with Jason, discovered that not only were gay relationships the same as straight relationships, but gay sex is really the same as straight sex. Different equipment maybe, the parts fit together a little differently, but it's still two people doing what works for them with the equipment they have. It's just not that big a deal. There's no need to talk about it constantly. Is the constant discussion of sex from some insecurity? Months after the Halloween gathering I realized that the Billys are not necessarily typical of all gay men and that their outrageousness and wildness are just part of the group's subculture.

For awhile the sex with Jason was better than sex with myself. There haven't been that many times in my life when I could say that, and it's probably an appropriate benchmark for physical intimacy with another person. And, while this assessment was true with Jason, it had also been true with some women (Cathy), although that was a long time ago. Although there's ample evidence I've been gay my whole life, it seems to have been intruding into my conscious daily life more and more over the last several years. Clearly, my body had become, over the last couple of decades, very reluctant to have traditional penis–vagina straight sex, and much more amenable to, and needing, gay sex. I have, however, been used to the idea that I can always give my partner an orgasm. With the idiosyncrasies of my own sexuality, I can have sex all night with a woman. This gives plenty of opportunity for her to climax. I can ultimately be satisfied, one way or the other, but I've been less worried about that in the last several years. Since my more typical midlife crisis in 2003, I had learned through my Buddhist practice that I am already truly complete. I realized that material possessions mean nothing; acquiring stuff now seemed pointless. I now know I don't really need anything, maybe just air, water, and food. This carried over into my sex life. I have been having sex with myself for thirty-five years; I've gotten pretty good at it, and know what works and what doesn't. If I'm actually having sex with another person (which happens less often lately), I want to give them a good experience. The only reason I can see to have sex with another person is for me to be able to give them that beauty, that pleasure. Being unable to do this for someone is uncomfortable for me.

Although initially the sex with Jason was good, at first outstanding, I began to think sex with men could be better and that chemistry was lacking. Both Kenneth, a gay technician at work, and Robert basically told me in terms of the mechanics of the sex act, that's pretty much how it happens so gay sex may not necessarily be better than what I experienced with Jason. Well, I thought, I'd had better sex with women. If that's as good as it gets, then I'm done with that.

It was a massive relief, a giant boulder off my chest, to break up with Jason and pull out of the gay community in every form. I was upset; I missed Jason in some ways; I really always liked affectionate physical contact, particularly with him as a man. I also missed him to some extent as a friend. One issue with the relationship that occurred to me after it was over relates to our potential future together. Within a few weeks Jason brought up the prospect of us moving in together. I was uncomfortable with that, believing even talking about it was premature. Jason always acted as if he was positive the relationship would last, "until death do you part."

Although that kind of optimism is basically good, realistically the odds were strongly against us. He was too young and I was too new to the gay thing. During our entire two months together, I always knew that if anyone or anything ever forced me to pit Jason against Cathy, Cathy would always win. There's just no way any relationship just a few months old could win out over twenty-two years of friendship, trust, and mutual support. He wouldn't have any idea what a lengthy relationship was really like. I do, and that was part of the problem.

Something that occurred to me a little later is that I may not have been ready for a real boyfriend at that point because it forced me to be "more gay" than I'm ready for. After breaking up, I can take more time getting used to my being gay. Cathy had come to realize she was gay slowly, over weeks or even months. I realized I was gay in one blinding instant and somehow had to learn to deal with it after the fact. There was no way I could deny the truth of the realization, and I only resisted it for a few days. It's just been really hard to get used to. A lesbian friend of Cathy's said it takes two or three years to get used to realizing you're gay. I think for me it was closer to three.

Also, the anger I felt toward Jason might be a defense mechanism on my part to keep from having to feel bad about hurting him. Near the end I knew our relationship was going down, but I kept trying to believe it would work because I didn't want to hurt him. I really am fond of him (from a distance) and I think he's a great guy, just not the right guy for me.

Occasionally still, during the ensuing two years, I pause and realize I'm thinking of my special someone being female. Even though I know I'm really attracted to men, I'm just not used to that yet. As my mentor Robert said at one point, related to why I'm still working with depression, "Well, it's not like when you were thirteen you really thought you'd be this way as an adult."

Weeks after the breakup with Jason, while I was getting my hair done, my stylist said that although it's true that the mechanics of gay sex are pretty basic, when the chemistry's right the sex will blow my doors off. He said this with the conviction of someone who knows what he's talking about and has experienced it himself, so I held on for the time when that'll happen.

30

Jealousy

One of the consequences of Cathy and I accepting that we're gay is the realization that we don't have to accept any of society's values; we have to be open-minded. We need to question the values we grew up with and that we brought into our relationship. Even though we felt we were living our lives according to what we believed, we were ultimately conventional and conformist in our attempt at living straight lives for so long.

One of the principles we had lived by that had to be discarded early was the generally taboo nature of sexual discussion. In all our years together, Cathy and I never openly discussed our sexual relationship in terms of what we liked or didn't like. We never discussed things we'd like to try or experiment with. The gay community tends to be much more open about sex.

For a few years before all this happened, Cathy and I had enjoyed attending an annual local gay-pride event that featured gay and lesbian comedians. I found it to be some of the best comedy I ever heard; good comedy can come from pain and the gay community knows suffering. It was also fun, as we were one of the token (allegedly) straight couples to observe how gays and lesbians act among their own. These performances were probably the first experiences of being within the gay community for both of us. Neither of us had very much exposure to gays and lesbians prior to moving out west, and none of that was in any kind of group setting. One thing immediately noticeable was the openness regarding sexuality. Straight people just don't talk about sex like that at all.

Neither of us had much difficulty with sexual openness. But another value we've been forced to question is the idea of fidelity. For a brief period of time, gay marriage was legal in California, and those gay marriages then formed are still recognized as legal.

While I was dancing essentially nude at the Billy Club Halloween gathering, another man came up to me, and, while dancing with me, reached over and grabbed my penis. The whole time this was happening, his husband was right next to him. The gay community demonstrates less commitment to fidelity than the straight community. This may be in part an honest appraisal of how people really function; just acknowledge it openly and accept it and fewer people are hurt. But I have also observed that there are many gay men who value monogamy.

In the straight world, infidelity can cause enormous pain, even though some people seem incapable of a lifetime of faithfulness to just one partner. There are some straight couples who don't practice monogamy and there are straight couples—swingers—who openly have sex with others.

Cathy, like me, has always believed in monogamy and neither of us ever cheated on the other. Cathy has struggled greatly in a relationship with a woman she is in love with. Although these feelings seem reciprocated, the other woman cannot let go of a woman in her past, even to the point of possibly sleeping with that woman if the opportunity presented itself. Cathy has to decide if she can accept that this woman may see and may choose to have sex with other women. The choice for Cathy, then, is either stay with this woman and accept her lack of monogamy, or refuse to accept it and lose the relationship. This is a difficult decision: suitable single gay and lesbian partners don't grow on trees.

Part of fidelity is emotional: the commitment to honor someone else's dignity, to not disparage the one you're committed to. Some studies of infidelity in the straight world reveal the perhaps startling concept that men cheat more for emotional reasons than for sexual reasons.[17] We don't have to accept society's value on fidelity, but that also means we may not be able to expect fidelity of a partner. Both Cathy and I find this concept difficult. While accepting open discussions of sexuality is fun; accepting that my partner may wish to openly see someone else is difficult.

I had a tiny taste of infidelity myself at the New Year's gathering in the big lodge in the woods.

> Went to main lodge for more coffee, found Jason
> with legs on another man's lap. He didn't say anything,
> but looked surprised and I left out a back door...
> —*Personal journal entry 1/2/10*

I felt jealousy when I witnessed this, although Jason probably meant nothing by it. He had gone out of his way in other situations to make sure I understood he wasn't fooling around on me. I wondered at the time if this was an example of how the concept of fidelity is a little looser in the gay community, and perhaps I shouldn't have been upset. This is probably another example of how naïve I can be this early in my gay experience.

In some cases jealousy can be masking feelings of lack of self-worth, fear that my partner is somehow better than me. Jealousy could also be homophobic guilt. Both of these issues would likely require introspection and possibly therapy to accept. Lack of self-worth may also underlie jealousy in the straight community; gays and lesbians don't have a lock on jealousy.

31

Anger

Anger is part of the evolution of this process for a variety of reasons. I experienced some anger early on as to why this had to happen to me. I had a convenient and complacent life. All this became a big disruption in what had been a calm existence. This anger was not long-lived, however, given how easily I could see the benefits I've gained from knowing who I am.

A constant, recurring source of profound anger, even rage at times, is the insinuation that I'm a newbie. I get furious frequently at this notion. I'm not sure I've ever been this angry about anything ever before; it's one of the defining emotions of my experience. It's like the gay community thinks I'm five years old because I just figured this out.

I feel bad enough that it took me this long to figure this out. I feel guilty enough that I could deceive myself for so long about something so important and fundamental. Being called a "newbie" hurts in part because maybe it's a little bit true and it feels bad, like I'm bad for not figuring this out sooner. But I also feel anger because I know that, fundamentally, I'm not a newbie. I'm a mature, sophisticated fifty-year-old.

I feel unaccepted to some extent by the gay community, and I think some of the community somehow thinks that I haven't suffered enough. It's pitiful to think that primarily what it means to be gay is to suffer and it's also pitiful that they can't understand how much I've already suffered because of this. This is the defining crisis of my life: the struggle for self-worth in the face of feeling wrong and inferior.

I have been gay my whole life. Just because I didn't know it all those years doesn't mean I didn't have to live it or suffer from it. I just didn't understand what was going on with me the way I do now.

Part of this anger is also that I often sense the attitude that I'm somehow not worthy, like, "There, there, you poor stupid newbie, just keep struggling along and maybe in thirty years you can be a real gay man like the rest of us." It seems I should get more acceptance from the people I consider my friends. It's as if I can't have validity right away, like it would undermine their authenticity as members of this exclusive club. I don't have this problem with the Billys; they accepted me immediately as a valid gay man. I've never felt I had to prove anything to them. I tend to get this condescending response from my non-Billy gay friends and I wonder what I have to do to be considered a real gay man in their eyes. I asked Robert about this and he said, "There's a bunch of shit you haven't gone through yet." Fair enough, but then is my colleague who just joined us after finishing training not a real doctor because "there's a bunch of shit that hasn't happened yet" to him?

If I ever found a guy who wanted to go out with me but who admitted not wanting to before because I wasn't ready, I'd tell him to fuck off. What is he waiting for? My dick to get bigger? Some horns on my forehead to fall off? I know from the boyfriend I've already had that gay relationships are just like straight relationships; it's the same interpersonal dynamics. I've had thirty-five years' experience with romantic relationships. I'm not new to romance. I have a lot more romantic experience than many gay men. When someone's gay and not out yet, they're probably not dating or seeing someone. If you have to wait until you're an adult to come out and then have relationships, you're missing a lot of experience. My relationship with Cathy lasted twenty-two years. Can any of my gay acquaintances say they've been in a single fulfilling relationship for that long?

Are they implying something about gay sex? Perhaps the idea is that I don't have enough experience in gay sex to be a good lover. That makes a little more sense, but how much experience do I need? I've seen that although I don't think I needed much training in straight sex, some aspects of gay sex do have to be learned. It's been suggested I utilize the services of a hustler (gay prostitute) to broaden my repertoire, but I'm not sure that's my style. Sex can be had through online hookups; I've received a thirty-minute tutorial on this by a gay friend, but I'm not sure that's my style either. Some friends have implied that the process of becoming a non-newbie will take years. So I can look forward to finally having companionship when I'm eighty; that's just wonderful.

One day it suddenly hit me: it's not that I'm waiting for some external approval that I'm ready, it's when I'm comfortable with who I am. In truth, that's a process I can hasten only to some extent. Couldn't I just go back to women? I'd be better at it now given what I've learned about romance and my sexuality. But the idea of dating women only seems attractive because I'm lonely. I'm too far into being gay now to go back to women. It's taking a long time to be a comfortable gay man, I can see that, but maybe I'm not ready for men yet. I realize, to my great frustration, that available appropriate single women far outnumber available appropriate gay men.

If I were straight, I'd have many single women to pick from, but it's very hard to find even one unattached gay man, let alone one that's age-appropriate. I have to be careful with women, though, because I can fall in love with a woman but wouldn't be able to emotionally follow through. If I dated women I'd miss sexual intimacy with a male partner. My problem with women in bed can be summarized with the tagline from the old Wendy's commercial, "Where's the beef?"

A more-recent example of being surrounded by eligible women occurred at work. I very much enjoy the company of my female coworkers, especially the all-female group that works with mammography and breast imaging. One day recently, I had an observation about straight men I wanted to share. I told the handful of female techs near me that I had an epiphany the other day. The two closest to me immediately sidled up closer to me and one said, "You learned that you're not gay, you're really bisexual?" Not quite understanding where this was going, I just said, "No, I'm still sure I'm gay." Both techs backed away a little and looked disappointed. "Okay," one said dejectedly, "what's your big news?" All I'd have to do is announce that I'm available romantically to straight women and I think I'd have my pick. I have, at times, felt I'm in that same situation to some extent with gay men, but unfortunately not with gay men who are truly compatible, who I'd have a chance of a long-term relationship with.

All my life I had lamented my lack of attractiveness to romantic partners. Now that I find I am attractive to them, it doesn't feel as satisfying as I thought it would. I end up feeling bad that I can't be there for them the way they want me to be.

I also have some anger that my friends seem surprised at my need to talk about all this. Some of my straight friends, even though they seem okay with the idea that I'm gay, still really don't want to talk about it. My mentor Robert is always willing to talk, but many other friends don't seem to want to be bothered or they seem disturbed by the conversation. Perhaps one of the downsides of living in a place where homosexuality is so well tolerated is that it doesn't seem like a big deal to many people, so they have trouble understanding why it's such a big deal to me. I don't want to talk about it too much and wear on my coworkers and family, but I need someone to talk to about it. Or perhaps part of the problem is that homosexuality isn't really as well tolerated as it would seem.

I think there are many individuals, usually straight men, who seem comfortable with the idea of some men being gay; they can have a perfectly fine conversation with a gay man, knowing he's gay, as long as gay issues don't come up. Pretty much everyone I know seems okay with the idea that I'm gay, but there's a much smaller subset who I can actually talk to about it, and it's virtually always straight men who are uncomfortable with it.

I also still feel angry over what my peers did to me. It wasn't really any one person, or even a specific group; it was just the milieu of the time and place. It's hardly anyone's fault, though, and the same situation has apparently occurred for many in the LGBT community. It's possible that being taunted and abused so much by boys (who were likely straight) is part of what makes me uncomfortable around straight men.

Fortunately, I don't have to be angry that my family doesn't understand. Luckily, I didn't inherit a religious tradition that shuns gays, so I don't have to overcome that. That can be a major stumbling block for many.

Anger can be felt for a variety of reasons, although in my case it primarily involves the feeling that I'm being looked down on by those who should be my peers. Over many months, my appreciation of this has matured. I don't think I am that much a newbie anymore and to some extent I'll always be a late bloomer, so maybe I'm a newbie in that sense. I think a lot of the anger came from the insinuation that I'm not ready for a relationship at a time when I really felt I wanted or needed one, both for companionship and for sex. I was being made to feel less worthy as a gay man because I was so stupid I couldn't see I was gay. Being gentler on myself, I realize it's really not a question of my stupidity, it was circumstances and the need for self-deception.

Over many months I've become more comfortable being alone and more comfortable with the idea of staying alone. I feel more self-assured in my gayness and don't have anything to prove anymore. This makes the accusation of "newbie" a lot less uncomfortable. Ultimately, I can't control others' behavior and attitudes; since gay men basically really only have one thing in common—sexual interest in men—there are going to be different attitudes and beliefs about everything.

Psychological defense mechanisms: "denial" prevents information from reaching the conscious mind, "repression" banishes them when they occur and "rationalization" seeks to justify them in an acceptable way
—*partially quoted from* Finally Out: Letting Go of Living Straight, A Psychiatrist's Own Story *by Loren A. Olson M.D. Kindle edition p.13*

32

Depression

It often seems Cathy gets all the fun and excitement of going out on her own and doing new things while I feel trapped and wallow in my misery. I felt this strongly at first, but I'm not sure this is fair. Maybe it just looks like she's having more fun. She assures me that she's not really having that much more fun. Maybe I just think she is having more fun because she can make most things fun and I can't. I often feel like a loser, for whatever reason. Isn't that what my transformation was for, to not feel like a loser? I'm going down. This isn't about issues anymore, it's about depression. I don't think I'd do anything overtly to actually commit suicide, but I see myself becoming more and more careless. Carelessness could do me in as well as purposefully causing a car accident.

In my forties, an insightful psychiatrist asked me how it is that someone as smart as I could repeatedly fail to actually kill myself. All my attempts were, in retrospect, carefully sublethal. When it's put that way, it's evident that I didn't really want to die.

I have always had a strong tendency toward depression, usually related to something going on around me, but occasionally it's been hard to be sure what the psychological issues are. Suicide, or at least attempting it, has been a major coping strategy. Without the tools to deal with feeling like a freak, and with my family's turmoil, I sometimes felt that suicide was the only way out when my depression became severe.

David L. Kaufman, M.D.

There is likely a family history of depression, and my issues with depression are probably too strong to explain only on the basis of immediate psychological issues; I think there must be an innate, possibly genetic, biochemical component.

At lot of big changes have occurred in my life recently in a short period of time and this alone could be triggers for emotional problems. The profound shift in my view of my sexual orientation, my neurologic problems, and the changes in my marriage all happened close together and these changes have provided a rich background for emotional upheaval.

At times, the issues would well up and become overwhelming, usually resulting in uncontrollable tears

> Another meltdown…The fatigue seems to correlate to feeling more emotional stuff.
> —*Personal journal entry 8/13/09*

During this particular episode, I became more and more agitated, feeling suicidal after about two hours. I was sitting on the floor of my office, hugging a wastebasket; I was crying so hard I was nauseous and thought I would vomit. I was feeling very overwhelmed by all my life changes recently and sad and depressed over my sense of loss. Although knowing I'm gay is wonderful from the standpoint of knowing I'm not a freak, knowing I'm gay also puts me in a small minority group that still faces considerable oppression. I need to be able to talk about it, but there are few people I can really talk to. Virtually everyone I know is okay with the idea of me being gay, but most just don't want to hear about it. I saw my Kaiser therapist at times at least once a week, but that isn't enough. This is just really hard to get used to: hard to get used to my new self-identity, hard to get used to the changes in sexual orientation, and hard to get used to being in a minority. It was overwhelmingly difficult to get used to seeing myself attracted to men instead of women and thinking about sex in terms of men instead of women. For the most part, I wasn't really against it, it was just really different.

Finally, in desperation, I pulled the phone down from my desk and called a colleague. I knew the number she was working from that day and I knew she was a solid friend who could help. Relying on skills she has needed with her two young children, she talked me down until I was breathing more normally and no longer nauseous. I said goodbye and called my therapist's office. Miraculously, she was able to answer the phone and we talked for quite awhile. This had been a very painful episode, triggered by issues with Cathy and probably feeling very left out. Afterward, I had cried so much I was so thirsty from dehydration I had to drink extra fluids.

I would often start crying spontaneously at work and it's embarrassing to cry in front of coworkers. I learned to try to have daily assignments that kept me largely away from coworkers and patients.

Cathy doesn't generally have these struggles to this extent; basically it seems that one day she just said to herself, "Okay, I'm a lesbian, now I'll have relationships with women." No big deal, just that. No lifetime of feeling weird, no deeply rooted feelings of unworthiness and shame, just, "Okay, now I'm a lesbian." I'm so envious.

More likely I felt lost and unhappy in the life I was leading for a very long time, so when I finally figured out why I couldn't wait to get on with the life I've been longing for.
— *Personal journal entry, with Cathy, in personal conversation*

Okay, I apologize for that harsh approach. I have the utmost respect for Cathy and the individual process she's going through. For a variety of reasons, it was much easier for Cathy to simply accept her gay status and move on, deciding to move out of the house, away from me, and start dating women, particularly the one she was initially drawn to. She's extraordinarily adaptable and resilient; I've watched her for more than twenty years and she just acclimates to new things quickly. For me, it was much harder to accept myself that easily. It's much more difficult for me to let go of the old and accept the new than it is for her. It's probably also harder for me because I don't have a specific man to be drawn to, so I just suddenly feel very alone. It may also have been harder, at least initially, for me because my experience was very sudden, a thunderclap moment, and hers was more gradual over time with more time to get used to it more slowly.

Had I been the one to bring up my gay status, and if she maintained that she was straight and didn't want to split up, I'm not sure I would have had the fortitude to actually leave and pursue a new life as a gay man. It wasn't even a matter of fortitude for her, it was as natural as saying, "Oh, it's raining today; instead of the park we'll go to the museum." For her, it was just, "Instead of romancing men, I'll romance women." Friends have advised me that Cathy has likely pushed all her doubts and anxieties aside and is probably not done processing all this and will decompensate later for putting it off. I don't think so; I have more than twenty years' experience with her, and I haven't seen her go through anything like decompensation yet over anything. She just adjusts to new conditions incredibly well.

The pain of losing Cathy is pain over the loss of something I've held for so long. It's hard for me to understand rationally, because I was very frustrated with Cathy as a wife at the end of our marriage, before our conversation. Close friends of mine recall many times I'd say I was leaving her, I'd had enough. My heart doesn't believe that or feel that way, however. Finally not needing all that anger to excuse sexual activity allowed the powerful love for her I'd been suppressing under the anger to surface. But the pain of feeling left, lost, and left out can be searing, so intense at times I have to stop and take deep breaths. This pain often motivates me to feel suicidal, sometimes enough so that I could do something to myself if there was a quick option. This feeling never lasts very long, but if it occurred in a setting where I could do something self-destructive, like in the car on the freeway, I'm not sure what would happen. I believe the pain comes from a very early perception that something was wrong in my immediate environment, which in a young child is interpreted as, "I'm a bad person." Children don't have the tools to understand that we can be different, or left out of a group, without being a bad person. Sometimes even as adults it's hard to take being left out of a group without feeling like it's a testimony to our badness. Young children also can't understand that it's not their fault if their parents split up.

Adjusting to all these changes has been a constant struggle to try to be okay with everything extraordinary that is happening with me. Struggling to cope, I was advised by a friend at work who has her own personal struggles to learn to just let go of what I can't have anymore. I can't pretend I'm straight, I can't have Cathy as a wife, I can't live in the same house with Cathy, some of my old friends can't deal with this. Ultimately, I just have to learn to let it go; there's really nothing else I can do about it.

Let the hurricane wash it away and don't dig through the garbage (conversation with female coworker).
—*Personal journal entry 10/29/09*

When my depression worsens, I start to hear things. At night in bed, wide awake, I can hear people walking, moving, and talking in the hallway. I hear their hushed voices, the footsteps, the clink of the ice in their glasses. I know there's no one there. If I was given to such ideas, I'd think my house was haunted. Perhaps built on an old Native American burial ground? No terrible murders are likely to have occurred here, the house is only eight years old; we bought it from the original owners and I don't think they were murderers. I see people, just standing there, at the edge of my vision. I turn to look and they're gone. A prescription for an antipsychotic seems to be helping. Great, now I'm in the company of schizophrenics. At least I'm not talking to people who aren't there (though that's not so odd these days; maybe I just have an invisible Blue-tooth). I'm already on two antidepressants, and the strengths of both were just doubled. I don't know for how long the doses can be increased. I also don't know how many different antidepressants I can take at once. The side effects are largely addictive from all the meds; the selective serotonin reuptake inhibitors have the most side effects for me. Impaired sexual function is not a happy thing for a newly realized, newly out gay man who's been feeling like a hormone charged teenager.

I have, however, realized how Prozac and its relatives have actually helped me with that. Their side effects of delayed ejaculation and generally diminished sexual response makes me acutely aware of what really works for me sexually, what really turns me on. Without Prozac, it would have been harder to see that I really do prefer men. Without Prozac, I could have continued to think that sex with women was good enough.

As time goes on, I'm getting more worried about more things. I'm not sure I'm going to be okay. How will this all work out? The people moving and hushed voices outside my bedroom door at night are very frightening. So far, the antipsychotic isn't helping much, I can still increase the dose, though. My support system is falling apart; no one wants to talk to me anymore. Cathy always has something else to do. I can't keep imposing on my friends, but I don't know what else to do.

It's almost funny; if I gave this manuscript to all of them, would any read it? I gave an earlier version to Jason after telling him I poured my heart and soul into this work. Ten days later I found the papers in the backseat of his car; he hadn't even brought them into the house, let alone read them. I felt betrayed and asked for the papers back, giving the excuse that I didn't think it was ready for anyone else to read it.

Lying in bed one night it hits me in a wave: I don't want to be gay anymore. I don't want to be different; I know I'm not a freak, but I don't want to be gay, either. I realize if I could change my sexual orientation, but didn't change anything else about me, I would be a really strange straight guy. But I'd really be back to feeling like a freak; maybe then I'd actually be a freak who fits in with gay men but is straight. I don't think I'd even make a good "metrosexual." I'd probably actually have to be able to talk about sports; that would be hard. So is this why I'm so depressed and upset? It's hard for me to admit I don't want to be gay; what happened to gay, proud, and strong? When I actually explore these feelings in more depth, I realize that the part of gay I'm most comfortable with is the men-liking-men part.

In the end I'm not sure I'd change being gay even if I could; truthfully it can be kind of fun sometimes. This feeling of not wanting to be gay only lasted for a day or two. Being with a man, Jason, was great and felt like finally coming home. No, I wouldn't change knowing I'm gay for a million dollars. This single realization is by far the most powerful piece of knowledge I've ever owned. If I had to choose between knowing I'm gay and being a doctor, I'd choose knowing I'm gay. I could find some sort of career. I wouldn't change being out either. It's good to have people know who I am, I don't have to worry about saying something to tip them off to my "big secret" if they already know. If they see me with a man, they already understand. If I'm not out and worried what they'd think, it would be my problem, my stress and anxiety. I feel strongly that being out puts the burden on them—either they accept me or they don't. If I'm out and they don't like me then it's their problem, not mine.

Always, when with Jason, from holding hands to kissing to sex, I really liked that he's a man. It makes him more attractive as a person and I never had the feeling that it was wrong or inappropriate in any way. It felt really right and natural. I am clearly really sexually attracted to men.

So what about gay didn't I want to be? I don't want to feel so different, I don't want to feel like an outcast, I don't want to be on the periphery of society, I don't want to be ostracized, I don't want to feel persecuted, I don't want my young son to be embarrassed about who and what his father is. Thankfully, these three years later, my son is okay with his parents' orientation and choice of romantic partners, but he's still afraid to have his friends know his parents are gay. Gay culture feels like some secret society. Sometimes that can be fun, but it implies that we're not mainstream. I want to be somebody who doesn't need code phrases to identify others in my group. Not being a singular freak and alone is very good, but now I have to face that I am truly different; there's no way around that now. At least before, while I felt like a freak, I could pretend I was a regular ordinary guy. I can't pretend anymore. I have to face who I am.

The morning after my "I don't want to be gay" moment, as I was about to get into the shower, a realization came to me. All I really have to do is just get used to being gay, get used to all this member-of-a-minority-group stuff. It's shouldn't be all that hard, it should be doable; all I need is to work on accepting it. It will take some time, but it can be done. That probably isn't as difficult as getting used to what now goes on in my head, thinking about sex with men, not women.

The antipsychotic medication is keeping the people outside my bedroom door away. I'm grateful they're gone, it was very frightening. But the depression is still there, and still bad.

When suicidal feelings increase, waves of intense emotional pain wash over me.

I told my mentor Robert that I was so depressed I was suicidal and hallucinating. He said I had to stay alive.

I said, "No, I don't."

He said, "You really do have to stay alive."

Again I said, this time emphatically, "No I don't!"

Finally he said slowly, in measured tones, "If you do try anything, I'll find you and drag you back."

"Even to the gates of Hell, which is probably where I'd end up?" I said.

He said firmly, "Yes."

On reflection, that was truly touching; my friends really do care about me. I can see that Cathy cares, too. During my struggles, she's been very busy, but I know if I really needed her, she'd be there for me.

I had found relief from the depression for a time, but in my loneliness after Jason, it came back with a vengeance. And when it worsens, it gets more medical: my colon stopped working, my brain felt full of molasses, and it feels like there's 100 pounds of weight on my shoulders. It's all just pushing me down. I don't need to kill myself, my body is dying all by itself. It's really a peculiar feeling; my body, brain, and mind just don't function, everything is slowed way down and it's takes enormous effort to do anything.

But this time there was no tendency toward suicidal thoughts or ideas. I think I've grown past this, understanding what a tragedy it would be. I just want to feel better. It occurs to me that I can probably learn to be whole alone faster than I can find someone. It's up to me.

Now the meds that were doubled are tripled and I'm considering ECT (shock therapy). I had ECT before and it really works. With my therapist, I understand that I'm struggling to find my identity. This is both trying to find myself independent from any romantic partner and also who I am after my awakening, marital changes, and medical problems. Trying to have an identity without a romantic partner is a very difficult thing for me. I have basically had at least the idea of a romantic partner since I was five years old. I'm just not used to being me, alone, just me.

Some two years after my awakening, I noticed odd neurologic findings and wondered if it was possibly related to brain damage from the hydrocephalus, associated mood disturbance. Cathy says I was doing everything slowly, like I was underwater. I could see the difference, aware that I used to be stronger and more resilient. I'd lost some of the strength I had gained, lost a lot of the fire I had before.

Testing was unable to pinpoint whether the changes were brain damage or depression but showed that I probably shouldn't be working. So I was off work on medical leave. Major increases in antidepressants were instituted (they had been lowered because I was doing well for a while). At least some of the old fire was returning with the medication changes.

But people who hadn't seen me in a while still noticed that I wasn't right, not my old self.

I could tell I was coming back, though, regaining my strength. I haven't lost the fire. The Lady Gaga song "Born This Way" still always chokes me up, brings tears to my eyes. I haven't lost the fire, it's just gone down a little.

My psychiatrist and I continued adjusting the meds and hoped for the best.

Over a few months, I began to feel better. The slowness went away after a time. There was a medical answer for the specific neurologic symptoms (oculomotor myasthenia gravis); the rest is apparently bad depression. I wonder why, with all my newfound knowledge and strength, I still have problems with depression. Ultimately, the answer that seems to consistently make sense is that I have a genetic predisposition, plus the habits of a lifetime in using depression as a way to cope with life's difficulties. My therapist repeatedly stresses that depression is a dysfunctional way of dealing with difficulty that I learned a long time ago and clung to ever since. I can see that Cathy's resilience and optimism can be learned, I just need to apply myself to the task. I understand that happiness is really just a decision, a decision to be happy no matter what; depression must also just be a decision, a decision to use it as a coping strategy.

33

Loneliness

I'm so lonely....................
—*Personal journal entry 8/8/09*

The loneliness is gut-wrenching. Is this what some single people deal with? No wonder people want to get married. When you're married you're a "couple"; you have an automatically assigned person to do things with. When you want to do something, you know who'll do it with you. After a while, you get to know each other, and you can anticipate what each other likes.

It occurred to me one day that since I met my first wife in high school, after all this gay taunting happened, I have only been without a romantic companion for a total of about three months. The entire rest of those thirty-three years before my marriage to Cathy, I had always had a girlfriend or wife. I have fashioned my identity from a significant other for as long as I can remember. The tendency to do so is probably related to my reaction to my parents' divorce, possibly something subtle, but powerful, that my mother said to me about romantic companionship. I may have picked it up from seeing both of my parents' reactions to their own split.

Suddenly, there's no one to share my life with; in the car there's no one to point out the beautiful rainbow or sunset to. Suddenly, in the innermost recesses of my life, I'm newly alone. Intimacy at its deepest and most personal level is missing. This loss of intimacy isn't so much physical, so much about sex—Cathy and I didn't really have that by the end of our marriage anyway. The missed intimacy is emotional, and we've always had emotional intimacy. Gradually, I began to realize that I missed the nonsexual physical intimacy, the hugs, hand holding, and cuddling. I've learned from my exposure to gay culture and from the romantic partners I have had that gays in a romantic relationship hug and cuddle and hold hands the same way straight people do, just not in public so much because some straight people will freak out if they see it.

This being alone is a whole other issue that came out of nowhere for me. I never saw this coming as part of the whole I'm gay, I'm dying, now I'm okay thing. This is, of course, a problem I've always had, and it's just now being forced to the surface as one more thing to deal with. The gay thing is forcing me to deal with all my hang-ups so I can emerge as a fully functional human being.

I need to learn to see that loneliness is part of who I am, a part of life. I'm starting to realize that to live life fully, I need to celebrate and live fully even the things that may initially seem bad. This is a predominantly Buddhist perspective. I can see that the good wouldn't be all that good without the bad. Obviously I'm not the first person to see that good/bad and happy/sad really are two sides to the same coin. When examined, sometimes the bad isn't really all that bad. I've learned that suicidal thinking can have a positive purpose. It can be a form of internal venting; it allows me to blow off steam without actually hurting anything or anybody. My therapist believes I'll never actually kill myself. After all, how many dozen times did I try and fail? Do I really even want to do it, or is just another form of self-expression?

I was instructed during a therapy session to allow the suicidal thoughts, don't try to push them away. It's funny how this works, but it makes that kind of thinking then seem less scary. These thoughts are just a part of me, who I am. There are still times I'm not sure I won't actually go through with it, though, and this is a very dark thing and can be frightening. When I feel good, I understand what a terrible tragedy my suicide would be for my family—so horrible, how could anyone contemplate such a devastating act? But when I feel suicidal, it just feels like the right thing to do; all those people really would be better off without me. Just think of how much money my wife would have from life insurance if I died. In the pit of depression, I may know my family needs me, but I'm in so much pain I think I'll do anything to make it stop, and this way of thinking is attractive because it's familiar. It would be so much easier; life just hurts, so much, so bad. How do I ever escape this pain? Is it even possible?

> My suicidal thoughts are the only familiar thing left because everything else that was familiar has changed, I have no other familiar places; the pain from distance with Cathy is because it was the last familiar thing. I hold onto it because it's very familiar having been there so long...
> —*Personal journal entry 10/2/09, with therapist*

Later on, though, as suicidal thoughts become more prominent, I can't stop thinking about it. I just don't want to be anymore. What's wrong? There's a dark saying in the gay community, "Better dead than gay." Unfortunately, many who've said it have committed suicide. Suicide is a leading cause of death in teenagers and a very large percentage of the guys are gay. In conjunction with my therapist, I realize I don't really want to die, I just want to feel better. There's just been too much pain for too long. When will it get better? Every time I think I'm done with the heavy stuff, more comes along.

Looking back, I realize that the closer to lethal a suicide attempt was, the better I felt afterward. It's like a suicide attempt is a form of punishment to me for being a bad person. I think some of the relief after a suicide attempt is that I feel I've appropriately drawn attention to myself and now there's a possibility I will get better. Maybe the physical illness resulting from an attempt distracts me from the real problems I had before it; it's like pressing the reset button.

I also realize that all my fantasies of suicide end with me surviving. I can see that I just don't want to inflict that kind of pain on my family and loved ones. I've learned through this process that I tend to get really depressed when I don't mentally acknowledge something that's really bothering me. Usually it's something that conflicts with the values I hold rationally. The price for cognitive dissonance is major depression.

My friend Ana is a great source of comfort in a world fraught with pain (sort of like mini-suicide).
—*Personal journal entry 9/29/09 4:00pm*

My friend "Ana" is short for anorexia nervosa. To not eat somehow conveys great power. At these times the tendency toward denying myself food becomes strong, somehow giving a sense of control. Eating is something I can control. The feeling of guilt after eating and euphoric elation when successfully avoiding food can be compelling. I try to counter this with the rational thought that calorie deprivation will break down the muscles I've worked so hard to pump up. This is the best counter to this line of thought I've come up with yet. Yet Ana haunts me almost constantly. I know the differences between various forms of weight loss. Weight loss from depression is silent; no sense of struggle or lost appetite, I just lose weight. Weight loss from dieting is accompanied by hunger and wanting to eat, but to lose weight, it isn't fun to not eat, just necessary. Weight loss from Ana is accompanied by the fun and triumph of not eating; there is hunger, but it's worn like a badge of honor. Ana is my friend I mustn't disappoint. And eating with Ana is so disappointing. Ana tends to encourage a very poor diet, mostly food deprivation, whereas serious dieting is usually a consciously appropriate healthy diet, consuming fewer calories.

I'm exhausted by the struggle; I'm tired of feeling so emotionally needy, of constantly requiring emotional support from those around me. Cathy always seems to have something pressing to do when I feel I need her. And I sense that many of my supporters are also tiring of my neediness; it seems to be wearing thin. Can I do this alone? Do I need their support?

The loneliness is far-reaching. I have to learn how to wrap my identity around myself. My mentor Robert has said that he can be comfortable being alone. The first guy I dated is alone and seems comfortable with it. How do I learn how to do that?

I think Cathy struggles with this as well. Given the differences in her family history, she probably acquired this tendency for a different reason, but still seems to struggle with it. This tendency in each of us to hold on may be part of what kept us together for so long.

After much reflection, I realize that maybe I don't really want somebody, maybe I'm just rebelling against a lifetime of being with someone and it feels wrong. I just want to feel whole. But how can I feel complete when I'm alone?

So there is an alternative to finding someone. I can be okay *without* finding someone. I just have to learn how to be complete by myself.

I find I'm affected by straight love songs, usually men singing about women. I don't want a woman, but what do I want? Okay, I'm pretty sure now, months later, I want a man. Can I feel that with a man? I want to feel what straight people feel in relationships. Is that possible?

> "I'll give up everything just to find you."
> —*Evanescence, Taking Over Me, Fallen*

I realized at one point something that surprised me: I've had a real hard time believing that not just "the right guy," but even "a right guy," is actually out there. I realized suddenly that my anxiety over this comes in part from the fear that there isn't anyone I'm attracted to that much. I mean, I want to be swept off my feet, don't I? But a little reflection helps quell this fear; I see really attractive men all the time. Of course some are straight, but there are definitely lots of gay men I find attractive.

I've also learned from experience not to fantasize about people I know. This is the game I played in adolescence, in school. Find a girl and attach myself. The problem is what to do when she's not interested, because then I'm devastated. It still happens with real people. I develop an attachment to someone, unjustified by anything previously said or done by them, and eventually, reality hits; then it hurts.

Months after our awakenings, Cathy and I were both struggling with how difficult dating really is and how hard being alone is. We're both in a similar place, trying to learn how to be okay alone. Is this part of what held us together? We probably always saw ourselves only as part of the couple and not so much as individuals.

I think both Cathy and I have gained enough experience in life to be realistic about relationships and we probably have a more than average level of maturity and sophistication. Society has a ways to go in understanding what love is. The popular media repeatedly presents the idea that there is one perfect person for me and that true love conquers all. This sets up expectations that can be impossible to fulfill. True love is a very powerful emotion. The reality, however, is that the vicissitudes of life can be challenging beyond what any amount of love between two people can actually overcome. In reality there are no romantic soul mates, just many people with varying degrees of compatibility. Or perhaps there are soul mates, but just because someone is my soul mate doesn't mean I'm supposed to be romantically attached to them for the rest of my life.

Different people will have different levels of compatibility in different areas. One person may be more compatible sexually and another may really share interests in music or specific hobbies. With any given person there will be issues, both positive and negative. Although I may feel a very strong bond with one specific person, whether or not the romantic interest is reciprocated, that doesn't mean I can't feel this same bond even more so with someone else. I have learned, however, that I need to feel comfortable with someone for a good romantic relationship to exist. I have also learned that it can be hard to let go of someone, or the idea of being with that someone, when the evidence suggests that ultimately it's not a good match.

I think everyone's struggle to let go is what drives the feeling that true love is most important above all else, and also the feeling that this one person is it, the one for me, even when they can't be. It's amazingly hard for me to let go of someone even when they don't feel the same way for me that I feel for them. This should be, rationally at least, the best example of incompatibility, but most of us have trouble emotionally letting go in that circumstance. Specific experiences both Cathy and I have had also demonstrate clearly that a mature, rational person can fail to see something wrong in a relationship that's painfully obvious to someone outside that relationship. We have become good romance counselors for each other.

Finally, I've learned that most, if not all, relationships contain an element of difficulty. A good friend who's been married for years is going through this, starting to feel like a separate individual with her own wants and needs separate from her spouse.

"Don't give up. Your problem gets better next month."

—From fortune cookie in Chinese takeout with Cathy, 1/17/10

Part IV
Acceptance

"Your intention to help others is the main cause of your salvation." (No Beginning, No End, Jakusho Kwong Roshi)
  —*Personal journal entry about 4/20/09*

Then he...swam toward the beautiful swans. The moment they espied the stranger, they rushed to meet him with outstretched wings.

"Kill me," said the poor bird, and he bent his head down to the surface of the water, and awaited death.

But what did he see in the clear stream below? His own image; no longer a dark, gray bird, ugly and disagreeable to look at, but a graceful and beautiful swan.
  —*The Ugly Duckling*, Hans Christian Andersen.[18]

34

Recovery

Therapy is like draining an abscess. The underlying emotional issues cause a constant dull distress; solving it, like draining an abscess, can be acutely painful, but then that constant distress fades.

With my therapist, I do an exercise to understand how cognitive distortions contribute to my depression. Underlying these recurring waves of pain are the emotions of hurt and shame that relate to specific situations. There are many cognitive distortions that underlie my incorrect assumption that this is because I'm a bad person. Ultimately, I realize I have a lot of evidence that I'm truly *not* a bad person. Over the next few days after this exercise, I see a marked reduction in the frequency and intensity of these waves of pain; over a longer period I perceive a decrease in the depression in general. I could see while we were doing the exercise that my therapist was waiting for me to state the answers; she already knew what the answers were, she was just waiting for me to say them. She said later that this exercise generally produces very similar results for most people. As young children, we don't have the cognitive tools to understand that when bad things happen to us, it's not our fault. We are not bad people.

This simple, although very intense, exercise has had a profoundly positive impact on me. Basically, all of my negative emotions, even those so strong as to compel me to feel suicidal, trace back to feelings of being a bad person starting from when I was a child. When I was five, my parents divorced. Then my mother got married again, then divorced again. Then she got married yet again, and then divorced yet again. In the meantime, my father got married again, then divorced again, then married again. I had trouble keeping track of who I was related to. There sure were a lot of step-siblings of mine at one time or another. In this context, it would be difficult to not somehow feel like I'm at fault, particularly when I was quite young. All this turmoil around me, it must be somehow my fault. My therapist had been suggesting I've had a difficult childhood all along but I never really understood it, or felt it, until after this exercise.

In fact, it's possible that I feel hopelessness about ever finding the right person or even any person at all because of my parents' trials and tribulations. They could never seem to find appropriate romantic partners, so I tend also to feel that I will not be able to find a good one. It's also possible that my parents communicated in subtle ways, without necessarily meaning to, a sense of frustration over the lack of compatible partners.

An additional strong negative feeling that traces back to this time is the feeling of being left out. I can be very sensitive to feeling so left out that it leads to suicidal thinking; it just feels so bad. But how much was I left out of as a child? My parents were divorced when I was very young at a time when very few kids had divorced parents; I didn't know any other kid at school whose parents were split up. There were many other reasons to feel left out. I'm left-handed—it's just another difference. We went to the Methodist Church and none of the kids I knew from church went to my school. I had serious health problems. I didn't know any other kid with problems as bad as mine.

I've noticed that since my awakening, I've occasionally felt sharp emotional pain that appears associated with thoughts of lesbians. Ultimately, I now realize because those thoughts mean two women together, I'm left out and I start replaying all those old intensely negative emotions related to feeling marginalized.

Probably the most intense feelings of being left out relate to my realization, at a very early age, that I was really different from the other boys. I was always marginalized, on the periphery of things because I didn't fit in enough to be a real part of any of the sports, the discussion about girls, the rough play. I was often left out of things. I liked it better to be with the girls, but that felt wrong. That has burned a lasting impression on the deepest parts of my being.

The waves of pain have largely subsided now, the occasional emotional discomfort is nowhere near provoking feelings of suicide. Also, three years out, I tend not to feel that old familiar pain related to thoughts of lesbians anymore.

I can usually directly see the connection of my current negativity to those feelings of unworthiness dating back to early childhood, my feeling like a bad person. Am I a bad person? Even in the pit of despair and severe depression, I can't believe I am truly a bad person. I'm a nice guy, a hard worker, and pretty smart. I'm probably more honest and altruistic than average. I came through eighteen years of college and training well, with occasional recognition for being well above average. I now have a respected medical practice; patients and other physicians occasionally seek me out specifically for my expertise. There is just no way I am a bad person. Sure, sometimes my behavior is a bit regrettable, but I am fundamentally, through and through, a good person. Part of what has kept me from suicide is the realization that I would be sorely missed by my family and friends and at least some of my coworkers.

Reflecting on the intensity of my suicidal feeling recently, I feel grateful to be past the worst of it. I don't think any of us really can know why we're here, but I still believe somehow that I have to do what my life is meant for before it can be over. As time goes on I find that, even with worsening depression, I'm not suicidal.

I decided to go to Disney World by myself. I needed to get away and be by myself and, having gone to Disney World as an adult with our children many times to escape the Michigan winter, it's a comfort, familiar vacation. On the way back it was a difficult flight, and the airline was way behind schedule. The flight attendants keep emphasizing that "It's a full flight, please take your seats."

I looked around, wondering where all the people waiting at the gate had been seated, when I realized the only two empty seats on the plane were next to me. Me, who's struggling with the idea of being alone. Even though I should have enjoyed the comfort of not having seat mates, I felt bad.

I was very stressed out; the flight was running very late, and I hade to work the next morning, after being off on medical leave and vacation. I decided to do a meditation thing: just expose myself to me and let it sit; just be, don't think, act, or do; just let it be. Everything is just raw sensation. I couldn't understand what people around me were saying, it was just sound.

Within a few minutes I saw a bright light up high with shadows in front, like it was shining behind a big gate or some people. Down below I saw what I knew was myself. I was like foamy red Jell-O. Below on me I saw a large festering wound, like a stinky abscess, moldy, fetid. I explored what it was and found profound pain.

I was sitting in my seat with my eyes closed and crying, tears running down my checks. Why this pain, what is it from? Then I saw myself being literally torn apart. It's me, trying to find my identity and feeling torn apart doing so.

While sitting at the gate, I had been noticing the pretty women around me. I sense that was part of the festering wound, a mistake. The me that's bad isn't the gay me, it's the me that's still trying to be straight. Suddenly, checking out women felt skanky, like it should be beneath me. On the plane I realize that I'm suddenly noticing men more than women.

When the takeoff seemed prolonged and the plane shot up and into a storm I briefly thought I was going to die. I feel ready, missed Cathy and Andrew, and then wondered if my life wasn't worth saving. That seemed really sad.

Continued therapy and a class in cognitive management of depression helps; I can see how distorted some of my thinking is, and how I've sabotaged myself since I was very young. I'm beginning to be able to see how Cathy's way of thinking is better at helping her cope than mine is; it's not so hard to believe that I can learn to be more resilient and optimistic. Later on, I read a book on resilience and discovered that it can be acquired; I can learn to be like Cathy. I'm also learning to be "Excellent!" when someone asks how I am. Cathy won't be the only one for whom life is fun. In the end I think it's like happiness—it's really just making a decision to be okay and to have fun. Life can be made fun and I can do it.

35

Buddhism

Several years prior to all this, I had a fairly typical midlife crisis. Gradually, over a period of a few days, I had the gnawing realization that I already had everything I'd ever wanted and I wasn't yet fifty years old. I had a lovely wife and child; I was a successful and respected physician in the community earning more money than I had ever dreamed possible. I had a nice house and a new car. I even had a big separate garage at home full of my toys.

Then I'm done, right? Can I die now? I wasn't even sure why I got out of bed in the morning; nothing made sense anymore. I had used all that income to buy stuff. I had so much stuff now I couldn't remember how it all worked. So I kept a file cabinet with all the different instructions and manuals. I had a huge pile of stuff I didn't even know how to use. And I didn't feel any better. Somehow I expected that when I achieved all this success that I'd feel better, somehow elevated, somehow happy, like maybe it would all come with a halo or something. But no, no halo, no feeling of satisfaction, no happiness, just that gnawing sense that none of it really mattered at all.

Way back in college I'd signed up for a Chinese philosophy course because I needed a 300-level humanities course. I figured learning about Confucius would be fun. On the first day of class the course professor said, "If you've signed up for this class because you need a Tuesday and Thursday morning 300 level blow-off humanities class, then drop out now, because I'm going to make you work."

"By the time this term is over," he continued, "you're either going to be Buddhist, or know enough to know why you're not Buddhist."

Okay, now he had me; throw out a challenge like that and I'm hooked. He was right about the 300-level humanities class thing; that was one of the reasons I'd signed up for this class. But now I couldn't let go. Buddhists, I thought to myself, aren't they the bald guys in robes in the airport? I don't think I want to be one of them.

We started in on Confucius, someone I had always wanted to know more about, but it turned out he was kind of boring. He was always going on about filial piety or governmental responsibility to the people or some such.

But when the second half of the class began, it was about Buddhism. "So when you're at the beach," my professor started out, "and you look at the lake, don't you see waves?"

Of course, we all nodded. We live in Michigan, we know about big water.

"A wave could look around," he continued, "and see other waves and feel like they're different, like people do with each other."

"But waves are all just lake; they have no defined start or end, they don't exist at all separately from the water. They just think they do."

He paused. "There really are no waves, only lake."

"People are like that."

At the beach we can observe waves arising offshore and moving toward the shore only to disappear at the beach and water's edge. Waves are constantly changing and only an illusion because nothing is actually moving toward shore—it's all just the lake, and the water itself is only moving up and down; no water is moving toward the shore.

—*Personal journal entry 1/22/04 lunar new year*

What?! A giant light bulb in my head lit up; this is powerful stuff. This explains how to see myself relative to others.

At that point the professor had me completely. We talked a lot about this stuff, and I wrote some papers about it (they were well received). We dabbled in meditation a few times. I had tried meditation in my early teens, sitting still for a grand total of about fifteen or twenty seconds before deciding that because nothing had happened, nothing was going to and the whole meditation thing was a bust.

Nevertheless, this class gave me a first look at something very powerful. I just didn't need it yet.

Later, in the grip of my midlife crisis, I remembered this class. My earlier experiences with religion had been based on Christianity and were not terribly fulfilling. I didn't necessarily think it was wrong, it just didn't appeal to me or help me at all.

I started reading about Buddhism and came to two conclusions: I needed to start meditating seriously, and I needed a teacher.

It turns out there are a significant number of Vietnamese refugees in southwestern lower Michigan. Many converted to Christianity, but some stayed Buddhist and the Michigan Buddhist Association set up local temples to support them. Tam Quang Temple, one such temple south of Grand Rapids, occupied a small, old, somewhat run-down house in a nondescript rural town. Monks from a monastery outside Saigon rotated through to meet the needs of the Buddhist refugee community. A couple of the monks spoke English reasonably well and were interested in teaching "the Westerners," as we were known. I found an Internet site referring to English-speaking services on Saturdays. This was only about an hour from my house. It took a couple of months for me to get up the nerve to go.

When I walked through the temple door that first Saturday morning, I left everything else behind. I left my wife, my children, my medical training, and my career as a radiologist. I walked in feeling totally naked, and scared.

Up a few steps was a darkened room with a giant Buddha figurine on an alter, a little intimidating. I heard some

213

commotion downstairs and went to check it out. A small man in saffron robes and with a shaved head was making coffee. Strong coffee, it turned out, and I took this as a positive omen. He realized I was new and we exchanged pleasantries. He asked what I wanted from this experience and I lied and said, "serenity." What I should have said was, "sanity." He looked me dead in the eye and said, "This will be very hard; are you sure you want to do this?"

He continued, "Once you start this path, you'll need to complete it."

I assured him I had every intention of following through whatever it would take. More people began to arrive, our conversation was put on hold until later, and I watched and waited.

We moved as a group to the upstairs room with the big statue and there was some chanting. We sat in meditation for over an hour. I knew this would be a part of the service and approached it with some trepidation. How can I possibly sit still this long? I could barely sit still for twenty seconds as a teenager. Interestingly, I just sat with my mind in as blank awareness as I could and suddenly the bell rang. It was over. Wow! I felt different, although it's hard to actually characterize what was different. This was followed by an informal tea break, with conversation among us. I recall saying to the monk that after this first real meditation experience of my life, I think I see why we people do this.

He was an excellent teacher. One of the challenges often repeated was to go to a lake, any lake, and look for the thing that doesn't move. I lived a few miles from the shore of Lake Michigan, one of the largest freshwater lakes in the world, so this seemed a convenient exercise.

Entrance to Buddhist practice and becoming open to their ideas happens for different reasons. My entrance, and probably that of many others, was through suffering. We see Buddhism as a potential answer to our suffering. There are a surprising number of gays who follow Buddhist teaching and practice, and meditation sessions are usually featured at Billy gatherings.

Buddhism is not a religion in the classic Judeo-Christian-Islamic sense, but more of a self-help philosophy. Buddhism provides the tools for immediate help for the sufferer. Suffering is the central focus of Buddhist psychology: the first principle is that life is suffering and the second is that suffering comes from our delusion, our not recognizing who and what we really are and aren't. The point of Buddhist practice, if there is one, is to see that we're already complete, already enlightened, already totally whole. We need to let go of the attachments, including to ourselves, that hinder our ability to alleviate our suffering. Ultimately, we get in the way of our ability to see who we are, our own enlightenment.[19]

Meditation is the core of essentially all variants of Buddhism to some extent. To be still and aware allows us ultimately to see our true nature. As a side effect, many ideas, thoughts, and feelings that normally exist below our conscious stream-of-thought existence will surface during this stillness. Our mind's job is to create stream-of-thought, which runs through our existence like a river, tumbled by rocks and rapids, and always rushing somewhere. We tend to believe the stories our minds tell us; to get to the root of them can be profoundly beneficial.[20] I've had many inspirations while meditating.

An often-used analogy to meditation is that if we're bending over the edge of pond in an effort to see our faces reflected in the water, the water must be still or we can't see our reflection. Likewise, for us to see ourselves as we really are, the waters of our minds must be still.

A significant piece of Buddhist philosophy is a form of radical acceptance: I'm already there, I'm already done, I'm already everything I need to be. I don't need to get anything, say anything, or do anything; I'm okay exactly as I am. The challenge is not to find or get what I need, but only to realize that I've already got it. I am, in essence, already a Buddha. What's stopping me is just not completely realizing this. In meditation practice, I'm not getting the pieces of what I need; I'm removing the obstacles within me that prevent me from seeing who and what I really am. We are all already enlightened; we just can't see it yet.

Another parable is that of the princess who believes she's literally lost her head. She looks everywhere to find it, then sees herself in a mirror and realizes she had it the whole time she was looking for it. Enlightenment is actually like that, we all have it already, we all already know what we need to, we just can't see it yet.

Buddhism is a very practical philosophy, very humanistic as a religion, for dealing with struggle and difficulties. That might be why there are a large number of gay Buddhists. The fact that Buddhism doesn't care in the slightest whether someone is gay or straight may also have something to do with it. It also doesn't matter if we're male or female, or even human. The term used to describe individuals who can benefit from this Buddhism is "sentient beings." Who or what counts as a sentient being is open to interpretation. It's possible that a cow, or even a mosquito, counts as a sentient being; it's not our place to judge other creatures. This is a factor in why many Buddhists are vegetarians.

The practice of mindfulness, particularly mindful meditation, is helpful for gaining insight into our struggles and ourselves. Although meditation is not done to accomplish anything in particular, it can be useful. Thoughts and ideas from just below the level of conscious thought can pop up during meditation practice. Occasionally, something useful occurs; I've had quite a few good ideas come to me during my times on the cushion.

A metaphor for how meditation works on our psyches is that of a person walking in the fog wearing a heavy overcoat. Not feeling any rain, he or she thinks that they're staying dry, but when they get to their destination they find the overcoat is soaked. Although, again, meditation is not done to realize anything, the effects of meditation on us can be both subtle and powerful.

The Buddhism teachings and the meditation practice helped me a great deal. I quickly was able to develop a new framework for my life, more about being of service to others than acquiring things (I do still like to shop, though).

216

I have continued the meditation practice, almost in continuity, since that first experience. I have found Buddhism to be very helpful in the form of suffering I experience. I often listened to Buddhist books on tape in my car while driving around. One set of tapes was by Jakusho Kwong, who I had never heard of. In the lecture series he referred to being on Sonoma Mountain. I had no idea where that was at the time; I didn't even bother to look it up.

Much later, I remembered the lectures and wondered if Sonoma Mountain was in Sonoma County, where I was moving. It turned out to be a short drive from my house, the Genjo-ji temple (Sonoma Mountain Zen Center).

After living in California for a few months, I looked up the Zen Center online and decided to check it out. Jakusho Kwong, or Kwong roshi as he is usually referred to ("roshi" is an honorary title that means "Zen Master") turns out to be a very kind and thoughtful older gentleman. It's a little unnerving talking to him at first because he's fully present in the conversation, paying complete attention to the person he's speaking with. The Zen Center is much more formal than Tam Quang temple, following the form (rituals) of Soto Zen closely. At first this took some getting used to. Many of us who come to Buddhism are suspicious of religious ritual, but over time I began to see the ritual as freeing. I don't have to think about how to do something, it's already figured out, I just have to remember it.

I joined as a member almost immediately. Membership includes occasional formal meetings with roshi, called "docusan," to discuss our practice. Actually, we can talk about anything, but Zen teachers are not psychotherapists. Initially, he helped me with my posture, to avoid backaches. At first, I found the Zen Center intimidating and I frequently felt foolish. After my realization and transformation, however, it now seems comfortable and natural.

Buddhism has continued to be a source of support and direction in my life. My therapist is a Buddhist, currently Tibetan, although the differences between Zen and Tibetan Buddhism aren't all that significant. She will frequently challenge me through Buddhism or advise me to seek answers in Buddhist literature. Buddhism can be remarkably helpful in my struggles and times of crisis.

36

Manuel

At one of the first monthly gay dinners I had attended I was introduced to Manuel, a tall handsome, older Latin. Manuel, incredibly, had also just realized he was gay, at about the same time I had. I have met more than a few men who realized they were gay later in life, as adults, but none who had figured it out recently. He attended one of the gay dinner groups and we were introduced. We exchanged simple greetings and that was all at that time.

At the Halloween gathering for the Billy Club, Manuel was there and he and I quickly became close friends. I sensed that the relationship was headed toward serious romance, but Jason assertively intervened and pretty much swept me off my feet.

Manuel was struggling that Halloween with coming out; he was out to only a very few people and not to his family or even his daughter. The emotional upheaval that occurs with the realization that one is gay is a very big thing and difficult to describe. For a person who's sexually aware at a constant conscious level, the sudden switch is vast in scope. I was past some of it, having come out to myself a month before Manuel had and having thrown myself into the process with vigor after my miraculous neurologic recovery. That coincident issue had a big impact on how I felt and continue to feel about being gay.

It was probably for the better that Manuel and I didn't form a couple at that time; we both had things to work through. And my experience with Jason was very helpful overall, but I think we both suffered from aspects of it, Jason mostly because we broke up and I because of my discomfort near the end. Manuel also had a romance with a younger man shortly after the Halloween gathering and we both felt these were worthwhile experiences.

Five months after breaking up with Jason I was ready to reenter the gay community. I felt ready to deal with Jason if he confronted me and I was lonely for the community, having only Robert and a few other coworkers as gay peers on a regular basis. I was also becoming quite lonely for romantic companionship and was unlikely to find it without involvement in the gay community.

I started by attending another dinner. The gay couple who organized the dinners would not be there but presumably the regular gang would be. On a whim, I looked up Manuel's phone number, not knowing if it was a cell or a home phone. Hoping it was a cell, I texted him that I would be at the dinner and he promptly texted back that he would go if I were going. This struck me as a positive omen to reestablishing our friendship and possibly starting a romance.

As I approached the restaurant I saw him outside waiting for me. He was alone and had a hopeful look on his face. We greeted with a hug and then entered the restaurant. Neither of us ate much that night and there were comments later among the others present that we were obviously becoming involved with each other.

I had to work the evening shift the following week, which gave us a breather. The Monday after my night shift we met at a coffeehouse and stayed until it closed, then talked outside until midnight. Just before we each went home, Manuel asked if I thought we'd ever have sex. "Eventually," I replied. I had been hoping we could be more than friends. The next night I met him at his apartment where he lives alone. Pretty much every time it's just the two of us alone together, we end up in bed.

Actually, I had manipulated the situation some, suggesting we go to a restaurant near where he lives, figuring that would bring an invitation to meet at his place first. I was barely in the door and we embraced with passionate kisses. One of us said something about "bed" and we made our way there, leaving a trail of clothes behind us. It felt very powerful and really good, like coming home, like this is where I belong. I learned from Manuel that sex with men is incredible.

The intimacy I experienced with Manuel was very powerful, some of the best of my entire life. I never really knew that sex could be this good and it was far better than sex with myself. Although his personality is normally reserved, even meek socially, in bed he's quite assertive. Later in the relationship he suggested that when we have our clothes on, I'm the more traditionally masculine one and when we have our clothes off, he is. I realized he was right and was startled I hadn't noticed this before. Later, I began to see how his masculinity in bed was what I needed and wanted in a relationship. I don't think I'm a weak person, I think I can be very assertive and usually I'm quick to stick up for myself and sometimes for others who are being wronged. But in a romantic relationship, I want to adopt the more passive feminine role. I've had other dating experiences since then, where my date was very much a man and I could just be like a girl. I loved it; it felt so right, so natural, and so innocent and unconstrained. I make that transition from strong authority figure to innocent girl without any difficulty and it feels wonderful; I thoroughly enjoy it.

Manuel and I had originally discussed our relationship as friends, then with the "eventually" comment, friends with benefits. At his proposal, we quickly decided to be official romantically involved and not see others. That wasn't a problem for me anyway because there was no one else for me to see.

Over the coming weeks, we saw each other frequently, generally at least once a day. Not generally very tech savvy, Manuel had figured out how to text message, not a small feat given his regular cell phone is without a full keyboard. We texted each other constantly all day long, usually twenty or so messages a day each. The relationship felt warm, safe, and comfortable. From the beginning it was clear that he was falling for me very strongly. I didn't completely share that, but realized that the experience with Jason made me pretty shy about another relationship. I had fallen in love with Jason very much at first, but this feeling faded only weeks later and I realized it wasn't working. I knew that left me reluctant to fall in love again.

Manuel and I discussed the difference in our level of feeling and he seemed comfortable with it. I was sure I loved him and said so frequently. When together, we often just stayed at his place or mine, preferring to cook in rather than go out. Manuel is an extraordinary cook and his talents give me pause in thinking I'm a kitchen queen. At times, I can't hold a candle to his talents.

Months went by and we began to refer to each other as "partner." We had tried to avoid calling ourselves "boyfriends" because that sounded too junior high school and we're much older than that. Plus, Jason and I always said we were boyfriends and at this point the term rubbed me the wrong way.

Over time I began to feel like I was falling in love. Friends often commented on how obvious our feelings for each other were. We tried not to show affection toward each other when we were with others, but subtle signs were still there. We knew that even if we weren't holding hands, anyone who watched us would realize we were a couple. At one of the dinners, which we continued to go to, someone across from us at the table picked up the signs of romance and asked how long we've known each other and been together. Not sure how to answer because we had been friends for months before romance, we paused and he asked, "Okay, so how long have you two been fucking?" That was a direct question we could answer.

Manuel had been very interested in entertaining friends for dinner, something I see a lot of in the gay community. We often discussed place settings, napkins, china, stemware, and flatware. I bought a book on fancy napkin folding and an etiquette book by Emily Post. We entertained some friends, were entertained by others, and I began to notice a pattern to Manuel's behavior around others. When we were in company that provoked some anxiety in him, he would unfortunately start to denigrate me. He'd recast the stories of our relationship in a different light. Somehow he was now the prim-and-proper reserved gentleman and I was a lascivious whore, bent on nothing other than ripping his clothes off and pushing him into bed against his protests. Finally, I decided to say something about it. I wasn't quite sure why he acted that way and the cuteness of it was fading.

One day I confronted him and he was devastated. "I only want your friends to know how much I care about you," he said.

I assumed the worst was past us when, at his insistence, he invited over one of my gay coworkers and his husband. I had a bad feeling about it, but couldn't really stop the dinner once Manuel had invited them.

The moment they walked in the door, I could see Manuel stiffen, visibly nervous, at least to me. He cut me down mercilessly all evening, and interrupted me every time I tried to say something. He even seemed to be gently putting our guests down. We were having a few glasses of wine and I had drunk so little that I couldn't really even feel it, but Manuel was clearly getting drunk, which only made things worse.

This event had been scheduled coincident with Cathy and her artist friends opening a new gallery to show their work. I had wanted to attend the opening to congratulate them, but couldn't because of our dinner plans.

After our guests left, I told Manuel that I had to go find Cathy; the opening was over, but I expected they'd be at a restaurant or bar to celebrate, and I could stop by and see them. Manuel ignored my comments, fumbling with my clothes, trying to take them off and pull me into bed. At this point he was really drunk, more so than I had ever seen before. I figured, to avoid hurting his feelings too much, I'd go to bed with him and then leave after he fell asleep, which I assumed wouldn't take long.

He fumbled a little in bed, then fell asleep. I got up to leave and he woke up, asking me what I was doing. I reiterated that I needed to find Cathy and her friends and he responded that he knew he had drank too much to go with me. He helped me dress and walked me to the door.

I found Cathy and her friends and had a wonderful time with them for the remainder of their meal. The next day Manuel texting me, asking me if I wanted to come over. I did, knowing I needed to talk to him. I was very angry.

He couldn't remember the end of the evening before, thinking I had just slipped out while he was asleep. He became very distraught when confronted; he has very sensitive feelings and I could appreciate that. He said again, "I just want your friends to know how much I care about you."

"By putting me down in front of them?" I countered. "That doesn't make sense."

He said he needed a few days away from me to find himself and I said fine as I didn't really want to see him for a while anyway. At this point, I was very frustrated by his behavior and was at a loss to deal with it. Also, after about four months my feelings for him had begun to cool off. I wasn't sure how to handle that part and hoped that the fire would come back. Manuel is a wonderful, thoughtful, and loving man and I knew I would really miss him if we broke up.

The next day I stopped in to the hospital to talk to Kenneth, the gay tech we had invited over, to get his take on the evening. I also wanted to talk to Robert, and I got the chance to talk to my new friend Jenny, the ultrasound tech.

Kenneth said they saw Manuel as a kind gentle man, but very eccentric. I mentioned being cut down and Kenneth said yes, he could see Manuel was nervous. Kenneth had met Manuel some time ago and really liked him. Then I mentioned the fire going out and Kenneth said, "Well, it isn't going to come back now, it's over." My mentor Robert reiterated the same points and Jenny had a powerful observation. She thought Manuel's' cutting me down sounded to her like insecurity, which would explain other things. When we were alone Manuel would fawn all over me, stroking my hair and rubbing my feet while telling me how hot I am. That could be insecurity as well. Suddenly, quite a few things made sense and I realized the romantic relationship had run its course and needed to end. Kenneth, Robert, and Jenny all counseled me strongly not to contact Manuel and let him contact me. Several days passed before he texted me and we exchanged some texts which let him know it was over.

At one point he invited me to his place for dinner with some friends of ours and I felt I could go as a friend. Manuel and I had always said if romance between us wouldn't work, we'd still be friends.

After they left we talked. I told him I felt he had some insecurities that accounted for his behavior which I didn't like, and he agreed. He asked if there was another reason the relationship had to end and I said, "Yes."

Very hesitant to say it, because I knew it would hurt him, I finally said, "The fire is going out."

He agreed immediately and said he could see that happening over the last week. Just as he's very sensitive regarding himself, he is also sensitive to others, and occasionally knew what I was feeling before I did. At that point we agreed the romance was over, but we would try to be friends.

The following days were difficult; he seemed irrational in his texts and his actions. After texting me that he understood it was over, he stopped by Cathy's house to invite her and her girlfriend for dinner (something we had talked about previously). Ultimately I realized he was feeling very angry and that was probably driving his apparent irrationality. I understand how powerful the feeling of being left or left out is and, overall, he actually handled it pretty well.

I felt sad about the loss, but relieved to feel alone and independent again. I realized from this that I really wanted to be alone. I missed a relationship, and would certainly miss the great sex, but I felt I needed to be alone for a while. I had been a slave to a perceived romantic partner for essentially my entire life and it was time for me to truly be myself, alone.

At the time Manuel and I first got together, I wasn't sure I wanted a romantic relationship, preferring we be friends with benefits. That changed quickly and made me a little uncomfortable. I also realized that, although I had known how I desperately needed to learn to be alone, and found so difficult initially, I was learning to be alone and I liked it. There are a lot of advantages to being alone, not the least of which is being able to spend more time with my son, Andrew. One of the issues between Manuel and me was that my life is very busy. I work full time and have a son to take care of, as well as a big house I'm finally trying to sell. He works more or less part time intermittently during the day and lives alone in a small apartment. He doesn't even have any pets.

This meant that while I'm at work, so busy with patient care that I don't have time to think about anything else, he's at home, pining away in my absence. He wanted me to spend every one of my spare moments with him.

There were many things that prevented that, like the several weeks I spent preparing and staging the house, but it meant I felt a lot of pressure from being so busy. Being alone again feels free. I'm even learning to believe that my life will be okay if I never find anyone else. That's a good perspective to have if I don't want to compromise. I'm now prepared to live the rest of my life without a significant other if I need to.

Manuel struggled with our separation and initially seemed very upset. Over time he calmed down and we started seeing each other as friends. While at this point I was feeling better about being alone, I was still lonely, and I realized that I truly loved him. I had missed him and, in particular, realized that I was attracted to him, though not as much as I would have thought possible. In all my travails with women, I had very rarely broken up with any of them; they usually broke up with me. My initial positive feelings about being rid of the bad things of the relationship gradually gave way to sadness over the loss of the good parts. Realization that there were a lot of good things and good times with him began to become apparent, and I began to regret the breakup.

We got back together, and our romantic relationship quickly reverting to what it had been previously. It only took about ten days for us to see that it still wasn't working. We may have great chemistry in bed but, for a variety of reasons we can't sustain a romantic relationship. The relationship now is very casual friends. We communicate by text and email. I felt bad that the romantic relationship ended, and I knew I'd miss the sex. However, it occurred to me that, with all the Prozac I'm now on, I never initiated sex, but if he initiated it, I was generally a willing partner. We get along pretty well socially and I knew I'd also miss the social contact; he had always been a good friend. But we seem to be functioning as friends without difficulty.

37

Bulimia

After about three years of my epiphany, I found my weight had slowly increased to an uncomfortable 219 pounds. With my mentor Robert I had gone clothes shopping in San Francisco, in the fitting rooms I felt and looked like a beached whale. Twice I found shirts I liked but couldn't wear because I literally couldn't fasten the buttons around my bulging midriff. This gradual weight gain has been pretty much my baseline state for the latter half of my adult years. Growing up and in my early adult years, finances limited how much I could eat. In my residency training food was unlimited and free; I gained weight. After I finished training I made enough money that cost was rarely an issue in the grocery store. Now, in California, there really wasn't anything that the supermarket sold that I couldn't afford. Every few years or so, I would realize that I was huge and begin to diet in earnest.

One of my first diets was during medical school. I had not gained that much weight, I couldn't afford to, but I was a little bigger and consumed by the idea that I needed to lose weight. I was, at the time, very stressed out by school and conflict with Cathy, who had moved out due to stress. I recall giving myself enemas in order to lose weight. I didn't understand then that the only weight you lose from an enema is the weight of the stool in your colon. Body fat comes from absorbed calories and that takes place earlier in the digestive system. By the time digested food makes it to the colon, the absorption of nutrients has already taken place, so the only thing left to remove is a lot of the water that would normally prevent dehydration. (Water is added to intestinal contents to enhance absorption and needs to be reclaimed or the individual will become dehydrated—hence, the colon's function as a water-scavenging organ.) At the time I didn't see my activities as indicative of an eating disorder, only great cleverness on my part, intrepid medical student that I was. There were no opportunities to work out and it never occurred to me to do that anyway. I ate very little when I dieted. My dieting came up in conversation with a female classmate and she asked, when told how little I ate, what I did for protein. I gestured to my flexed biceps muscle without a word; I was using my body's own protein. I recall seeing the shocked look on her face but it didn't register that my behavior was dysfunctional. I was just happy to be losing weight; I couldn't see that my overwhelming focus on weight loss was dysfunctional.

At the time of this escapade, Cathy and I were separated and struggling, mostly due to my stress from school. Cooler heads ultimately prevailed, probably in the form of strong advice from Cathy, and I stopped dieting. Even though we were separated, I still spent most of my limited spare time with her and we never broke up.

In Michigan, a few years before moving west, I saw a picture of myself at Disney World, with Eeyore. My gut clearly hung over my belt and I was disgusted. At this point I connected with the idea that I needed to work out, but I couldn't stand to do anything like exercise and doubted I could find something I liked. A friend and colleague, who was a runner, talked about running as if he actually liked it, rather than doing it just because it was good for him. I decided to give it a try. I started running in my neighborhood. The flat Michigan streets were no big deal, I just had to dodge the ice patches on the road in the wintertime. I absorbed what I could about the basics of running from a book, bought some shoes, and gave it a try. I discovered that I liked it. In particular, if I was preparing myself for an upcoming race, not to compete against others, but to compete against myself, I felt I had a higher purpose than just working out to lose weight. I mapped out a course in our neighborhood that was exactly 5K, to prepare for a race. I bought a few tops and some shorts and kept at it. In the meantime, I was dieting heavily, using computer software to log my food intake, daily weight, and workout information. From this data, the program could figure out my baseline calorie burn rate. I gave the software a target goal weight and date to shoot for and the program, every day, told me how many calories I could eat. As I logged in the food that I ate, it showed how many calories were left that I could eat that day. This provided a powerful incentive to me and I stuck with it.

All in all, I lost about sixty pounds, stopping when Cathy insisted I was thin enough and shouldn't lose any more weight. At the time I thought I was just successful at losing weight, but, in truth, I was obsessed with it. My morning weigh-in began to be a very important part of my day. Friends and coworkers were impressed with my diligence and I never thought about how hard I worked, how obsessed I got, and how much my weight mattered to me.

After being in California for a few years, my weight had crept up again and I felt compelled to diet again. I used the diet software again and worked out on my treadmill at home. I became more and more obsessed with weight loss, pushing myself harder on the treadmill and also to eat less and less. I still only worked out for thirty minutes a day, however.

At this time, I was a practicing vegan, ostensibly for weight-control reasons, but ultimately I had begun to feel a sense of moral superiority over my lack of contribution to animal suffering. I had also had braces put on my teeth, finally able to afford the orthodontia I should have had as a child. I found being a vegan and wearing braces to be mutually exclusive; there wasn't much I could eat that was both vegan and braces friendly, particularly the food in the hospital cafeteria. As I lost more and more weight, people began to notice. I started getting more comments that I'd lost enough weight and it was time to stop dieting. I continued to diet, unable to stop, and blamed the problem on my braces. My teeth hurt too much to eat was my excuse. I continued until I was so sick I couldn't work. Deep down inside I knew I was addicted to dieting. I couldn't stop; dieting was my life. I knew how many calories were in everything, how many calories I'd burn doing a run for thirty minutes, and how many calories I needed, at least in theory, a day to survive. I cut it pretty close. Finally, at the point of emaciation, rail thin, I decided to abandon the vegan thing and go back to eating all foods. I stopped dieting. I think again it was Cathy telling me in no uncertain terms that I needed to stop that convinced me. I knew then that I had some kind of eating disorder. When I started dieting it became all-consuming and was very hard to stop. But I did stop and went back to slowly gaining weight.

Two and a half years after my epiphany, it happened again. I found myself in a fitting room at Macy's in San Francisco feeling again like a beached whale. I couldn't wear the clothes I liked in the store because my belly was so big. This time there was a difference though. This time I was a part of the gay community and most of my friends were gay men. Overall, having so many gay friends was a tremendous blessing. Now that I had finally found my people, I naturally wanted to associate with them. This meant, of course, that I was exposed to the culture of gay men, which is largely positive for me, as they generally share my values.

The gay male culture is very body-weight centered and appearance conscious; I had gotten many comments from gay acquaintances about my weight; one man patted my stomach and asked when the baby was due. In the past, Cathy could tell me I'd lost enough weight, but now we had a different relationship and no longer lived together. She told me on several occasions that I was thin enough and needed to stop dieting. A few of my closer friends at work also said the same thing. This time Cathy's insistence that I stop losing weight wasn't enough; neither was the insistence of friends. I became frightened. My friend, "Ana," anorexia nervosa, had become very powerful and she had a very strong hold on me. My internist is also a board-certified pediatrician and because she works with teenage girls, she's very attuned to eating disorders.

When I had blamed my weight loss on braces, I think she was suspicious. I finally worked up the nerve to contact her, by secure email, with my concern. It took several tries before I was able to compose myself and send the message. She responded immediately and has been very supportive ever since. Eventually she told me I needed to get rid of the bathroom scale. This is a really big step because weighing myself was a central point of my day. If I lost weight from the day before, I was in a good mood all day; if I gained weight, I was in a sour mood all day. My life revolved around the bathroom scale. I tried to take the scale to my storage facility with the other stuff left over from the house but conveniently forgot to bring the scale. I think my friend "Ana" made me forget it. So I gave it to Cathy and asked her to hide it. Getting rid of the scale originally freed me to be able to eat more without horrendous workouts, but after several days, I became really anxious about it and wanted it back. Sure enough, in a few weeks, it did bother me. I felt panicked, not knowing how much I weighed. I sensed my pants were getting tighter, but it could have just been a pair of skinny jeans that were snug to begin with getting tighter because they were washed for the first time.

I started working out again. I had stopped in a move to be kinder to myself and to try to stop the vicious cycle of eating and extreme workouts. I had asked my internist if I could work out because I missed them. I proposed just going for thirty or forty-five minutes. She is a big proponent of exercise but understands well what exercise represents to me in my illness. She said I could "stroll" for thirty minutes. Well, I did cut my workouts down from two hours to thirty minutes, but I couldn't make myself work less hard. Walking uphill fast, drenched in sweat and gasping for breath, was how I usually did it. Finally, I cut down the intensity, but then went for sixty minutes one day and two hours the following.

Kaiser takes eating disorders seriously and provided a special therapist, in addition to my general therapist, as well as a dietician with experience in eating disorders. I really needed the help. I had learned a fair amount about nutrition (on my own; it's true that medical schools don't teach much nutrition) and knew all about how many calories and how much salt is in everything. I kept track of salt because it made me retain water and then I weighed more the next day, a major crisis. I knew all about carbohydrates, proteins, and fats. What I didn't know, actually had no idea about, was how to structure a meal plan for the day that was nutritious and healthy, not fattening. I realized well that part of my eating disorder was eating just my normally a little too much and slowly gaining weight when I'm not dieting. If I could stop gaining weight when I'm not dieting I wouldn't need to diet, and my friend "Ana" only bothers me when I'm dieting. I can make her go away otherwise.

There are a lot of myths about eating disorders and a general lack of understanding on the part of nonsufferers. I discovered quickly from the few people I told, that besides being surprised that I had this problem, they didn't know much about eating disorders. When I didn't eat much and would be losing weight, they'd say, "What's the problem? I'm jealous." This sentiment was also common from gay friends. One of the biggest myths is that eating disorders are about being too thin. It's true that a classic anorexic is usually rail thin, but that's a side effect of the eating disorder. What eating disorders are really about is unhealthy behaviors regarding food and eating. What's healthy is a balanced, nutritional diet of just enough calories, and working out in reasonable moderation. Drastic reductions in calorie intake (anorexia) and self-induced vomiting (bulimia) to control weight are unhealthy behaviors.

Even though people with bulimia tend to be normal weight, there is still an eating disorder because they're engaging in unhealthy behavior. My eating disorder probably best fits a form of bulimia. Instead of vomiting to lose weight (I had tried to do that before, but couldn't make myself throw up), I exercised excessively to burn off calories. As I got more panicked over the loss of the bathroom scale, I was tempted to try the vomiting routine again. I generally restricted calorie intake, not binging very often at all. But eventually, I realized that every time I ate anything it was like a binge. I couldn't ever eat anything without feeling very guilty. This is an example of the dysfunction of an eating disorder; I should be able to eat without horrible guilt. I also had a distorted body image, feeling hideously fat when the bathroom scale and all my acquaintances say I'm normal weight.

Anorexics generally have drastically reduced calorie intakes; a regular day's ration of food for a true anorexic might be two almonds and a piece of lettuce. I didn't restrict food that much. My computer software kept track of how many calories I actually burned and any calories it thought I could have that I didn't use it would put in my "calorie bank." After a few months I had almost 90,000 calories in my calorie bank. I usually got anywhere from 1,000 to 1,800 calories per day. The software calculates my baseline daily calorie burn rate and the amount of calories I burn just being alive plummeted from almost 3,000 per day to less than 2,000 per day.

Along with the decrease in metabolism, I became intolerant to cold and got really dizzy when I stood up. These are both common side effects of excessive weight loss. I had been concerned the dizziness when standing was a return to the orthostasis that had prompted my shunt placement. Fearing that the shunt was malfunctioning, I got a brain scan and contacted my neurosurgeon. He was convinced that there was nothing wrong with the shunt, and my internist was convinced the orthostasis is secondary to my too-rapid weight loss. My orthostasis was documented clinically by physical exam testing in the doctor's office, and a couple of lab tests were abnormal in a pattern consistent with anorexia.

I also had constant fatigue. I could only do the big workouts after a lot of caffeine and stimulants. I had been using supplements for weight loss, but most were metabolic modulators, not directly stimulants. I took stimulants to get me through the workouts, though. This was more unhealthy behavior. Needing stimulants to do a workout was excessive.

I felt that I was controlled by an external power, my

friend "Ana." Eating disorders are like an addiction; I was addicted to losing weight. It's also much like obsessive compulsive disorder—the excessive dieting and working out is a compulsion. I don't think dieting is really any easier for me than anyone else, I just lose a lot of weight quickly because I'm extremely compelled to diet. At times I was frightened by the changes I saw in me. I wasn't sure where this was going, but it didn't appear to be heading to a good place. Also, since my epiphany, I had been feeling much happier and much better about myself.

Now comes along this dysfunctional, disturbing pattern of dealing with food and I couldn't tolerate it. I want to be strong and free, to feel good about myself without restrictions. I needed help. My internist and my eating disorders therapist have been very supportive and very helpful. My regular therapist, who has been with me through all the ups and downs of my gay thing, suggested that the eating disorder is a combination of attempting to bundle together all my insecurities and lack of control over my romantic life and shift it to something I do have control over. I realized immediately that she was right and after that discussion, my friend "Ana" pretty much went away. I still felt a compulsion to diet and work out hard, but I could see that it was driven by the unhappiness in my life, the loneliness that I had been afraid to accept and confront.

Although I realized how much my loneliness bothers me, most of the time I'm apparently in denial about what a big deal it is. Listening to some new music, I heard a song about a woman longing for her lover who's away. The lyrics could be construed to be about someone looking for love, knowing that the right person was out there somewhere, but just not knowing how to find him. This resonated so strongly with me that hearing this in the car driving, I started to cry. I realized then how much the loneliness really bothers me. I really do believe that out there somewhere there's a man for me. Where is he? What is he doing now? How do I find him?

I can see that my general therapist is probably right, the eating disorder is about my attempt to control something when another part of my life feels out of control. I had spent almost half of my life with Cathy and I really thought I had found my life's companion and I wouldn't ever be looking again. My life was pretty much all settled and then the gay thing turned everything upside down. Upside down and on fire, that's how I had said it early in the process. Well, now the fire's out and things don't seem quite so upside down.

Three years after my epiphany, I'm pretty comfortable with being attracted to men. I love women as companions, I want us to be like sisters, I just don't want to sleep with women. Sex with men is fantastic and I can see that romance and romantic love could be very good with the right man. I just can't find him. Everyone tells me to be patient, that I really deserve a wonderful man and I'll find him someday. But when will someday come? Just writing about this brings tears to my eyes and a lump in my throat. I like some aspects of being alone; I can do what I want, when I want, most of the time (I still have to work for a living). I can decorate my apartment the way I want, I don't have anyone else's opinion I have to consider. But the bed is starting to get lonely at night. I'm missing that special someone in all the quiet, still small places in my life.

At the beginning of my romantic time with Manuel, he had once taken my hand and said, "Let me fill the small spaces, the private spaces that others never see. Let me be the one who knows you best, who sees your innermost self." I don't remember my reaction exactly, but I think I cried.

38

Gay and Sexual Orientation

The Kinsey report for male sexuality was first published in 1948 (the report for women was first published in 1953). This was revolutionary for several reasons, in part because it legitimized discussion of these topics. Finally, our repressive society could at least talk about it. In other cultures, homosexuality was more accepted than it is even today in ours, and we've made a lot of progress since the 1950s.

The Kinsey data made a couple of very important points. First, it's not all-or-nothing, straight or gay; it's a continuum. Second, a lot more of us than we think aren't strictly heterosexual; bisexual and gay is actually common.

Current thinking in the scientific community suggests that all humans and all animals are bisexual. The whole idea of hetero- and homosexual may be spurious; individuals just live according to circumstances and their genetic makeup.[21]

It probably appears to straight people that being gay is just about men who like men; in truth it's far more than that. It turns out that "gay" is much more than sexual orientation, it's values, interests, a whole different community, a new language, new places, and new people. At this point in my development as a man who now knows he's gay, I think the men-who-like-men aspect is really a small part of what being gay means to me. In some ways I feel so different from straight men, it's like I'm a different gender, yet in other ways, I'm clearly still a man. I like reading tool catalogs, doing projects with power tools, and riding my Harley.

In terms of language, every large cohesive group with a long existence has its own lexicon. There are a few gay terms I've learned recently. I realize there are many more, and I don't want to be excommunicated from the gay culture if I reveal too much.

A term used to refer to an individual, couple, or group that's gay or lesbian is "family." For example, to ask if someone is family means, Are they gay? This is very helpful when confronted with individuals who are suspected to be gay. If asked directly, "Are you gay?" and they are gay, fine. If they're not gay, they may be very offended by the question. On the other hand, asking, "Are you family?" is much safer. Gays and lesbians will generally know that they are and answer in the affirmative, whereas straights will generally be dumbfounded, unable to understand how an otherwise stranger thinks they're related. This is much safer, particularly in a context where the hostility provoked by being wrong could be severe.

There is a secret code phrase dating back to gay clubs in the pre-Stonewall era, when it was basically illegal to be gay, in order to gain admission.

"Do you know Dorothy?" was the initiating question.

"Yes, in fact I'm a friend of Dorothy's," is the correct response.

The Dorothy mentioned here is Dorothy of *Wizard of Oz* fame. Not only Dorothy, but Judy Garland herself are great heroines to the gay community; plucky, innocent optimism in the face of grave danger rings true to members of a minority only recently allowed to legally exist and still usually not allowed to marry.

The rainbow symbol for gay is attributed by some to derive from a line from the song in the *Wizard of Oz*: "Somewhere over the rainbow." Other origins have been suggested, but the Oz connection may help explain why it's popular.

Like any other group with an extensive history, gays may interact with straight people in the world at large, but to some extent we're still separate, we still keep to ourselves. There's the us we'll present to everyone, and the us we save for family, our community.

The whole gay thing is so big, it's sometimes hard for me to understand it, to grasp the whole of who it is I've turned out to be. In terms of knowing who I am, it's wonderful. In terms of knowing I'm not a freak, it's incredible. In terms of dealing with all the consequences and implications of what it means to be gay, it's formidable. Nevertheless, the whole gay thing resonates through my entire life, my past, as far back as I can remember. It's one of the most defining characteristics of who I am, and I only found out in middle age. It is also the defining crisis of my life. It led to severe major depression that started around the age of eleven; my first (of many) suicide attempts at age thirteen; the feeling as a young boy that I was very different; and progression of those thoughts into feeling that if I'm that different there must be something wrong with me, I'm a bad person. This led to profound shame at my mere existence.[22] Is it a coincidence that depression started around puberty and that my first attempt at suicide was a little later in my sexual development?

The guilt felt over feeling subhuman can be intermittent and expressed in different ways; my compulsion from an early age to be a nice guy could be from guilt, possibly from feeling like a freak.[23] Just seeing how I feel in a group of typical gay men is enough to convince me I'm gay; my whole life I've looked for my people, and clearly these guys are the ones.

Our culture and society wants us to think that there are two genders, male and female, and that it's all very cut and dried. Even people who are more open and accepting of gays and lesbians seem to think that gay and straight are a "black or white" kind of dichotomy. In reality, I think it's really more a spectrum; in some ways gays and lesbians seem somewhere in between straight men and straight women. Then again, in some ways we're just different, not even on that continuum. There is also gender identity. Some of us cannot identify with the gender we were born as and believe we are meant to be the other. And some transgender individuals are attracted to the opposite gender whereas others are attracted to the same gender. There are also intersex individuals, whose physical gender (and possibly gender identity) is somewhere between male and female. And there are, no doubt, other criteria or measures of human sexuality, like how strong an interest in sex one has, or how big a role sex plays in one's life.

Ultimately, the whole concept of gay and straight, the concept of sexuality, is more complicated than it first seems. There has been a gradual shift toward acceptance and understanding in our culture, but there is still a long way to go. The religious right continues its oppression and gay marriage is still illegal in most states.

39

Gay History and Stonewall

Homosexuality has been around since the beginning of human history. Different cultures in different times have had a different take on it. In the mid 1800s, the German scientist Karl Heinrich Ulrichs advanced the theory that gay men are a third sex, male bodies with female brains. Ulrichs believed that homosexuality was congenital. Although this characterization has some practical merit, this is a gross oversimplification. I was pretty sure I didn't have a female brain. I can be very feminine, based on traditional feminine values, but I was pretty sure I'm not a woman.

One of the first known gay civil rights events occurred in 1869 when a Hungarian physician, Karl-Maria Benkert (also known as Karoly Maria Kertbeny), published a letter to the Prussian Minister of Justice to counter legal punishment of homosexuals.

Benkert had come up with the terms "homosexual" and "heterosexual"; the medical diagnosis previously was "contrary sexual desire," or "moral insanity." Legally homosexual activity was known as perversion, sodomy, or buggery. Gays of the time preferred to be known as "congenital inverts," in part to imply that it was of biological origin. This term originated with the German neurologist, Richard von Krafft-Ebing.

An American organization, the Society for Human Rights, was started in the 1920s but was of limited impact.

David L. Kaufman, M.D.

The revolutionary Kinsey studies brought the idea of homosexuality to the forefront, and paved the way for open dialogue. Discussion is a necessary first step in the progression to understanding and acceptance. In the late 1940s and 1950s, homosexuality was still considered a disease, a perversion of nature, and oral and anal sex were illegal. Gays were frequently harassed, even arrested, by the police. Anti-gay sentiment swept through the country. In the 1950s, homosexuality was seen as being somehow associated with communism; the McCarthyism witch hunt prevailed against gays and lesbians, as well as communists.

Homosexuality, in the science literature, didn't always mean what it means now. In many early animal behavioral studies, when an animal acted during sex like the opposite sex, that was often referred to as homosexual. If a male rat having sex with a female rat acted female, that would be considered homosexual. In 1948 Kinsey recommended referring to this behavior as inversion, and reserving the term "homosexual" for a sexual encounter between two individuals of the same sex.[24] This meant that any sexual encounter between members of the same sex is homosexual. If a man is receiving oral sex from another man, that's a homosexual encounter, even if he's fantasizing that the other guy is a woman. A man giving anal sex to another man is homosexual, regardless of his own view of his sexuality. Inversion is often seen with homosexuality but the two are independent. There are many gay men who are very masculine and in sex roles never act female.

At the time of Kinsey's research on male sexuality, there was much less sexual orientation data from observation of animals in the field, or even in captivity. True homosexual behavior had been observed in animals, but with the anti-gay cultural overlay on the researchers, they couldn't or didn't accept it. When two male animals were seen engaged in sexual activity, it was assumed to be some sort of anomaly and that observation was ignored. As times have changed and homosexuality has become more culturally accepted, it's now more accepted within science to report these observations.

Additionally, DNA testing has now made it possible to map out the relatedness and genders of groups of animals. Particularly in birds, it's been observed that two male or two female birds will build a nest and raise young. In these cases, a separate male or female will provide the needed sperm or eggs.[25]

It has also been seen that as many as 1,500 different animal species exhibit homosexuality.[26] The evolutionary purpose for this behavior has been speculated. Homosexuality, at least in males, may be genetic. How this could be supported evolutionarily is a little tricky. It is possible for gay men to have children; I do and I know many others who do. Nevertheless, homosexual men would generally be less likely to have children than straight men. So how can this persist as a genetic trait? Wouldn't it be eliminated by natural selection? It would, unless it provided some other benefit. Only men have a "Y" chromosome and there isn't much genetic material there. If being gay is genetic, it's likely on another chromosome that women would also have. This means that women could carry the gene as well. Looking at relatives of gay men could be revealing. There is ample scientific evidence that relatives of gay men have more children. It's not really "the gay gene," it's "the fertility gene."[27,28,29,30]

Research has shown that, compared with heterosexual controls, homosexual men have a later birth order, an earlier onset of puberty, and a lower body weight. Homosexual men have a greater number of older brothers than do heterosexual men.[31]

This is similar to the situation with sickle cell anemia. Obtaining copies of the sickle gene from both parents is fatal at an early age without advanced medical treatment. The gene is preserved, however, because having only a single copy causes no significant health problems and protects that individual from some species of malaria. Then, it's not "the sickle cell anemia gene," it's "the anti-malaria gene."

Additionally, homosexuality among males of a species in the absence of females preserves both the behaviors and the sperm-producing ability for when females become available.

Homosexuality in animals, as in humans, has been observed in captive populations when few of the opposite sex are available. All this research contradicts the assertions by anti-gay forces that homosexuality is not natural or is a choice.[32] Homophobia constitutes multiple different psychological etiologies. Some people are fundamentally anti-gay really only because they don't know anything about them or have no familiarity with them. This is the form of homophobia that can be overcome by having more of us come out; the more common gayness is, the more normal it appears. Specific anti-gay attitudes often come from religious teachings; the fundamentalists in many religious faiths decry homosexuality.

Kinsey saw the significance of whether homosexuality occurred in significant numbers in the animal kingdom; if it is present, it puts human homosexuality in a whole new light.[33]

By Kinsey's data, about 50 percent of men are exclusively heterosexual in sexual contact and about 6 percent are similarly exclusively homosexual. Because about 10 percent of men live homosexual lives, that implies that about 40 percent of all men who are living straight are actually bisexual.[34]

Homosexuality has been present for the history of humanity, although at times more accepted than others. During the 1940s and 1950s it was not accepted and being gay or lesbian during that time was quite difficult.

Gay rights probably got started in this country with a series of meetings taking place around the Los Angeles area in the early 1950s.[35] The meetings were an attempt to join forces against the discrimination and police harassment that was occurring. One such organization, the Mattachine Society, was founded in 1950.

ONE magazine, dedicated to gays, began publication in 1952; the thought behind it was, "You can be proud of being gay."[36] You can look in a mirror and say, "This is what I am, and so what?" The idea of gay pride in that era was new; the struggle for many of them was just to accept who they were and understand that gay is not some psychiatric disease or perversion. Before gay rights could accomplish anything, gays had to recognize that they deserved rights. *ONE* struggled in publication; the post office often seized copies on the grounds that it was pornographic. Simply promoting gay interests was considered pornographic because homosexual acts were illegal. Ultimately, the publishers of *ONE* fought all the way to the U.S. Supreme Court and won, but they still faced opposition.

Laws were often unfairly applied; oral and anal sex were illegal, but this was essentially never enforced against heterosexual couples. Entrapment by police officers was common, so was lying about what actually happened. A simple touch could be construed as soliciting an illegal sexual act and therefore that person could be arrested.

In 1960 the Daughters of Bilitis, a lesbian organization founded in 1955, held its first convention in San Francisco; the police were watching very closely and impersonating a male could be cause for arrest. The women could be arrested for wearing fly-front jeans.[37]

In 1966, *Time* magazine published a scathing editorial on homosexuality, depicting it as a perversion and a sickness. Although the tone of the article was homophobic, it paved the way for discussion about the subject. Ultimately, much of the negative press was actually beneficial for the gay and lesbian community; it showed that there were others in a similar situation.

Individuals in the early organizations were often split on the group's function. One side wanted to push for gay rights with protest and political pressure on legislators. The primary goals were to stop police harassment and allow out gays and lesbians to be able to keep their jobs, both within the government and outside.

The other faction was probably intimidated by the idea of so much exposure, given conditions at the time with harassment and discrimination. They were more interested in support for the community of homosexuals, both male and female, to fight the insecurity and poor self-esteem that plagued their community. This is a problem still today, but was much worse in the '50s and '60s. The word "homosexual" couldn't even appear in print. With society telling them that they're sick immoral perverts, it was difficult for many to maintain a sense of personal dignity. Early in this time period there was so little said about gays that many gay men and women in more-isolated communities knew of no others like them and felt they were alone in their differences. This is something I can relate to; not knowing there were others like me was demoralizing, often to the extreme. Many stories of these early experiences are similar to my struggle.

> We're not like everybody else. I don't think or feel like a heterosexual. My life was not like that of a heterosexual. I had emotional experiences that I could not have had as a heterosexual. My whole person, my whole being, my whole character, my whole life, differed and differs from heterosexuals, not by what I do in bed.
>
> [there is]…a body of language, feelings, thinking, and experiences that we share in common…we used certain language, certain words…
> —*Direct quote from Chuck Rowland, interviewee*[38]

The gay community often felt forced into hiding; an arrest at that time could be devastating. Names were often published in newspapers and being forced to come out could cause loss of job, home, and credit. It was a very difficult time.

In 1964 the first organized gay protest took place. It was a humble beginning: ten picketers marched at a U.S. army induction center in New York City. In 1965, there was a large confrontation between police and gays in San Francisco. Like other examples of how negative publicity still helped the gay community, this helped establish San Francisco as the place to be if you were gay or lesbian. Hearing even negative accounts of events like this alerted gays and lesbians that there were more people like them and ultimately had positive aspects. Just knowing that we as gay and lesbian individuals are not alone is a very powerful thing, and something I can relate to strongly.

Many of the individual groups began to band together—
North American Conference of Homophile Organizations
(NACHO: "nay-ko")—in 1968 held a convention promoting the
idea that "gay is good" to promote pride.[39] This was another
attempt to bolster the self-confidence of the gay community
and reverse the perception that being gay is a disease.

A major turning point occurred on June 28, 1969. This was
one day after Judy Garland's funeral, and as both Dorothy in
the *Wizard of Oz* and Judy Garland herself have been heroines
to the gay male community, there was a strong sense of loss
and gays everywhere were upset and in mourning. Not seeing a
connection, police staged a raid at the Stonewall Inn, a grungy
bar in New York City's Greenwich Village. They went in and
rounded up the people they intended to arrest, including the
cross-dressers.

Throughout this time, transvestites had been bolder than
other gays, more willing to take chances. Even going to a bar
in drag was risky. Although many gays not into cross-dressing
looked down on the drag queens, many transvestites were
generally more willing to take a stand. The cross-dressers
probably also suffered at least as much as non-cross-dressing
gays because they were obvious targets in bar raids.

The police were not prepared for what happened. The
bar patrons fought back and it turned into a riot. It started with
throwing coins, but escalated to breaking windows, fire, and
slashing tires on the police vehicles.[40] This continued for a few
days. The gay patrons at the bar that night were no longer
willing to accept police harassment and the ultimate result was
revolutionary in scope.

Gay rights was suddenly propelled into the modern
era, and eventually there was some success in reversing laws
against gay sex and ending discrimination against gays in civil
service. Although many barriers remained then and still remain
now, the previously widespread homophobia was starting
to abate. Gay activists were becoming more militant as their
earlier hesitancy to make waves changed to a tendency for
greater activism.

Gay-rights organizations were probably also spurred on to more-dramatic attempts at change by the generally more activist atmosphere in the country. There were groups at this time protesting the Vietnam War, and the Black Panthers were protesting for civil rights for African Americans, for example. Not many gays at the time saw the significance of this atmosphere, but it acted as a springboard to give those interested in advancing rights the incentive to be more direct and assertive. This was a pivotal moment in gay-rights history. It was also a tumultuous time in American history in general as many traditional mores were falling. This made it easier for gays and lesbians to begin to be more accepted.

Another strongly positive sign of the changing times was when the American Psychiatric Association, in 1973, removed homosexuality as pathology in the Diagnostic and Statistical Manual of Mental Disorders. This work is the official canon for psychiatry, and although the move was controversial, it marked a major change in thinking. During a time when organized medicine, specifically psychiatry, was claiming homosexuality was a disease, it was difficult for the gay community to believe otherwise. It takes a strong person to be okay with themselves when doctors are telling them they're a pervert.

A large aim of the gay-rights movement is for the gay and lesbian community to achieve and maintain self-esteem and personal dignity. This is the essence of gay pride: We can and should be proud of who we are.

Increased visibility of gays and lesbians over the last decades has improved public perception of our community. The more of us who come out, the better off we'll all be because as society sees that there are so many of us and we are normal people, then gay rights will be a natural evolution of the understanding that we're really just regular people. This has been a major point of the gay-rights movement. First, we need self-respect, and then we need to come out so people will know who we are. Coming out is a complex issue. On the one hand, it's a personal decision and no one should be forced to come out. On the other hand, it is making a political and social statement: "I'm gay and I believe it's okay." We need as many of us out as possible so the straight world can see that we're just normal people like them.

Homosexuality has been a significant part of human sexual activity ever since the dawn of history, primarily because it is an expression of capacities that are basic in the human animal.[41]

Gay rights has come a long way in a relatively short time. The struggle is not over yet; there are more hurdles ahead of us. The right for gay and lesbian couples to marry and the elimination of any form of discrimination are primary goals.

The Clinton administration advanced the cause of gay rights to some degree, even though the "Don't ask, don't tell" policy for the military was a disappointing policy. But legal marriage rights remain elusive in most parts of the country. A case in Sonoma County highlights the difficulties gay couples face without legal marriage. The following is taken from *Out for Justice*, the National Center for Lesbian Rights blog (http://nclrights.wordpress.com):

> Today, NCLR launched a national media campaign to bring visibility to a tragic new case where Sonoma County, California, officials separated an elderly gay couple and sold their worldly possessions despite the measures the men had taken to protect their relationship.
>
> "In the 33 years of our organization's history, this case is perhaps among the most tragic NCLR has ever been involved in," said NCLR Executive Director Kate Kendell. "Clay and Harold had taken all of the necessary precautions, including living wills and powers of attorneys, to protect them in a time of crisis. Not only were their relationship and legal documents ignored, Clay and Harold literally lost everything. These appalling events demonstrate how urgently same-sex couples need full equality rather than a patchwork of rights that can be dismissed and ignored in a culture that still treats LGBT people as second-

class citizens. This never should have happened to Clay and Harold."

Clay Greene and his partner of twenty years, Harold Scull, lived in Sebastopol, California. As long-time partners, they had named each other beneficiaries of their respective estates and agents for medical decisions. As 2008 began, Scull was eighty-eight years old and in deteriorating health. Greene, eleven years younger, was physically strong, but beginning to show signs of cognitive impairment. As Scull's health declined, it became apparent that they would need assistance, but the men resisted outside help.

In April of 2008, Scull fell down the front steps of their home. Greene immediately called an ambulance and Scull was taken to the hospital. There, the men's nightmare began. While Scull was hospitalized, Deputy Public Guardians went to the men's home, took photographs, and commented on the desirability and quality of the furnishings, artwork, and collectibles that the men had collected over their lifetimes.

Ignoring Greene entirely, the county petitioned the court for conservatorship of Scull's estate. Outrageously referring to Greene only as a "roommate," and failing to disclose their true relationship, the county continued to treat Scull as if he had no family. The county sought immediate temporary authority to revoke Scull's powers of attorney, to act without further notice, and to liquidate an investment account to pay for Scull's care. Then, despite being granted only limited powers, and with undue haste, the county arranged for the sale of the men's personal property, cleaned out their home, terminated their lease, confiscated their truck, and eventually disposed of all of the men's worldly possessions, including family heirlooms, at a fraction of their value and without any proper inventory or determination of whose property was being sold.

Adding further insult to grave injury, the county removed Greene from their home and confined him to a nursing home against his will—a different placement from his partner. Greene was kept from seeing Scull during this time, and his telephone calls were limited. Three months after Scull was hospitalized, he died, without being able to see Greene again.

"Because of the county's actions, Clay missed the final months he should have had with his partner of twenty years," said Greene's trial attorney, Anne Dennis of Santa Rosa. "Compounding this horrific tragedy, Clay has literally nothing left of the home he had shared with Harold or the life he was living up until the day that Harold fell, because he has been unable to recover any of his property or his beloved cats—who are feared dead. The only memento Clay has is a photo album that Harold painstakingly put together for Clay during the last three months of his life."

Greene is represented by Dennis, along with Stephen O'Neill and Margaret Flynn of Tarkington, O'Neill, Barrack & Chong, in a lawsuit against the county, the auction company, and the nursing home. NCLR is assisting Greene's attorneys with the lawsuit. A trial date was been set for July 16, 2010 in the superior court for the County of Sonoma.

The case is Green v. County of Sonoma et Robert, Case No. SPR-81815.

The case ended with NCLR clients Clay Greene and the estate of Harold Scull, Greene's deceased partner of twenty years, reaching a settlement on July 22, 2010, resolving their lawsuit against the County of Sonoma and other defendants. Greene and Scull's estate will receive more than $600,000 to compensate for the damages the couple suffered due to the County's discriminatory and unlawful conduct.

"What Clay and Harold lost can never be replaced, but this settlement brings a measure of justice to their story," said Amy Todd-Gher, Senior Staff Attorney for the National Center for Lesbian Rights, which represented Greene with The Law Office of Anne N. Dennis and Stephen O'Neill and Margaret Flynn of Tarkington, O'Neill, Barrack & Chong. "This victory sends an unmistakable message that all elders must be treated with respect and dignity, regardless of their sexual orientation, and that those who mistreat elders must be held accountable," according to the NCLR Website.

40

Reflections on Being Gay

Recovering from my explosive first take on being gay and the gay community, I began to take stock of where I felt I was. I completely withdrew from the community, attending no gay events, and talking about related feelings only with my immediate circle of gay friends. One really good friend, one of my coworkers at the hospital, said not to worry about it. When I expressed embarrassment about how exuberant I had been, he laughed and said, "You may have singed your feathers a little but you didn't do anything you need to feel bad about. We all thought it was cute."

"You didn't just come out of the closet," he continued, "you flew out like a jack-in-the-box."

Introspectively, I realized another reason for my coming out so avidly. I went through a profound personal transformation when I knew I was going to live after my near-death experience and I knew then I *had* to come out. Much later, I began to realize how much the timing of my illness and recovery influenced my feelings about being gay. On a very deep and not entirely conscious level I feared that my terminal diagnosis was a punishment. Having a miraculous cure convinced me very strongly that there is nothing wrong with me. I was made this way and I was, like all of us, made perfectly. I feel very proud of who I am; I feel that being gay contributes to my being a good person, an interesting person. I wouldn't be straight now even if I could.

The outward changes were sudden and difficult to ignore: dressing different, standing taller, looking ahead instead of down; and being much more self-confident. This led to people wondering what the hell happened to David; by coming out, I offered an explanation. Now we don't have to talk about why I'm suddenly so different.

I finally realized, about a year after I came out, another reason I was so adamant about doing so, about being out to everyone who knew me. I was proud; proud of who I really am, proud to be a normal gay man. It was such a change from how I felt as a straight man (weak, inadequate, flawed, broken) that I wanted everyone to know who I am and to share in my joy of finally being okay and whole as a person.

Ultimately, the gay thing totally rocks. I can finally be who I really am. I can finally be as feminine or as masculine as I feel. I can finally express how I really feel about things without fearing it won't seem masculine enough. And, truly ultimately, I can finally accept that I'm really attracted to men more than women.

I am really proud of who I am now. I think I'm much more colorful and interesting as a person. I'm adventurous, not just one more guy who likes football and big tits.

Many coworkers attributed my changes to the marked improvement in my health, but I've been through a lot in my life and nothing else ever changed me like this. I graduated from medical school and became, "Dr. Kaufman" without any perceptible changes in my demeanor. I believe that what truly underlies all of this is the relief of knowing I'm not some mutant freak of nature, I'm just different and there are others like me. And I'm going to live. Yes, gay is hard, but I'm still part of a large community, and there are perfectly good explanations for my behavioral differences from typical straight men. All of my thoughts, fantasies, feelings, and behavior that seemed weird before are now easily understood as perfectly normal for a gay man.

I have a big message to send to the world: I'm totally normal, and I'm gay. Not, "but I'm gay," not, "even though

I'm gay," but just, "and I'm gay." I am a normal man. Part of what is remarkable about all this is that I can thoroughly enjoy being able to explore who I really am. Knowing I'm gay means I can do what I want; I'm not bound by society's long-established behavioral expectations of masculine and feminine. Although it's true that I didn't think I was really all that bound by convention before, there were layers and layers of expectations, standards, and traditional values for straight men I felt I had to uphold. This was too much to overcome without a massive push. Finding out I'm gay was the really massive push. Now I'm free; shot free of the bonds of conventional thinking, I can be whatever and whoever I want to be. I'm pretty sure I don't want to wear women's clothing, but I could and would if I wanted to. I could never have even thought about it before, never even considered the possibility before. It would have been totally off-limits.

Sometimes I feel bad for straight men; they have so many rules to live by. In fact, there seems to be a rigid script that straight people follow for their lives. Do well in high school, graduate from a good college, get married with so many bridesmaids and a rehearsal dinner, get a job, get a dog, buy a house, go on vacations to where ever is trendy with your peers, have children. If the script isn't followed, the couple is viewed with suspicion or even contempt. Although some gays and lesbians feel compelled to try to replicate that script, many realize it's a lost cause and we just live our lives the way we want to.

I do acknowledge that being gay is hard; that's been a recurring theme throughout this whole process. It's painful to be marginalized, to realize this process has cost me some civil rights. I realize I'm no longer going with the flow; I'm a salmon swimming upstream. The challenges are great; gay couples can't really even hold hands in public without repercussions. Jason and I occasionally held hands, and even in liberal Sonoma County we sometimes felt the sting of rejection (one elderly couple, upon seeing two men holding hands, bolted in opposite directions, with horrified looks on their faces). Yet I feel so liberated, so free. It's amazing how something can be so hard, yet still so good at the same time.

As the process continues, I can see that the difficulty of being gay is not a sense of decreased worth; I've grown to like it, actually. Most of the time I feel it's really fun to be different, to be bold and adventurous. The difficulty is in the struggle just to get used to who I am. Sexuality is a big part of how I see myself, who I think I am. I would have thought I'm sexually conservative, meek and mild, but apparently I'm not. Sexuality plays a significant role in my daily life. Do I think about sex a lot? Maybe once every fifteen minutes, possibly more. Do I think about sex more than the average guy? I have no idea. Has this change in how I see my sexuality turned me upside down? Absolutely. Some of my friends seem startled at what an incredibly big deal this is to me. Either I'm more sexual than they are, or they don't realize how much it would affect them if it happened to them.

Straight men have no idea what they haven't had to go through. When you look at all the collective suffering in the LGBT community it's truly staggering. Clearly I've really struggled, but my experiences are, unfortunately, not unique.

My father often quoted some lines in a long-since forgotten movie he saw a long time ago. Two male police officers are patrolling in a car, one white, the other black. The black guy turns to the white guy and says, "Do you ever think about being white?" The white guy says, "Of course not, why would I?" The black guy then says, "Well, I think about being black every day."

That's what it's like for many of us gay men—we think about it every day. It's a constant presence. We live constantly in the shadow of our own uniqueness. In contrast, I doubt that straight guys ever give their sexuality a second thought.

Many months after my epiphany, I find my difficulties adjusting to a new life were less troublesome and it occurs to me that some day, some time in the future, this will all be okay and will seem totally normal. I'm gay and it's okay; I've got a tube in my brain and it's okay; Cathy and I live separately and it's okay. This is a profound idea, a very powerful tool. At the three-year anniversary of my first conversation with Cathy, I'm pretty much there. I'm gay and it's okay. I can see the parts of me that didn't change—my love for things electronic and mechanical, my fondness for motorcycles. I can also see the parts of me that did change. I'm not only much less shy, but now something of an exhibitionist. I'm clearly sexually attracted to men. And I feel a lot of femininity within me, a tendency to feel like a girl.

So what words do I think describe me? I like "gay" and "queen," I'm okay with "queer." "Homosexual" is fine, but clumsy to say. I don't like "fag" or "faggot," probably because of the taunting I received as a child. I'm not very happy with "fruit" or "fairy" either. The "q" words are okay with me, but the "f" words are off-limits.

Occasionally someone says to me, "You're so gay."

My response is, "Thank you."

When people say, "That's so gay" to someone who's not gay, I perceive that as an insult to gays, as well as the person it's said to.

I've thought about what it means to specify how gay someone is. This can really be interpreted in different ways.

In terms of being gay, saying a guy is "really gay" can mean different things. "Gay" can refer to effeminacy; in this context a "really gay" guy is just really swishy.

A related continuum is flamboyance; a man could be nonswishy but flamboyant. This is less likely as swishy and flamboyance tend to go together, but it's probably possible for a guy to not be swishy but still be flamboyant. For example, in attire, I'm probably more flamboyant than swishy. My mentor Robert is neither. People meeting him might be surprised that he's gay, but then people meeting me might be surprised, too.

"Gay" can also refer to the well-publicized Kinsey continuum with gay at one end, straight at the other, and bisexual in the middle. In this scheme, "really gay" means really close to the gay end, totally uninterested in women. So a man could be really swishy and totally bi, or very butch and strictly at the gay end of the continuum.

Another categorical form is perhaps more subtle, it's how a man sees his own body sexually. Presumably, the anatomical body part straight men center their sexuality on is their penis (not being a straight man, I'm not actually sure; it's something of a guess). In this way of looking at it, a man who sexually identifies with his rectum instead of his penis (this guy would really be a "bottom" man) could be construed as "really gay."

Another way to be more or less gay is related to how long the person has known they were gay, how long they've been out, and or even how involved they are in the gay community. Someone like me who's new to this can seem "less gay" than someone who could be my age but has been out for decades and is very involved in the community. Some guys have known they were gay for years, but came out late and are not involved in the community at all. Some gays are involved in the community at large on multiple levels, involved in social events meeting others, even involved with political groups and gay-rights activism. This category is probably not so much "how gay," but more properly, "how involved in gay" the person is.

All of these categories can be mixed and matched; there may be trends, but I think these categories are really fundamentally independent.

Cathy and I have a unique perspective as gays because we're very familiar with the straight world and point of view. This is an advantage in some ways. We can see our relationship to the straight world and understand how the straight world views us. We've spent a great deal of time around people who would feel free to voice their homophobia if they had any. We've seen the gay world from the straight perspective, and from the point of view of straight values and expectations.

A straight community value that can carry over into the gay community is the idea of family. I've seen that many gay men really want to have a family, kids, minivan, and the whole white picket fence thing. I believe that we, as humans and even as animals, are hard-wired to want families, otherwise the species would disappear. I've been through the family thing twice, and, from my perspective, it's really hard. Without some instinctive desire for this, we humans would go extinct.

From even before this whole gay thing, my own observation and opinion, although admittedly biased, is that I sense that gay and lesbian couples probably make better parents than straight people. Many straight people seem to take parenthood for granted whereas gay and lesbian couples consider it an honor to be able to raise children. Having children is not a natural result of same-sex relationships and requires a great deal of time, effort, and money. I know two gay couples who moved to California specifically because they were from the Midwest, which didn't allow adoption by gays.

This desire for family may be, in part, a value from the straight community that many of us have internalized. Do some of us want children out of hard-wired instinct or is it out of a desire to look like everyone else? I see a longing for this kind of family partly as an attempt at being "normal," a desire to live like a typical straight couple. Ultimately, hard-wired instinct probably plays a strong role. It's been observed that although gay men, who by definition should have fewer children than straight men, often demonstrate personality characteristics that are quite nurturing. The presence of many (admittedly stereotypical) gay attributes may indicate the persistence of a genetic trait, that is, men who have these characteristics but aren't gay may have more children than average.[42]

Typically, for a straight man, and true to the habits I'd learned in thirty-five years since puberty, I've been an observer of women. I'm sure I started this pattern before puberty; young children often talk, in terms of fantasy, of marriage and family. Of course, as a boy I was expected to grow up and marry a women and have children.

Partly related to this habit, I have struggled somewhat in my relationship to women. As a gay man, technically I don't "need" them. I could still live my life with romance and sex even if I despised women. Some gay men apparently do dislike women for some reason. The problem is that I personally do need women. I love women intensely; it's just that now I finally realize that I mean that only for companionship. When I could finally stop the pretext of trying to get sex out of the relationships with women, I found I'm suddenly free for very rewarding friendships. Women who know me, and know I'm gay (which is virtually all of them), know that they're safe around me; I won't hit on them, grab their butt, or fall in love with them. They know when I'm being friendly I'm not just manipulating them for sex. They know that they can be touchy-feely with me and not worry that I'll get the wrong message. What I really want is for us to feel like sisters. It's fun to feel like one of the girls, it's truly wonderful. Wow! It actually feels good to be gay!

Initially, I found that I generally noticed women and not men. This was disturbing because I knew from my epiphany that I wanted men sexually, but in public I'm not attracted to them. My first exposure to a whole group of gay men came fairly quickly after my coming out, and in that setting I did feel sexual interest in the men. Maybe I'm just not attracted to straight men. After all, there's really no point in being interested in straight men, and, besides, they do dress like schmucks. They wear baggy clothes and I can't see their ass; if you're a straight man and you don't want gay men checking you out, wear baggy clothes; it's a real turnoff.

I think the average straight guy dresses as much as possible out of comfort; he wears the first thing he picks up that's comfortable. Men's clothing in general is driven far more by comfort than women's clothes. Most women go to great lengths to look attractive in the clothes they wear. Just look at high-heeled shoes and panty hose. I've actually worn panty hose on a few occasions, but not to look like a woman. In order for a wet suit to work properly, it has to fit tightly, which means it's hard to get that neoprene suit on. Wearing panty hose makes the legs go in much easier and so I wore panty hose several times when scuba diving. So I can say from personal experience: Panty hose is ungodly uncomfortable. There is no way the average guy could be convinced to wear panty hose on the basis of looking good.

Gay men, at least some of us, seem to care more about

our appearance than a lot of straight men. We tend to have, I think, a sense of style.

Something I noticed later in my process is the change in my reaction to a few people. There was a young man who worked at the hospital who always bugged me. It wasn't that he ever said or did anything offensive, I just didn't like him. Finally, I figured out what the problem was. He's gay, and he's really cute. He bothered me because I was attracted to him, but at that time I couldn't consciously accept being attracted to a man. After thinking about it, I can remember other men who have irritated me like that, and I was also probably actually attracted to them. Come to think of it, there are a few men I see regularly in my life who are attractive and used to disturb me. I think Cathy noticed this phenomenon also in her life, but hasn't experienced it as much.

The recurring issue of noticing the women around me rather than men has been disturbing. I have very strong evidence I'm gay, possibly a "little" bisexual, but why don't I notice men? Why only women? In the past, I played up my attraction to women because it's all I had. At the supermarket recently, for the first time, I realized I wasn't noticing or looking at women, just at men. At work a male coworker described a female coworker as pretty (I can see that) and with a nice body (I have no idea, I can't tell at all). I can see that some women are pretty, but women's bodies are pretty much lost on me at this point. I think noticing women was a habit learned from my peers around puberty. When it came to women's bodies and how hot they are, I realize I never really got it; I was pretending, telling myself as well as others that I could see a certain woman as hot. It takes a lot of time and effort to unlearn a lifetime of self-deception.

> "Someday I'll have everything, even a pretty girl
> like you;" my heart wants a pretty girl. [or does it?]
> —*Jonathon Coulton, "Code Monkey" 3/12/10*

Do I want a pretty girl? I don't think so. I think I'd like

a strong relationship with a strong man. I think what I really want is what straight people, what everyone, wants. I want someone I'm excited about, someone who makes my heart beat faster, someone who makes my palms sweaty.

Months later I had a realization. When I'm thinking about a woman I think is attractive, I'm picturing her as I saw her, dressed and all. When I see an attractive man, I'm thinking immediately about being naked in bed with him; I'm thinking about his penis. At times, on rare occasions, I still do feel drawn toward a woman, but I know it's just a relic of my past and doesn't mean anything. I have many women friends, and thoroughly enjoy their company, without sexuality.

Cathy admitted at one point that she has caught herself kind of flirting with men without thinking about it, then realizing and wondering what the hell she's doing. I can relate to that.

Recently, I had a long talk with my older son by phone and we were comparing our taste in music. I like Lady Gaga and so does he. Then I brought up Katy Perry; he agreed he liked her music, too.

"Plus," he said, "She's really beautiful."

"Yes," I immediately responded, "I can see that, she's gorgeous."

"And she's really hot," he continued, "She has a great body."

"She does?" I answered. I couldn't recall noticing that or finding it all that sexy if I had.

I later recounted this conversation to Cathy.

She quickly said, "Oh yeah, Katy Perry has a really hot body."

Yes, some gay husbands and wives have conversations that go a bit differently from the norm, like a wife noticing a woman's hot body that the husband can't see! I have been able to let go of many of my previously held convictions, and it's been a wonderful relief. One thing I've let go of is the idea that sex is some mysterious, off-limits, taboo subject. It's not; it's just sex. I observed even before my awakening that the gay and lesbian community seems much more open about sex. It seemed like a good idea to me even then, even if I wasn't able to be completely on board.

Now I'm not hesitant at all to talk about sex. If it came up (and it most certainly won't), I could easily have a conversation with straight friends about the intricacies of gay sex, the key to giving good oral sex, and tricks for receiving anal sex. It's really no big deal; it's just sex, another body function, like eating. I suspect that if the straight community could be more open about sex, they would experience less pain and suffering.

A conversation rarely heard among straight couples but not all that rare with gays is;

"You want to have sex?"

"Sure, come on, let's go."

"Okay."

In the process of losing the habit of noticing women and thinking about men, I've come to ponder my sexuality as me alone, by myself. Discussing how I've dealt with this in the past, and my relationship with common household objects with phallic characteristics, my closest gay friends advised me that I really should have some toys.

Previously I wouldn't have been caught dead in an adult bookstore; no way, that's just against the rules. In particular, I couldn't admit any thoughts, feelings, or behaviors related to sex that go against cultural norms. Well, now it's not "an adult bookstore," but "the toy store," and I like the toys. On a whim, I bought a blow-up transgender sex doll. She's basically an elongated beach ball with arms and legs. She has a photograph face printed on the plastic head and stringy hair attached only to one spot on the top. She came with an attachable penis and two orifices. The blow-up doll turns out to be completely useless for sex, but she's nice to have in bed at night, just as a sort of companion to keep me company.

Prior to buying the doll, on my first trip into the toy store, I perused the gay DVD section carefully. I made what looked like a good selection and then asked the salesman if they had any dildos with suction cups on the back.

The salesman saw the video in my hand and leaned toward me.

"You can't have that," He said.

I mumbled something like, "Why not?" as we walked toward the extensive selection of dildos.

"You can't have that one," He said again, indicating the video.

"Why?" I asked again.

He stopped and turned toward me, pointing at the case. "This guy is so fuckin' hot!" he exclaimed.

Now I got it; he liked to borrow the DVD and couldn't if I bought it. Well, then, it looks like I made a good selection.

We stopped in front of the dildos and he pointed to one model.

"This one has a suction cup," he said.

"My God, that's huge!" I exclaimed.

He leaned closely over my shoulder and said quietly, "Chicken... chicken...."

"Don't you have anything smaller?" I asked

"Nope, that's it," he said, more quietly, "...chicken...."

I bought the DVD and some other things, deciding to think about the monster dildo.

There's a lot here to think about, a great deal more than just being a man who likes men. For me the easiest part of all this is the I'm-attracted-to-men realization. That is, after all, the part I can see I had before my revelation. I can see now that I was attracted to men, and I clearly knew that I wanted men sexually, I just didn't have a context to put that in, a way for that to make sense for me as a person. I have that context now and it's a great relief to have found it. Where I fit in my culture and society in the grand scheme of things, who I am as a person in many different ways, is the big issue. I like to ride my big Harley and work with power tools, but I also like arranging flowers and shopping for crystal stemware.

In a conversation with my father, a gifted retired therapist, we explored a novel concept regarding homosexuality, at least in men. Given that male homosexuality demonstrates characteristics suggesting that it's a genetic phenomenon,[43] we discussed a model for explanation how the sum total of what gay is represents more than just homoeroticism.[44] Many of the typically feminine qualities present in gays—kindness, sensitivity, empathy, and tenderness—could be inherited individually.[45]

In the medical world some diseases are considered syndromes, a collection of symptoms that can be seen in a disease process, although all symptoms are not necessary for the diagnosis. In this pathophysiologic model there are a number of signs and symptoms produced by the disease, but most patients have only a subset of these. Syndromic conditions are often specified as needing eight out of the ten total symptoms in order for the patient to qualify as having the disease. Multiple sclerosis was a syndrome in this fashion, although now there are more concrete objective measures.

Homosexuality, at least in men, could be a syndrome. Effeminacy would be one of the defining characteristics; some homosexual men demonstrate this, but many do not. An interest in cross-dressing could be another characteristic that's variably present. Other tendencies that could be part of the syndrome are: gentleness, being noncompetitive, and the tendency to express more creativity. Some of these characteristics could be secondary effects from primary genetic traits. Proclivity in the arts could just be what effeminate, gentle, and noncompetitive men like, rather than, for example, football. (To be fair, there are gay football players; the stereotypes aren't all-pervasive)

Homoeroticism, the men-who-like-men part, would be considered a required characteristic of being gay. A man with many of the other features, but heterosexual, is probably possible and would explain the metrosexual (looks and acts gay, but is straight).

> "You're so gay, and you don't even like, you don't even like, you don't even like... ...penis."
> —*Katy Perry, "One of the Boys," Ur So Gay*

There is a suggestion from the scientific literature that many of the stereotypical characteristics of gay men may increase a man's chances of reproducing if he lives as a straight man.

Note that ascribing homosexuality in men to genetics often meets with fierce resistance from the gay community. That implies it's a disease, some say. I don't think so; being male or female is genetic and I don't think either of those conditions qualifies as a disease. My blue eyes are genetic and I definitely don't consider that to be pathologic.

Another criticism is that if homosexuality is genetic, then it could possibly be tested for. This is more problematic; what would we then do with an individual who tests positive for homosexuality but insists they're straight? Is that legitimate? What about the other way around: Does an admitted gay man who tests negative lose veracity? All this opposes my own value that everyone is entitled to believe in who they are sexually.

A serious criticism to the genetic argument is testing young boys or even fetuses. Would routine gay testing be performed on early gestations, allowing for therapeutic abortion if found positive? What does that say to the gay community: that we're defective and would have been aborted had our parents known? The deaf community has faced similar issues regarding whether being deaf is a disease or an alternate form of human being. Not being deaf, it's hard for me to have an opinion about this. I, of course, believe very strongly that, just like being a man or a woman, gay is a normal variant of humanity. The possibility that fetuses with gay genes would be aborted is really disturbing. The irony of this is that, theoretically, only people who can accept abortion would consider this, in other words, liberals who should be okay with gay offspring could be okay with aborting an allegedly gay fetus but conservatives wouldn't. That means that all or most gays would therefore be born into conservative families. Now that's just the cat's pajamas! I have to admit I feel some perverse satisfaction in that.

I have, of course, encountered at least a few people who are uncomfortable with the whole gay thing. They're almost always straight men. When ostensibly straight men seem uncomfortable with the gayness, or me as a gay man, it occurs to me that they may be partly bisexual and seeing some of me in themselves.

The gender theory of homophobia says that homosexuality as a social role, rather than a sexual practice, is what's upsetting. This makes some sense, given that gays are something of a mash-up between straight men and straight women. We often don't fit well into the little boxes or categories that our society has created for men and women. In some ways gays are like straight men and in some ways like straight women.

The part of being gay that's hard is that others may not be able to see gayness as another form of normal. It is sometimes difficult for me when my gayness interacts with other people, particularly straight people. I have a personal history of being treated very poorly, ostensibly for being gay. Although it's probably likely that the bullies who taunted me didn't really care or even know about the gay thing, they still did what they did. Being repeatedly called a fag and beaten leaves emotional scars. Even realizing it's true and in some ways feeling liberated by it can't block the fear and uncertainty about how others see me. I feel proud of who I am and I like myself now. The part of being gay that's directly inward and personal, that drives my inner experience, desire, fantasy, and intimate behavior, is totally glorious. I feel set free. Although gay individuals are not completely like straight individuals in some ways, the differences are trivial. We're still people, we basically still feel the same, have the same joys, sorrows, hopes, and dreams. Gays function like everybody else. Gay relationships, and even gay sex, involve the same interpersonal dynamics as they do for straights. The differences between straight and gay individuals is not bigger than the variation among straights.

Anyone could be uncomfortable with the whole gay thing from a lack of exposure to it. I think some racism comes from this same basic lack of experience. Unfamiliarity would likely be a source of distress. The more discomfort someone professes, the more I tend to think that they're just trying to cover something in themselves, to protect their own view of who they are. To just understand and accept that they may be a "little" bisexual would probably go a long way toward alleviating that discomfort. But I suspect that would be hard for them.

Just because someone is a little "bi" doesn't mean they have to do anything with it, it just would explain why they sometimes feel the way they do. Learning to accept this is probably the difficult part for most people. Being a little bi is not an insult to their masculinity, nor does it imply that somehow they're not attracted to women. In this light I am less put off by their attitude, which can actually seem comical.

An additional point regarding the characterization of human sexuality: there are other metrics besides the gay–straight continuum. Degree of sexuality is variable among individuals, although stereotypically greater in males than females. I know I think about sex constantly. I always have, at least since puberty. I used to think about sex in the context with women and now I think about it with men. This has been a big struggle because thinking about sex with men is new and different for me. It feels more right and more true than sex with women but it still feels very different. Cathy admits to not thinking about sex anywhere near as much as I do and has not struggled as much with the same feelings. Just as there are those of us wired for sex and romance with the same gender, there are those of us wired for high intensity and those of us for whom sex doesn't really matter all that much.

My desire for a romantic relationship without sex makes a lot more sense now. I think it's interesting that part of what this means is that I never really fell in love with a woman, only with men. I even believe that the reason girls didn't like me in school was partly because I picked girls who wouldn't like me so I wouldn't have to go through with anything sexual. My problems with physical intimacy in my first marriage may be at least partly my fault for being gay. If I was straight I might somehow have been more attractive to Barbara.

With my transformation, I do seem to be seen as attractive by both men and women; perhaps it has something to do with confidence, as my older son thinks. So now I wonder, can a relationship with a man match one with a woman? I think so. Can it match what I felt when I truly fell in love the first time? Probably not, and for my sanity's sake, I hope not.

About a year after my epiphany, it's not seeming so insanely weird anymore, it just feels more normal and natural. I notice more attraction to men and less to women. I think it's reasonable to say that I don't think of sex with women as bad, I just prefer men.

> "The only way to really know is to really let it go."
> —*Ingrid Michaelson, "Maybe," from the album*
> *Everybody*

About eighteen months after my epiphany, I've pretty much gotten used to being alone. It's very refreshing to not feel I need someone. I may want someone, but I don't need someone. I'm actually feeling pretty good about being single. After nearly a lifetime of going from one romantic attachment to the next, I'm free of that cycle. I can decide if I want to have a partner or not; I can decide whether I want to pursue a relationship with someone instead of taking them because they're there and they want me.

So where am I three years out? I'm definitely feeling a lot more comfortable about the whole thing. I still like being gay, now it doesn't feel so weird anymore.

I had observed for many months that I'm not so attracted to straight guys, only gay ones. But I can see now that I can be attracted to straight men, if they're attractive. That includes how they're dressed; most straight guys have no sense of style or fashion and probably wear whatever is most comfortable. Show me an attractive straight guy in a sharp suit and I'm all over him; he's hot. I heard the ZZ Top song, "Sharp Dressed Man" the other day in a store and thought, "Yup, I'm locked on that."

The relief I feel at knowing I'm not a freak is because I have a different identity than I thought; I fit well in the gay world. I was trying to be the wrong thing. I'm much more comfortable being a gay man than trying to be a straight man. It's true that I could pretend to be a straight guy and still have my values, likes, and dislikes, but I wouldn't fit in very well there while I fit in great in the gay world. I didn't fit well in the straight male world because I wasn't a straight male. It's more than my values, ideals, likes, and dislikes, though, it's my fundamental identity. For example, no matter how much I like African American culture, no matter how hard I try to embrace it, I'll never really fit in because I'm not black.

I struggle a lot with femininity; I often feel very feminine. I think sometimes I walk like a girl (I often catch myself swinging my hips) and I talk like a girl. I have a regular man's voice, but my word choices are more feminine, the way I compose sentences seems more feminine to me. I don't think I'm effeminate in the limp-wristed sense; I'm told that I'm pretty butch for a gay man, and I doubt that most people who meet me at first think I'm gay. Only a very few of my current friends and acquaintances really thought I was gay before I did, though a few really did know before I did.

But there's still a lot of girl in me. I don't think I want to look like a woman, maybe because I don't think I would be very good at it. Truthfully, I haven't tried to do so since I was about twelve years old. One day, shortly after puberty, my Mom was out shopping or something and I tried on some of her clothes. Mostly what I remember is that it felt really bad, really naughty. That would be my peer group influence, I don't think my parents would have been that upset if I were a cross-dresser. Since that time I've felt that I don't want to cross-dress. Maybe, though, I don't want to do it because as a twelve-year-old boy, I felt ridiculous trying on my mother's clothing. So I might like it now if I could do it well.

Actually I'm happy to be a girl inwardly most of the time. Now that I know and accept that I'm gay, I can celebrate the feminine within me. Previous to my epiphany, I found the feminine in me deeply disturbing and tried mightily to suppress it. Consciously, I thought I was accepting my feminine side, but, in truth, I had little overt recognition of how feminine I really am, and I worked very hard to suppress any conscious appreciation of it.

Part of the femininity struggle is how I relate to or fit in with women. I want us to be like sisters. I believe I identify with women, at least in some ways. I can tell, though, that like the African American analogy, I'll probably never completely fit in with women because I'm not one. That's probably the key to the transgender issue. If I was truly a transgender male-to-female I would truly and completely identify myself as a woman and therefore would feel like I fit in. I identify with gay men and, most of the time, feel like I fit in and truly belong in that group.

From my association with the many gay men I now know, I think a small percentage feel the same as I do about the femininity thing. I definitely know gay men who don't have a sense of themselves as feminine and I know gay men who genuinely don't seem to like women. I don't understand that, but I know it's true.

So where exactly do I fit in? I'm a man, but I don't identify with, and occasionally don't feel comfortable with, straight men. I'm definitely gay and I now identify that way. I don't think I'm a woman even though sometimes I feel like one and I love them as friends. I don't think I'll ever identify as a woman. My identity is that of a gay man. At least that's what I think so far.

But I'm definitely a lot less convinced now that I don't want to look like a woman. It's possible the reason I haven't wanted to try is because I fear I'd make an ugly woman. Recently, on vacation, I looked in the hotel bathroom mirror. At first my reaction was the usual one I've had since my epiphany, "You're an OK guy." Then, it suddenly struck me that I look really masculine, much more masculine than I feel. At this point, I'm truly not 100 percent sure if I'm a gay man or a straight woman. I feel like a woman a lot. I think I can relate to women, but there are aspects of womanhood that escape me. Especially for a gay man, I'm really not that much into decorating. The part of the Sur La Table catalog with all the aprons, napkins, and other linens holds no interest for me; perhaps a typical straight woman is more interested in it than I am. But then all straight women probably don't get into that either.

So I'm staring at myself in the bathroom mirror thinking I look way more masculine than I feel and I start wondering what I can do about it. The vacation happened to be an all-gay vacation in Mexico so I had the chance to observe a lot of gay men. Earrings, I thought. I could get my ears pierced. That would give me the chance to look a little more feminine and if I didn't like it later I could just take the earrings out and the holes would heal over. But I wasn't sure I wanted to get my ears pierced in Mexico and, anyway, I figured I should take a few days, at least, and think about it.

As soon as I got home, I went to the jewelry section of Macy's and asked if they pierced ears. "No," the saleswoman said, "we don't, but there's a kiosk in the mall a little ways down that does."

I found the kiosk, but the saleswoman was at lunch. So I went to a nearby jewelry store and killed time by buying a pair of diamond stud earrings. Back at the kiosk, the saleswoman was very friendly, really helpful, and said they do pierce ears. Only a few minutes later, I walked away with newly pierced ears. I have to say it hardly hurt at all, much less than a shot at the doctor's. The bummer is that I have to leave the original studs in for a long time before I can take them out and wear the diamonds I bought. Over the next few days I reflected on my courageous act of femininity and decided something more was in order. I vowed to grow my hair long, like a woman (I could wear it in a ponytail at work). The next time I see my stylist, we'll talk about it.

This far out I realize that the loneliness bothers me more than I was giving it credit and I needed to be sensitive to my own wants and needs that way. I think my loneliness is coming from two different things. One is inherent loneliness that stems from the human condition and this form of loneliness is appropriate. The second form is the part about my not used to being alone and that's something I need to work on. I've never really been without a special someone for any length of time before and I need to learn how to be okay by myself. I have friends, I just don't have a special someone, a romantic partner. It still feels like a big loss, a huge gaping hole in my life that needs to be filled. Rationally, I'm not even sure it can be filled; I'm a unique gay man, possibly, at least in part, a straight woman, and it may be hard to find a complementary mate. Part of the reason I need to learn how to be alone is because I may be alone for a long time, possibly the rest of my life.

41

Conclusion

> The reason I feel free to be whatever I want is because I've realized that to go from wanting women to wanting men is upsetting everything I always thought I believed in—if I'm not sure about that, then I'm not sure about anything and everything I like or don't like is up for grabs.
>
> —*Personal journal entry 9/25/09, in conversation with a coworker*

The enormous power of my realization rarely fails to impress me. Through all the ups and downs, particularly the downs that have happened since, the personal power that comes from my awakening has not left me. Through all this, the core of my transformation has remained constant. I continue to stand tall and proud, holding my head up, with strength and dignity. There have been times when I've feared I was losing it, but it always reappears. The most reasonable explanation is that now I am completely sure that I'm an okay person; I am not a freak, I am a normal man. Yes, I'm different, but there's a legitimate explanation, there is nothing wrong with me, I'm not a bad person. Just being able to stand seeing my reflection is incredible; the increase in self-esteem is so powerful.

I spent almost all of my life so far trying very hard to be something I'm not, and the cognitive dissonance that produced was torturing me. I can now look back and see the agony I suffered for not really knowing who I was or why I am the way I am.

About eighteen months after my epiphany, I realize something profound: I'm basically there. I'm gay, I know, and it's okay; I have a tube in my brain and it's okay; Cathy and I live separately and it's okay. It's all okay. I don't go around in a constant state of confusion about my sexuality, about all the other big changes. I feel strong, connected, comfortable with who I am and ready to face what life brings. I look around and think, I really like who I am, I'm comfortable with it. I like my life. This whole gay thing totally rocks!

I started out knowing I'm sexually attracted to male anatomy, but not necessarily attracted to men otherwise. I didn't think I could kiss a man, let alone did I want to kiss a man. I was uncomfortable with pictures of men kissing each other, even just with their faces close together. As far as I could tell, I was still attracted to women. I couldn't even imagine a romantic relationship with a man, still only women. This made me wonder if I could be transgender. Gradually, over time, I realized I could kiss a man, and maybe actually wanted to. When Cathy beat me to the punch and kissed a woman first, I knew I was past due; I needed to kiss a man and find out.

When I finally did kiss a man and was amazed at how good it was, I actually got weak in the knees and almost had to sit down. The feel of a man's beard stubble on my cheek now is intoxicating.

I still wasn't sure I was really attracted to men, though. Women still held a certain appeal, even though I knew that my body's sexual response had been and still was changing, and it was unlikely the appropriate body parts would cooperate in an attempt to have sex with a woman. I wasn't sure I wanted a romantic relationship with women or men. It's like in my mind I'm bisexual, but my body is totally gay.

Then gradually I began to notice that, when out in public, I'm often more attracted to men than women. I began to realize also that it's not that I used to be attracted to women and now I'm not, it's that previously I had been suppressing my attraction to men. I'm not immune to feminine charm, it's just that before that was all I had, and now I can allow myself to feel the much stronger attraction I have for men. It took months from my awakening to get to this point.

So now, after all this, do I wish I wasn't gay? I don't have a choice; this is who I am. There have been times I've felt that I don't want to be this, but I generally like it. It feels comfortable; it feels like who I really am. It's an enormous relief to know I'm not a freak; the relief feels like waking from a bad dream. It has been hard to get used to, though, and being gay can be difficult. There is still societal pressure to not be this way. Our society is set for all of us to be straight. Advertising to men sometimes uses women I'm supposed to find sexy to help sell the product. For obvious reasons, that never worked well on me and now I find it annoying. Motorcycle ads often use scantily clad young women and it annoys me, they're blocking my view of the bike. Greeting cards I see are all oriented toward straights although somewhere there must be gay cards.

I have had many more insights, corrections of stereotypes, and wrong thinking. In discussions with Cathy and my mentor Robert, and in retrospect, it becomes evident I must be at least somewhat bisexual. I don't think I could have lasted living a straight life for almost fifty years had I been totally gay, with no interest in women altogether.

Am I feeling better than I ever have before, better adjusted? I feel better about the gay thing; being a man who's attracted to men seems relatively natural now. Robert has helped me understand occasionally being attracted to women; it doesn't mean I made a mistake and am not gay; it just happens sometimes. I can and will be attracted at times to women, it doesn't mean anything…

—*Personal journal entry 01/23/10*

Robert helped me to understand that there will be times when woman are appealing to me not just as friends, but as potential romantic or sexual partners. This doesn't mean I'm straight, or that I made a mistake about being gay. It's just a normal part of life. I've found that, without getting down on myself about it, not consciously fantasizing about women makes being gay feel easier. It's probably just as okay for a man who thinks he's completely straight to occasionally find a man attractive or curious about sex with a man. I've found that, three years out, I have no desire to fantasize about women, I'm just not sexually attracted to them at all now. Truly beautiful women are moving to me, but not sexually attractive.

I suspect that those feelings give the average straight man more trouble than the feelings I've had about women give me. The Kinsey data suggest that about half of the male population is exclusively heterosexual and only a few percent exclusively homosexual. This implies that close to half of the men who live straight have some bisexual component.[46] I've come to view discomfort with homosexuality in men I speak with as a sign that they may be in that bisexual half and that they're uncomfortable about it.

Cathy helped me to understand that bisexual can mean not just wanting sexual contact with *both* men and women, but could also mean wanting *either* men or women. It's whomever I fall in love with. I could possibly fall in love with a woman again; it wouldn't be a huge crisis. But pursuing it could be a bad idea.

> If I dated a woman, I'd still be waiting for the man.
>
> —*Personal journal entry 10/13/09*

At one point early on I commented to my mentor Robert that I was considering dating women for companionship, given the lack of available gay men. He responded that it was a bad idea.

"It's not fair," he said.

To lead a woman on when ultimately I'm not capable of a typical long-term sexual relationship with her would be unfair. I have to be careful with women because I can probably still fall in love with a woman, but ultimately can't follow through sexually. To start a relationship I'd probably abandon if the right man came along would not only be unfair, but cruel. After a powerful date with a man I realize that I really don't want a woman at all, I want a man. He just has to be the right man. I have an appreciation for effeminate gay men, but I'm not attracted to them, they're generally "bottoms" and I really need a "top"—a very masculine top. My minimal interest in women after my epiphany is just residual from a lifetime's worth of habits and the lack of an appropriate gay man. When I find the right gay man, women will be a moot point.

Soon after my epiphany I noticed that I still looked at women, and never noticed men. Everywhere I went, all I could see were women. Why wasn't I looking at the men? After all, I'm gay, aren't I? This continued for months and was very unsettling. Over time I realized that I'd learned to look at women, not men, starting from puberty. For the last thirty-five years I'd only sexually noticed women because it was a habit, and one not easily broken. Even after I was convinced I was really attracted to men, I still noticed women and very rarely men. I would often find myself caught up in a woman I'd see and then think, "What do I really want to do with this woman?" The best I could come up with was: coffee, maybe we could get coffee. I didn't really think I wanted anything else. At times, while being distracted by a woman, I have pondered her body and thought about what was in her bra and panties. Do I want that? Not really, not at all. Then why do I keep looking at them, why can't I stop? What's wrong with me? Will I ever figure this out?

I've thought about this a lot; it's very perplexing. I also think it's related to my difficulty accepting change. Noticing women is familiar; noticing men is new. I have also, since my awakening, had sexual or romantic feelings for women and wondered if that's what I really want or am I just feeling that because it's comfortable and familiar. I may revert to women when I feel overwhelmed or lonely. I can also see, as time goes by, the walls go down that I built to protect myself from being attracted to men. This process of building walls probably started even before puberty and was well established by adulthood. I can see occasionally, when I let my guard down, that I can be intensely attracted to men sexually, far more than I think I was ever attracted to women. In a flash of epiphany months later I realize I can't date women, I would miss the rectal stimulation part of sex. Sex with myself with toys would always be better.

Skimming through a department store flyer recently, looking for men's clothes (that in and of itself a new habit), I pass women's images clad only in underwear. "She's kinda cute," I think to myself and wonder. Then I see a man in his underwear and I melt completely. I'm still finding deeper and deeper understanding of how strong my homoeroticism is; there's a serious phallic worship thing going on.

Others can see their past and project themselves into the future. They can see what they'll want ten or twenty years from now. This is useful, say, for retirement planning. My life has changed so much, so many times, that I don't feel that I can plan like that. I have no idea where I'll be or even what I'll be twenty years from now. I assume I'll want a romance and down the road I may find one. I assume I'll still be working as a doctor. Although there have been very big changes over the last many months, things have been settling down and my life seems much calmer. The crazy roller coaster ride that was 2009 seems to have ended, and in a very positive way. I finally like who I am; I'm finally truly proud of who and what I am. But I still don't know what's in store; I still can't see the future. That leads to a certain amount of excitement. Who knows what the future will bring?

Throughout this process, I've had difficulties understanding what I want my role with women to be. I'm aware that a few gay men can be strikingly misogynistic. Not me; I love women, but only as companions. I wanted to hang around with the girls as a child, and with the women as an adult. I like being one of the girls.

Really good time with [friend from dinners], liking women is okay, knowing some are attractive is okay, it's actually better when gay because have more contact with them. Also said, "to thine own self be true," and talked about that; have to be me and let everyone else deal or not.

—Personal journal entry 8/25/09

I have noticed the phenomenon of women, particularly female coworkers in my case, feeling more comfortable with me than before. Now we're free to really be friends. It's really wonderful.

In the wake of the Jason experience, I have again begun to feel that what I want in a relationship is not possible. I reread my journal entries about the beginning with Jason to bolster my beliefs that it really can happen again, that I could feel that way again. I have doubts about my ability to connect with a man, even though I already have, several times. I know I can connect to women romantically, but I also know it won't work long term. It feels like being between a rock and a hard place. Three years out I have a date that really appeals to me and I know it's possible, it just may take a while.

I still reflect on how I've obviously always been gay, and the role fantasy plays in showing that. Fantasies are a profound insight into what someone really wants or needs. Fantasies about gay sex, fantasies that I'll survive a suicide attempt, fantasies that Cathy will come back, these speak volumes about who and what I am deep inside. Learning to pay attention to what I fantasize about has been deeply insightful.

My suicide fantasies always involve me surviving an attempt. This implies that I really don't want to die, I just want to feel better. My history of multiple (obviously) sublethal attempts bears that out. But it's still possible for someone like me with this history to feel compelled enough to either actually kill myself or make an attempt that accidentally works. This is a significant risk and my psychologist and psychiatrist are constantly on guard about it, as I am. I have specific directions to follow if it gets that bad.

My fantasies about working it out with Cathy come from the difficulties we've survived over the years. There have been so many times I've thought it was over and we still worked it out. My having been divorced already before Cathy and I got together is insidious; there's always that idea, in the back of my mind, that if this really doesn't work, I can leave.

During some of the many arguments between Cathy and me early in our marriage, out of anger I occasionally said I was leaving, that we were getting divorced. The last time I said it, years ago, Cathy started crying.

She said, "Why do you say that when we fight; I never say that. I'm not willing to give up so easily,"

"I'm sorry," I said after some thought, "you're right, I never thought about it that way. We've fought many times, but we always stay together."

Well, yes, we've always stayed together, no matter what. My mind understands that this time is different; this is beyond our ability to smooth over and fix up. We can't maintain a relationship as a married couple anymore. My heart still has a hard time believing it, though. So many times in the past, I was sure it was over and yet we worked it out. It's hard to accept that this time, there's no fixing it.

Oddly, I still feel this way even though I know rationally that Cathy and I are much better off finally living who and what we really are. We actually get along better and are more supportive of each other. Rationally, I know it would be detrimental to go back to the way we were. The power and permanency of my transformation shows how much better off I am now. Clearly, Cathy is better off, too. Surely we have a much better relationship now than we ever had. I can feel how much better it is, how much we're now able to support each other, far more than we ever could as a married couple.

Ultimately, my fantasies have evolved into more and more directly gay experiences. No matter what it is that provokes doubt, I can't deny fantasies that have become more and more, totally and completely, gay over the last several years. Obviously, this awareness is a process that has been ongoing for some time. I have probably, at a level below conscious thought, been preparing and arranging my life to allow for this. How could I go so long without knowing I was gay? Probably self-deception based on peer pressure. How much longer would it have taken without the Internet images? Probably not all that much longer.

I've observed that I'm less worried about the really bad things, like physical injury and pain. I feel less obsessed worrying over less-dramatic things, like financial problems and losing the house, for example. Part of my exuberance is related to a sense of fearlessness. With what I've been through, what's there to worry about? I've had a tumultuous life, but this last few years I've been through more turmoil and personal upheaval than I could have ever imagined. It would seem that sexual orientation shouldn't be all that big a thing, but it is. It defines who I am at a fundamental level. I've had to change who I think and feel I am in a basic way; things like losing my home seem trivial by comparison. Even the idea of dying seems less important. I faced that this last year and got through that, too. I never used to fear death, feeling that when my time came, it would be okay, a relief, to surrender my consciousness. I believed I had so many flaws that death would be a relief. Even when I wasn't depressed or particularly unhappy, I still was okay with the idea of dying. The idea of being able to live longer than a typical human life span was not a positive concept for me. Even when I was really sick and told I was dying, that wasn't the part that bothered me. How it would affect my family bothered me. And I wanted a chance to be better, and enjoy it, before I died. I got that wish. Now I kinda like the idea of being able to live longer; now I really don't want to die anytime soon.

More darkly, I sometimes found myself feeling that, because I'm gay, it doesn't really matter what I do. It felt like I can never again be the well-respected pillar of the community, a shining example of humanity, kind of person again. If I can't be such a wonderful person anymore, than it doesn't matter if I have a few faults. For example, it doesn't matter if I smoke;

I'm gay, so what. This feeling passed after many months; I can be a well-respected pillar-of-the-community kind of person. It's really okay to be gay. This was hard to see for a long time. I could see that there was nothing wrong with me, but I felt so different. Two years out I don't feel that different anymore. I'm gay, but so what? Lots of other people are gay, it's not that weird to me anymore. I'm still a human being with the same basic wants and needs. A friend of Cathy's had said that it takes two years to get used to being gay. I think she's right; three years out and it just doesn't seem that weird anymore, it's just a part of who I am. In a way I'm different, but not inferior.

That line of thinking, that I'm inferior because I'm different, represents another stereotypically negative attitude about homosexuality, that I'm somehow less human than my straight counterparts. Some of this is undoubtedly cultural, but most probably comes from the feeling that my differences with other boys and men means I'm a bad person. This is a form of internally directed homophobia. Many months later this feeling largely vanished; I believe I'm already well respected at work by colleagues and coworkers and for the most part, no one really cares that I'm gay. I not only can be but I am still a wonderful person.

There have been times when I've felt I'm not the same person anymore. Of all the people startled by my transformation, I think I may have been the most shocked. It was unsettling to see myself thinking and feeling differently on all those different mundane things, like how I dress, how I take care of my face, and how I act.

I need to stop thinking "I'm still the same person" because I'm not—not even close.
—*Personal journal entry 9/25/09*

At first it was difficult to see where all that came from. It seemed to me that I was suddenly channeling some long-deceased flamboyant gay man (Liberace, perhaps?). I can see now, however, that I'm very much the same David I always was. The differences that seemed so profound are actually relatively superficial and, on introspection, can be found in the pre-awakened me. I liked to dress well before; I just didn't allow myself to do it very often. Who I am on a deeper level is really unchanged. I still like basically the same hobbies, and I think I'm still a nice guy and a hard worker.

I've lived through the resolution of the dominant personal crisis of my life and a profound shift in my identity. There is tragedy in that it took something this profound to show me that I can be what I want.

Any man, gay or straight, should be free to act and be as he pleases without concern over what is "masculine" and what is "feminine." There is no reason why straight men can't be involved in traditionally feminine ideas or activities. A straight man doesn't have to be interested in professional sports, he can crochet instead. A straight man can take dancing lessons (his wife or girlfriend would probably appreciate it). It's ridiculous to think that somehow that would make him gay or mean he's less of a man. It's ridiculous to think that being gay means he's less of a man.

It would be good for all of us (me included) to understand and believe that gay isn't less than straight, it's just different.

Even after Stonewall, even with more-recent advances in gay rights, many of us still struggle with who we are. We—the gay and lesbian community—have to come to terms with our own homosexuality; we have to accept it and make it our lives. We have to "live our gay" with pride and strength. We need to be proud of who we are: interesting people with something of value to add to society. We need to be strong in our conviction that we are normal, good people.

It would also be helpful to consider the possibility that describing activities, beliefs, or values as feminine or masculine can be detrimental to the mental health of all of us. Crocheting isn't "feminine," it's just a hobby. Riding a motorcycle isn't "masculine," it just something some people like to do. And my personal nemesis, professional sports, isn't the sole purview of straight men or necessarily "masculine."

We should champion the blurring of these boundaries. This

can be seen to some extent in the gay and lesbian community. Cathy went from me, with no interest in professional sports, to the company of lesbians, some of whom do follow it. I went from Cathy, with minimal interest in feminine fashion, to men, some of whom are all into makeup and female clothing. There is value in mixing up feminine and masculine; we can find ideals and activities that have real meaning for us.

One of many powerfully positive aspects of my transformation is that now I think I understand romance. I understand the power of a gentle caress, the joy of holding hands, a gentle touch on the check. Before, when caressing and hand-holding was just a prelude to sex, I just really didn't get it. It took all this for me to understand that. I sometimes wonder how many other (straight) men don't get it either. Is that common to straight men, or just common to gay men who think they're straight?

In the gay community there is much talk about pride. Well, we all deserve to be proud of who we are; whether we're Latino or white, black American or white American, gay or straight, differently-abled or not, we all deserve to proud of who we are.

I believe that we in the LGBT community need to be strong as well as proud. From pride can come strength. We should be known by our conviction and our strength.

Ultimately, I've gone through a powerful experience that is truly life altering. I will surely never be the same. Overall, it's been profoundly positive; a hard road to follow, to be sure, but still overwhelmingly positive.

> By definition, as a gay man, I'm unconventional; I no longer wish to be bound by convention at all for anything. This is why I feel that being gay, I can be anything I want.
> —*Personal journal entry 10/5/09*

A searing instance of profound personal insight was forever burned into my consciousness. This addressed what has been the most fundamental and defining crisis of my entire life: I am not a freak, a weirdo, subhuman, or an aberration of nature. I am not a bad person. I'm just a gay man, a normal gay man; a normal man who happens to be gay. The strength necessary to fight the shame of being a freak can now be turned to positive use.

> He had been persecuted and despised for his ugliness, and now he heard them say he was the most beautiful of the birds. Even the elder-tree bent down its bows into the water before him, and the sun shone warm and bright. Then he rustled his feathers, curved his slender neck, and cried joyfully, from the depths of his heart, "I never dreamed of such happiness as this, while I was an ugly duckling."
> —*The Ugly Duckling*, Hans Christian Andersen.[47]

With self-knowledge comes authority, certainty. From self-validation comes personal power. No longer suppressing a very large part of who I am, I am no longer living a lie. I am now, for the first time in my life, proud of who and what it is that I am. For the first time in my life, I can be truly happy.

This understanding yields immense force and power: I am gay, I am proud, and I am strong. Very, very strong. No one can take that away from me. There has been and there will be opposition. There are those who will despise me without even knowing me, and there could be violence. But even if they kill me, they can't take this strength away; if my life is ended, then I will die, gay, proud, and strong.

Epilogue

> Spiritual warriors see everything that happens to
> them as a challenge; ordinary people see things as
> blessings or curses.
> —Jack Kornfield: *The Inner Art of Meditation*

It turns out there's more; I'm still going through the phases of gay. I originally saw myself as the "G" in LGBT but now realize I'm the "T." I'm transgender or transsexual. Initially, I felt I didn't want to look like a woman, but later on I had to address that issue. I think I struggled so much with identity as a gay man because it was really my identity that was changing, I just hadn't completely realized who I was. Thinking I'm gay was a big deal to me because I'm really transgender and all this is about my identity as well as my sexual orientation.

During the first year or so after my epiphany, I really felt much more masculine than I ever had. I also, however, often felt feminine and I understood that some of my favorite activities, like cooking and flower arranging, are generally seen as women's work. It's true that top chefs tend to be men, but routine cooking in a household tends to be women's work. Men bring home the bacon, but it's the women who usually cook it. In hindsight, I could see that my original euphoria in being gay was because it meant I could be more feminine, and my femininity increased gradually over the three years. I couldn't see it then, but another transformation was in store.

I went on a blind date to a movie; through the entire movie I was so giddy I could barely stand up, just to be next to such a wonderful, masculine man. He is very much a man, not macho at all, and a total gentleman. All during the movie, I kept looking over at him and feeling waves of attraction.

Also during the movie, I kept having waves and waves of feeling that I was a woman. I didn't just want to be a woman, I felt I really *was* a woman. Not only that, but this feeling felt so good, I couldn't remember feeling this good in years.

The lead woman actress in the movie we saw was someone I had not seen or heard of before and she was ravishingly beautiful. In some scenes, in skimpy clothing, I thought she was sexy. Partway through the movie, I began to wonder: What did I see in her? What did I want with her? I was essentially too giddy to stand up from sitting next to an incredibly attractive man, why was I attracted to a woman?

Near the end of the movie it finally hit me, in an epiphany as great as my realization three years before, that I didn't want her, I wanted to be her in every way—I overwhelmingly wanted to be a beautiful woman in absolutely every way, even anatomically.

Three years out, after initially feeling more masculine than ever following my initial realization, I read a very good book about a cross-dresser and another outstanding book about a male-to-female transgender person. I was startled to learn that there are resources to help trans-women (as male-to-female transgender individuals are called) learn how to walk and talk female. I had previously assumed that if I was really a woman in a man's body all that would come naturally. I didn't know anything about putting on makeup, therefore I can't be a woman.

Apparently all that feminine behavior doesn't come naturally. A lot of what we consider to be feminine is actually learned. It was obvious when I seriously thought about it; I just never consciously thought it through. The problem then is that I assumed I wasn't a woman in a man's body because none of that came natural to me, I just felt really feminine most of the time. This really changed everything; this was a really big deal. So maybe I am a woman in a man's body. In truth, I had wanted to be female, to be a girl, when I was five years old. The more I thought about it, the more it made sense. Could I really be a woman? I knew I felt like a woman and assumed that the more I did to look like one, the better I'd feel.

So I decided to find out what it would actually feel like to dress as a woman. It wouldn't be hard, I just needed to buy some women's clothes and try them on. So, the next day after work I stopped at a drugstore and bought some panty hose. I put on the panty hose and discovered that it didn't feel weird or bad or naughty at all, it just felt totally natural.

As a thirteen-year-old, I had cross-dressed in my mother's clothes, but stopped because it felt bad. It felt bad to be a boy wearing women's clothes and it felt bad to be rummaging around in my mother's private things when she wasn't around. I had made a semiconscious decision that it was wrong for a guy to dress in female clothes and I wouldn't do it anymore.

So I clearly have a strong desire, or even need, to dress like a woman. Initially, I thought I would only dress female at home in my bedroom with the door shut. I quickly understood that I needed to be able to go out in public as a woman. Ultimately, I knew that I needed to fully transition to being outwardly a woman all the time. The more I did to make myself outwardly a woman, the better I felt.

Gradually, I began to see that I could wear woman's clothes and still present as (look like) a man. I ordered a pair of silicone mastectomy breast prostheses, for women to put in their bras post mastectomy. The day they arrived I took the box to Macy's, to the lingerie department, and asked for a bra that would fit them and me. The first time I put them on, it felt a little weird. A few days later, I tried again and it just felt wonderfully normal and natural. Inadvertently catching my reflection in a mirror and seeing breasts, my immediate gut emotional response was, "Yeah, that's what you're supposed to look like."

The official term for negative emotion over being in the wrong gender body is called "gender dysphoria." By then I knew that I had suffered from this for as long as I could remember and it was very strong now. To be stuck in a man's body really hurts. This is an aspect of transgender that's not immediately obvious to other people—the pain of being in the wrong body is real and compelling.

A metaphor occurred to me: Say one day you just start noticing that your foot hurts. Kind of a vague pain, no remembered trauma, it just kinda hurts. Finally, after a few days of this, you inspect the area. "Aha!" you see suddenly, I've picked up a splinter. Now, upon knowledge of the cause of pain, two things occur. First, it hurts worse somehow, for knowing why. Second, you know the sliver has to come out.

I have had a giant splinter wedged deep in my soul for essentially all my life. Now I see it and it hurts even worse and I have to remove it. I don't have a choice, it has to come out. I understand, I think, the magnitude of the task before me. This will be the hardest thing I've ever done, harder by far then medical school. It also, however, feels really, really good to be a woman outwardly, to have my outward appearance finally match my innermost feelings of identity.

After a while, I came to understand that the social boldness I had acquired in my gay transformation serves me well. My employer, Kaiser Permanente, sponsors those employees, queer or queer friendly, who wish to march in gay-pride parades. We get banners and signs to carry and T-shirts. During gay-pride month, the Sonoma County pride parade is held in nearby Guerneville. A woman I've worked with is co-chairperson of the KP Santa Rosa Pride Committee. She has been wonderfully supportive and helpful to me. I emailed her and asked if I could march in the parade with the Kaiser group as Danielle. She replied, "Of course, as far as I'm concerned you're already Danielle." That was a wonderful experience, the first time I was out in public as Danielle (although it was "safe" because it was pride day). People weren't pointing fingers at me and giggling. In fact, I ran into several people I knew as David and essentially nobody recognized me.

I signed up to march in the much bigger San Francisco pride parade later in the month with the Kaiser people. On that day, I started using the woman's room when dressed as Danielle. It's much more fun than the men's room. Women, even strangers, actually talk to each other in the bathroom.

At the beginning of my transition the whole process seems daunting and almost impossible. And during my darker, bleaker moments, it still does seem impossible. It was certainly much, much easier just to be a gay man. It seemed like such a big deal at the time, but now being gay seems pitifully easy compared to everything involved in being transgender. While it took three years to get used to being gay, it only took a couple of days to get used to being transgender. I think I really always knew for years I was trans; I just didn't completely accept it. I have actually encountered people who think this is a choice. Anyone who thinks transgender is a choice has never had electrolysis!

There is no question that this is the biggest thing that has ever happened to me. Medical school and training pales by comparison, as does being a parent and my parents' divorce. I did make a stop at gay on the way to transgender, however. The intervening time and mental processing was critically important to my being able to accept that I'm transgender. So the thing to do now is to move forward with it.

Cathy and I continue as best friends and gay buddies. I believe we are some of the best romantic advice counselors for each other that we have. We know each other better than pretty much anyone else and we still clearly love each other and care about each other at least as much as we did before. We just can't be romantic partners and we know it, but we easily discuss each other's romances without a trace of jealousy or other negative feeling.

Cathy and I remain romantically alone. I've learned to enjoy my singlehood. I have many friends, but, during my transgender transition, I need to be romantically alone.

Here's my last tip and a final note: The G-spot for men is the prostate gland, just inside the rectum and toward the front.

It feels like a walnut under the rectal lining.

And, yes, I went back a few days later and bought the giant dildo.

Appendix

The Devil is in the details.
Anonymous

Phases of Gay

Cathy and I have both observed that there are different phases we both have gone through in our process of understanding and accepting who we really are. Although in some ways our paths have been very different, in other ways they're still the same. The similarities between us regarding these phases are impressive. In retrospect, what we've experienced is:

Shock and amazement: What and who am I?

Feeling weird: "I like who?" Sometimes I can feel this attraction, but other times it feels very foreign. How can this be me? Could this be a mistake? No it's not a mistake. Ultimately, the difficulty lies not with the idea of gay, but simply the difficulty in accepting how different it is. This was a bigger phase for me than for Cathy.

Thinking, just thinking: This phase is when there's a great deal of internal processing that needs to be done. During this time we just need to think, alone. Even eating is a distraction; we both lost weight during this phase. I went through this phase later than Cathy. I couldn't tell for sure what I was thinking about, just that I needed to process. It was probably happening below the conscious level of thought. I could see occasional progress; something that had bothered me before would suddenly make sense. I could see evidence that my mind was doing something very intense; I just couldn't see what it was as it happened.

Teenage exuberance and outward adjusting: We experienced a strong desire for sex and romance. This can be very strong; life itself is approached with the enthusiasm, impatience, and possibly the lack of judgment, of a teenager.

Mental/emotional vomiting and the need to write this stuff down: We've both been through times when we feel very compelled to write things down. We have each kept a journal.

Finding same-sex romance/sex: At some point the teenage intense desire and impatience will find fruit in some sort of relationship, from serious long-term (not likely right away) to just hooking up (be careful, but it can be helpful for development). The teenage lack of judgment may speed up this phase, hopefully in a way that does not result in extra pain or sexually transmitted infection. This phase doesn't necessarily follow the others and can occur earlier in the process.

Pulling back, uncomfortable with the connotation of "gay" and inward adjustment: As the exuberance fades it's replaced with a more-mature viewpoint. Post-exuberant embarrassment is possible. The, "Look at me, I'm gay," excitement turns to reservation. Now not so quick to come out to anyone that we haven't come out to already. I don't always want to talk about it, although I frequently feel compelled to discuss it with people who already know.

Feeling more comfortable/reconciliation: Over time the weirdness of the whole thing starts to fade. For both of us this took months. For me this really took three years before I began to realize the whole gay thing doesn't seem so weird anymore, it just feels normal. I just think, "So, that's just me, it's just who I am, it's normal." At this point we begin to reconnect to the pieces of our prior lives that still have validity. We find we want to be back with old friends, old associations, old hobbies, and some of the music we used to like. This represents a reconciliation with our prior life experiences.

Ultimate complete acceptance of who we are: We're not there yet, but we're getting there. Perhaps this is a process that will take the rest of our lives.

Time

Throughout all of this, there is an odd phenomenon both Cathy and I have noticed that is not so much a phase, but a general overall observation. Our sense of time passing has slowed greatly. Something that happened yesterday feels like weeks ago, and something that happened a week ago feels like weeks and weeks ago. Our gay process after about a year feels equivalent to the last ten or so years of our prior lives. It sometimes feels like half of the twenty-two years with Cathy has been all this gay stuff; everything before that has faded into a gray haze. This time distortion faded after several months.

My Lists

My Rules of Gay

I wanted to think of more rules of gay, but I guess my list is pretty short and simple.

1. My sexual orientation is my call. I'm straight if I say I'm straight.
2. Who I come out to and when is also my call, totally my call.
3. My gender is totally my call as well. If you think I'm a man and I say I'm a woman, then I'm a woman.
4. Never, ever, force someone, especially your own child, to come out to you.
5. You can ask a gay guy anything.

Things that Have Changed:

In addition to the phases, I have noticed some fundamental apparent personality changes. I have kept lists on my BlackBerry of things that have changed and things that haven't. Most of what's changed is difficult to trace to any idea other than feeling freer to express myself and what I like or don't like.

Over many months, I've observed all this and watched how some of the changes have stuck whereas others have faded.

I thoroughly enjoy being unconventional, standing out from the crowd, and being extroverted. Previously I tried very hard to fit in, be just like everyone else, and not stand out. This appears to be a profound and fundamental change, possibly the greatest single change…

—Things that have changed 12/1/09

I totally changed regarding personal style; I clearly (even when sick or upset) prefer to be different, to be unconventional. I'm not just tolerating it, I'm embracing it wholeheartedly. This is a very big powerful change.

—Things that have changed 10/15/09

Previously, I could be characterized as a little brown field mouse, scurrying here and there, trying to hide in the underbrush. Trying not to stand out or be noticed, I wanted to blend in. The goal was to be middle of the road, even though I realized a bit before we moved to California that my social and political beliefs were too left of center to be middle of the road.

After my transformation I wanted to be a peacock. To be flamboyant and to stand out were my goals. This was most apparent during my exuberant phase, and did not abate much after. I kept thinking I was done being flamboyant, but the next day I'd still pick a fancy shirt to wear to work. Months later, in a conversation with my father, he offered a possible explanation for this change. Prior to my realization, I didn't want anyone to look at me too closely, they might figure out who and what I really am. This idea has validity, but I think I also wanted to blend in because I didn't like who I was. I have to like who I am to want people to notice me.

I need to be really edgy (at least in attire); this has really changed a lot…I need to live life a little on the edge, that is, risky…

—Things that have changed

The desire to be edgy involves more than clothing, but that's probably where it shows the most. Fundamentally, I think it represents what happens when I no longer feel the need to please everyone. I needed to be middle of the road to make as many people around me as happy as possible. I would have thought I wasn't trying to please, but the extent to which I felt this became apparent after I didn't feel it anymore.

More rebellious in general; it's fun to just be me and let everybody else deal… not afraid to piss people off; not worried about it at all…realize there are now some people who will never like me because they can't accept gay, so I don't need to try to make anyone else happy.

—*Things that have changed*

I'm more open to and tolerant of social situations, not intimidated by them.

—*Things that have changed 11/21/09*

I can dance?!? (10/13/09. I noticed at least a week ago.)

I'm less driven to do any of "my stuff" (hobbies) in general; I actually occasionally look for non-my stuff to do. It doesn't need to be my stuff. I was probably obsessed with my stuff before; this makes sense. (10/7/09)

What I'm willing to do or like has changed; I kind of like washing dishes by hand and am less driven to do what I want for me such as hobbies. (10/5/09)

My whole self has changed; I like very much who I've become, but I often don't even recognize myself. (I'm not "the same Dave.")

Listen to different music, months later still like this music, but don't play it so loud.

Much more concerned with my appearance (it's fun to be well dressed) and much more preoccupied with hygiene

Feel much less inhibited about showing my "feminine side."

Feel much less inhibited regarding open discussions of sexuality

I said "fuck" a lot more often; a few years later this faded.

Less interested in nature and more interested in people

Things that Haven't Changed:

Love for family (Andrew, Cathy and extended) (10/21/09)

Still a maker, still like the milling machine, welding, and metal working (10/21/09)

Still like the motorcycle (10/21/09)

Still like to cook (10/21/09)

Bibliography

[1] "Stopping the Bullies." *Scientific American Mind.* June 2005. pp.76–81.

[2] Alan Downs. *The Velvet Rage: Overcoming the Pain of Growing Up Gay in a Straight Man's World.* DeCapo Press, 2005.

[3] Hans Christian Andersen. *The Ugly Duckling,* paragraph 17 from http://hca.gilead.org.il/ugly_duc.html.

[4] Hans Christian Andersen. *The Ugly Duckling,* paragraph 27 from http://hca.gilead.org.il/ugly_duc.html.

[5] Hans Christian Andersen. *The Ugly Duckling,* paragraph 30 from http://hca.gilead.org.il/ugly_duc.html.

[6] Robert Bauman. *Making Gay History,* by Eric Marcus. Harper Collins. 2009

[7] "Equal right to kiss? Why you may be disgusted by gay behavior without knowing it." *Scientific American.* June 18, 2009.

[8] Alfred C. Kinsey. *Sexual Behavior in the Human Male,* Indiana University Press 1948, p. 638.

[9] "Jesus Loves the Little Children." Lyrics by C. Herbert Woolston, music by George F. Root.

[10] Franz Kallman. "A comparative twin study on the genetic aspects of male homosexuality." *Journal of Nervous and Mental Diseases* 115 (1952):283 quoted in *Being Homosexual,* Richard A. Isay, M.D., Vintage Books, 2009, p. 20.

[11] Alfred C. Kinsey. *Sexual Behavior in the Human Male,* Indiana University Press 1948, p. 638.

[12] "Bisexual species." *Scientific American Mind.* June 2008.

[13] Attributed to Ralph Waldo Emerson.

[14] Reference for this section of this chapter is *Harrison's*

David L. Kaufman, M.D.

Principles of Internal Medicine, Mcgraw-Hill, 2008.
[15] "I Guess That's Why They Call it the Blues." Lyrics by Bernie Taupin, music by Elton John, from the album *Too Low for Zero*.
[16] "...light will come again." Lyrics by Ingrid Michaelson, "Everybody" from the album *Everybody*.
[17] Gary Neuman. *The Truth About Cheating: Why Men Stray and What You Can Do To Prevent It*. BBC 2008.
[18] Hans Christian Andersen. *The Ugly Duckling*, paragraphs 32–36 from http://hca.gilead.org.il/ugly_duc.html.
[19] Talk by Shinko Kwong, Zen priest, at SZMC on November 28, 2009 in conjunction with the Jukai ceremony.
[20] Personal therapy session with Georgia Meyer, PhD on February 10, 2010.
[21] "Bisexual species." *Scientific American Mind*. June 2008.
[22] Alan Downs. *The Velvet Rage: Overcoming the Pain of Growing Up Gay in a Straight Man's World*, DeCapo Press, 2005.
[23] Alan Downs. *The Velvet Rage: Overcoming the Pain of Growing Up Gay in a Straight Man's World*, DeCapo Press, 2005.
[24] Alfred C. Kinsey. *Sexual Behavior in the Human Male*, Indiana University Press 1948, p. 615.
[25] "Successful same-sex pairing in Laysan albatross." Young LC, Zaun BJ, Vanderwerf EA. *Biol Lett*. 2008 Aug 23;4(4):323–5. Unrelated same-sex individuals pairing together and cooperating to raise offspring over many years is a rare occurrence in the animal kingdom. Cooperative breeding, in which animals help raise offspring that are not their own, is often attributed to kin selection when individuals are related, or altruism when individuals are unrelated. Here we document long-term pairing of unrelated female Laysan albatross (Phoebastria immutabilis) and show how cooperation may have arisen as a result of a skewed sex ratio in this species. Thirty-one per cent of Laysan albatross pairs on Oahu were female-female, and the overall sex ratio was 59% females as a result of female-biased immigration. Female-female pairs fledged fewer offspring than male-female pairs, but this was a better alternative than not breeding. In most female-female pairs that raised a chick in more than 1 year, at least one offspring was genetically related to each female, indicating that both females had opportunities to reproduce. These results demonstrate how changes in the sex ratio of a population can shift the social structure and cause cooperative behaviour to arise in a monogamous species, and they also underscore the importance of

genetically sexing monomorphic species.

[26] "Bisexual species." *Scientific American Mind.* June 2008.

[27] "Maternal inheritance and familial fecundity factors in male homosexuality." Rahman Q, Collins A, Morrison M, Orrells JC, Cadinouche K, Greenfield S, Begum S. *Arch Sex Behav.* 2008 Dec;37(6):962–9. Epub 2007 Jul 31...aimed to...test the so-called "fertile female" hypothesis for this trait in a contemporary British sample. ...we found that white...and non-white...homosexual men (n = 147) had a significant excess of maternal but not paternal line male homosexual relatives compared to heterosexual men (n = 155). We also found significantly elevated fecundity of maternal aunts of white homosexual men compared to white heterosexual men, whereas non-white heterosexual men showed elevated fecundities of almost every class of relative compared to non-white homosexual men. No significant excess of older brothers was found in homosexual compared to heterosexual men, irrespective of ethnic grouping.

[28] "Biodemographic and physical correlates of sexual orientation in men." Schwartz G, Kim RM, Kolundzija AB, Rieger G, Sanders AR. In: *Arch Sex Behav.* 2010 Feb;39(1):93–109. Epub 2009 Apr 22 Gay men have both more relatives, especially paternal relatives, and more homosexual male relatives.

[29] "Genetic factors increase fecundity in female maternal relatives of bisexual men as in homosexuals." Ciani AC, Iemmola F, Blecher SR. *J Sex Med.* 2009 Feb;6(2):449–55. Epub 2008 Jul 15. We present evidence of an X-chromosomal genetic factor that is associated with bisexuality in men and promotes fecundity in female carriers.

[30] "A comparative twin study on the genetic aspects of male homosexuality." Franz Kallman. *Journal of Nervous and Mental Diseases* 115 (1952):283 quoted in *Being Homosexual,* Richard A. Isay, M.D., Vintage Books, 2009, p. 20.

[31] "Biodemographic comparisons of homosexual and heterosexual men in the Kinsey Interview Data." Blanchard R, Bogaert AF. *Arch Sex Behav.* 1996 Dec;25(6):551–79...Compared with heterosexual controls, homosexual men have a later birth order, an earlier onset of puberty, and a lower body weight...homosexual men have a greater number of older brothers than do heterosexual men.

[32] "Do Gays Have a Choice?" Robert Epstein. *Scientific American Mind,* Feb/Mar 2006, p. 51.

[33] Alfred C. Kinsey. *Sexual Behavior in the Human Male,* Indiana University Press 1948, p. 611.

[34] Alfred C. Kinsey. *Sexual Behavior in the Human Male*, Indiana University Press 1948, p. 616.

[35] Eric Marcus. *Making Gay History* Harper Collins. 2009

[36] Jim Kepner, *Making Gay History,* by Eric Marcus, Harper Collins. 2009

[37] Billye Talmadge, *Making Gay History*, by Eric Marcus, Harper Collins. 2009

[38] Chuck Rowland, cont., *Making Gay History*, by Eric Marcus, Harper Collins. 2009

[39] *Making Gay History*, by Eric Marcus, Harper Collins. 2009

[40] Morty Manford, cont. *Making Gay History*, by Eric Marcus, Harper Collins. 2009

[41] Alfred C. Kinsey. *Sexual Behavior in the Human Male*, Indiana University Press 1948, p. 666

[42] "Genetic factors predisposing to homosexuality may increase mating success in heterosexuals," Zietsch, et al. *Evolution and Human Behavior*, 29 (2008) 425. Many of the typically feminine qualities present in gays; kindness, sensitivity, empathy, and tenderness could be inherited individually.

[43] "Genetic factors predisposing to homosexuality may increase mating success in heterosexuals," Zietsch, et al. *Evolution and Human Behavior*, 29 (2008) 424–433. Suggesting that it's a genetic phenomenon.

[44] "Genetic factors predisposing to homosexuality may increase mating success in heterosexuals," Zietsch, et al. *Evolution and Human Behavior*, 29 (2008) 424–425 How the sum total of what gay is represents more than just homoeroticism.

[45] "Genetic factors predisposing to homosexuality may increase mating success in heterosexuals," Zietsch, et al. *Evolution and Human Behavior*, 29 (2008) 425. Many of the typically feminine qualities present in gays; kindness, sensitivity, empathy, and tenderness could be inherited individually.

[46] Alfred C. Kinsey. *Sexual Behavior in the Human Male*, Indiana University Press 1948, p. 616

[47] Hans Christian Andersen. *The Ugly Duckling*, paragraph 40 from http://hca.gilead.org.il/ugly_duc.html.

About the Author

David L. Kaufman, M.D., is a radiologist at Kaiser Permanente in Santa Rosa, California, where he is chief of nuclear medicine and radiation safety officer for the hospital. He is board certified by the American Board of Radiology.

He received his medical degree from the Wayne State University School of Medicine in Detroit, Michigan. Graduating in the top third of his class, he received the honor of distinction in biomedical research for work done in reproductive endocrinology. He published papers from this work and presented at the American Association of Anatomists annual meeting. He served as a tutor in biostatistics and epidemiology.

Dr. Kaufman completed an internship and diagnostic radiology residency in Grand Rapids, Michigan through Michigan State University, where he completed research in neural networks. He also completed a one-year fellowship in vascular and interventional radiology at Henry Ford Hospital in Detroit, Michigan. A graduate of Michigan State University with a bachelor of science degree in psychology, he participated in social psychology research.

During his career, Dr. Kaufman worked for three years in private practice for a multispecialty group practice in Defiance,

Ohio; he served as a staff radiologist at Muskegon Mercy Hospital in Muskegon, Michigan for five years, serving as chief of vascular and interventional radiology for two years.

Dr. Kaufman's personal interests include cooking, computers, electronics, music, and metal working.